MW01627677

The ARTISAN JEWISH DELI at Home

Made Fresh Daily!

Michael C. Zusman and Nick Zukin

Photography by Caren Alpert

Andrews McMeel Publishing, LLC
Kansas City • Sydney • London

Andrews McMeel Publishing, LLC
an Andrews McMeel Universal company
1130 Walnut Street, Kansas City, Missouri 64106

www.andrewsmcmeel.com

ISBN: 978-1-4494-2007-9

13 14 15 16 17 WKT 10 9 8 7 6 5 4 3 2 1

Library of Congress Control Number: 2013937457

Design: Tim Lynch

Photographer: Caren Alpert

Photo credits: page 125 courtesy of Michael C. Zusman;
page 169 courtesy of Nick Zukin; pages 162, 235 Library of Congress

Photographer Assistant: Marzette Henderson

Food Stylist: Heidi Gintner

Prop Stylist: Carol Hacker/TableProp

Assistant Food Stylist: Michelle DePietro

www.artisanjewishdeli.com

ATTENTION: SCHOOLS AND BUSINESSES
Andrews McMeel books are available at quantity discounts with bulk purchase for educational, business, or sales promotional use. For information, please e-mail the Andrews McMeel Special Sales Department: specialsales@amuniversal.com

"As it is written, Let all who are hungry come and eat. Nobody likes to dance on an empty stomach. If you give us borscht, fine. If not, I'll take knishes or kreplach, kugel or dumplings. Blintzes and cheese will suit me, too. Make anything you like, and the more the better, but do it quickly."

—Sholom Aleichem, "The Bubble Bursts"
(the second story of Tevye the Dairyman; 1899)

To my dad, who let me destroy a fridge-full of ingredients as a five year old.

To my mom, who can stick a chile relleno to the ceiling like no one else.

To my wife, whose lack of skills in the kitchen made me expand my own.

And to my friends John and Scott, who never seem to mind indulging in second dinner . . . or third dinner.

—NZ

To Gracie and the family

—MCZ

Contents

Foreword by Nach Waxman

For me, America's delis are, in the very best sense of the word, museums—collectively, a sprawling network of cultural institutions in which we can view and sample the edible artifacts that evolved within one particular New World immigrant population. As they surged ashore in the late nineteenth and early twentieth centuries, the Jews of Europe, and of Eastern Europe in particular, brought with them a host of gastronomic preferences, kitchen techniques, lore, foods permitted and foods not permitted, and theories as to what constitutes a fit and proper diet. Romanians and Poles, Russians, Latvians and Lithuanians, Hungarians, Czechs, Germans, French, and other immigrants from dozens of nationalities settled in, each with its own history and its own ideas of what it wanted to find in markets and what it expected to encounter on its tables.

Almost from day one, processes of cultural change went, inevitably, to work. For example, the newcomers, living cheek by jowl with each other, were exposed to each other's tastes and ways of preparing food. Further, they found themselves, in their various communities, spread from New York and Boston to Galveston, Santa Fe, and Seattle, brought face to face with local traditions, which would come, in time, to exert influences on the way that they ate. And, beyond all that, they discovered that the range of ingredients available to them was quite different from that of the world they had left behind; this, too, opened the door to change, as they were forced to find substitutes for what they could not get and to develop uses within their traditional culinary idiom for what was new.

Although the national foods continued to have some place within the homes of the Jewish immigrants, quite early on, other contrary social forces soon came into play. As with the American population as a whole, more and more immigrant women began to work outside the home, and traditional cooking skills were rapidly diluted or even lost. And the broader society, anxious to assimilate the new arrivals, took steps that served to accelerate the process of acculturation. Public schools began to provide lunches to the children of poorer immigrant families, and the food they served was mainstream American—tomato soup and macaroni and cheese, not borscht or knishes. The emergent field of home economics offered courses—for adults and for children in the schools—that stressed American-style food. And cookbooks, such as the *Settlement*

Cookbook, intended for the use of the newcomers, offered a mix of American home cooking and largely homogenized European dishes, most not identifiable with any particular tradition.

By World War I, although the tastes and the food memories remained in the immigrant communities, many women could no longer reproduce the old-time dishes, and more and more the specialties they knew were available only from butchers, bakers, and fish-mongers, and in a breed of retail shops known as "appetizing stores" or delicatessens. These outlets produced (or acquired from producers) their own versions of everything from kishke and pastrami to smoked whitefish, baked farmer cheese dotted with black pepper, and rugelach filled with walnuts and cinnamon. In time, such foods were also increasingly to be had in restaurants or at catered celebrations.

These new channels of accessibility were certainly of real value in preserving what might have been lost completely, but at the same time the entire body of foods was taking on a new character. First, most of the new entrepreneurs were not particularly concerned with the regional and local differences that had served to make Jewish food a richly varied folk cuisine. The resulting "deli food" was a little bit of Romanian, a little bit of Polish—an amalgam of food traditions, perceived broadly as Jewish but not further identified. Second, this generalizing process was accompanied by the active incorporation of elements taken from the culinary milieu of the host country—foods that did not originate in the world of the Jewish Europe but were nonetheless welcomed by the nostalgia-seeking second generation with the kind of enthusiasm they were beginning to feel for the dishes of their parents and their grandparents. Now included on the menu could be found a welter of "deli foods" including hot dogs, Reuben sandwiches, scrambled eggs with lox, sticky buns, Danish pastry, all washed down with Dr. Brown's Celery Tonic (later to be known as Cel-Ray). Third, by the end of World War II, one of the most fundamental features of deli—kosher observance—began to fade. In many establishments, cheeseburgers appeared on the menu, along with shrimp salad and challah French toast served with a side of bacon. A crucial link with the past was being severed.

But something else was going on as well. Many of those who made themselves the custodians of this peculiar mishmash of "Jewish food" also did with their loosely traditional cuisine just what is done by good cooks everywhere: they sought to improve, to innovate, to bring fresh thinking to old models. Cooking does not stand still any more than does language or science or the arts. Whether passively through the natural processes of evolution or more actively by playful riffing or earnest experimentation, change does happen, and more power to the people here who are willing to try, to adventure—to look for what is better rather than for what is dutifully the same as it always was.

So, as is true of almost every facet of our many American hyphenated cultures, pure and authentic this food is surely not. And while it is true that delis have been in decline in both number and in distinctiveness for some years, they are nowhere near dead, as this very valuable book attests. They remain with us as important museums—repositories of many of the foods of the past, from pickled tongue to chopped liver made with real schmaltz, to matzo balls, whole-sour dill pickles, herring in cream sauce, and dozens of other gastronomic treasures. They surely do offer an atmosphere of appreciation for a tradition that has earned its right to be preserved. And they do offer inspiration for a new generation to begin making these foods once again, sometimes in new and fresh ways, but also, as always, with love, with care, and with a sense of the history of an amazing migration that arrived here empty handed. And when the arrivals found out that our streets were not, in fact, paved with gold, they dug deep, worked hard, and brought forth gold where none had been.

Introduction

Why a Cookbook About Jewish Delicatessen Food?

For all my true-blue Jewish credentials, I never considered myself religious, didn't keep kosher, and lacked even the foggiest notion about the history of the Jewish delicatessen. All I knew is that I liked the food: pastrami on rye; chewy, malty bagels with a schmear of cream cheese and topped with lox or smoked whitefish; blintzes; and potato latkes with a dab of sour cream. With the 2007 opening of Kenny & Zuke's Delicatessen—co-founded by Nick Zukin and partner Ken Gordon—I had a place to go in my Portland, Oregon, hometown to indulge my deli food fancy.

Kenny & Zuke's fits neatly into a developing local paradigm. Budding bakers, brewers, chocolatiers, charcutiers, cheese makers, and other culinary artisans earn credibility and raves by looking back in time to rediscover traditional flavors, textures, and sensations and express their craft in small-batch, freshly made foods. They choose local ingredients whenever possible, elevating quality over convenience and mass mechanical production.

In his book, *Save the Deli*, David Sax traces the rise and fall of the Jewish delicatessen. He concludes that a new breed of Jewish deli—one that looks back to the deli's roots but is sensitive to modern dining preferences—might salvage a great, but floundering, culinary culture. Kenny & Zuke's was not included in Sax's book as the archetype for what a modern Jewish deli could be, but after Sax stayed and ate there for several days in a row, he extolled the deli's virtues in later articles and on his blog. He also talked up the handful of other such modern-style Jewish delis around North America.

The next logical step, I figured, was for someone to write a cookbook picking up where Sax left off, detailing the recipes of the modern Jewish delicatessen and placing them in their proper cultural and historical context.

The Origin and Evolution of the Jewish Delicatessen

As anyone who grew up steeped in Jewish culture can attest, persecution is at the heart of the Jewish experience. The customs, laws, and practices that set Judaism apart from other religions and cultures have for millennia made Jews a target of oppression, expulsion, and attack, from the Hebrews of biblical times to nearly the entire Jewish population of Europe during the Holocaust. It has also meant that Jews have moved around a lot, with small insular communities shifting from place to place over time depending on the relative tolerance of local governments and neighbors.

The widespread persecution and resulting dispersion of the Jews have had a profound effect on Jewish culinary culture. One abiding historical theme has been impecuniosity and innovation. With limited opportunities as strangers in unfamiliar lands, Jewish populations often lived in poverty and had to make do with inexpensive ingredients and the bits and pieces left over by their betters. They also had to find ways to stretch what little was available to feed themselves and their families. Especially for the Ashkenazic Jews—those who found their way to the northerly climes of central and eastern Europe, the Slavic nations—this meant lots of potatoes, onions, and root vegetables, some dairy, and the consumption of the cheapest cuts of meat, including offal, when meat was affordable at all. Chicken and fish were favored over beef. Rye and buckwheat were primary grains because they were cheap and abundant compared to wheat. Preservation by drying, smoking, or pickling with vinegar or salt allowed foodstuffs that would otherwise spoil quickly to last longer.

A second main theme in the development of Ashkenazic cuisine was the adaptation of local foodways while remaining faithful to kosher dietary laws. Derived from the Old Testament, kosher rules are complex and, even now, can be the subject of interpretation and disagreement. Most non-Jews are aware that pork products are strictly prohibited, but the list of restrictions and rules is much longer. Also banned are all forms of shellfish and certain fowl (sorry, no lobsters or predatory birds in the kosher kitchen), though consumption of chickens, duck, and geese is permitted. No animal blood of any sort may be consumed, so rituals and practices developed to assure that otherwise acceptable meat products are not tainted. Salting to remove residual blood and skillful knife work are the stock-in-trade of the *shochet*, the kosher butcher.

Beyond the outright prohibitions, kosher foods are divided into categories of meat, milk, and pareve. Milk and meat cannot be consumed together. In fact, those who keep strictly kosher must use separate meat and milk dishes, utensils, and even storage spaces. Pareve foods are considered neither meat nor dairy and may be consumed with either. Layered atop the primary regulations are rules for certain holidays, such as no foods with leavening during the

Jewish Passover holiday, and differing levels of oversight for maintaining kosher status, with the most stringent known as *glatt kosher*.

As the Ashkenzic Jews moved around Europe, they drew inspiration from local specialties, substituting compliant ingredients for those they could not eat. This gave birth, for example, to the German frankfurter (*vurstshtlekh* in Yiddish), which ultimately developed into the all-beef hot dog. As Gil Marks says in his exhaustive *Encyclopedia of Jewish Foods*, "Sausages, *vurst* in Yiddish, became a mainstay among central European Jews." The rarely seen today delicacy called *kishke* (page 164), a "classic example of Jewish soul food" according to Marks, was a kosher adaptation of a non-kosher Slavic blood and barley sausage. Derma, beef intestine, substituted for pork casing and was stuffed with a combination of meat scraps, chicken fat (schmaltz), onion, and matzo meal. Similarly, Jews in Romania borrowed local preservation techniques that relied on spice-rubbed dried meat to create the predecessor to pastrami. Jews who settled in and around the Baltic States became aficionados of the ubiquitous herring that took well to salt-preservation methods such as kippering or pickling in vinegar brine.

When the first waves of German Jews immigrated to America in the mid- and late nineteenth century, there was no singular Jewish cuisine. But as more Jewish immigrants from throughout the conflict-torn, frequently inhospitable Slavic lands arrived, two things happened. First, a large proportion of the émigrés settled in New York City, the most expedient point of entry and already a bustling big city. Second, the distinctive dishes that had once dotted different areas of Europe began to concentrate and meld as the Jews from all over Europe came together and shared meals. The earliest Jewish immigrants crowded into the Lower East Side, eventually spreading out to the Bronx and adjacent boroughs.

The Jewish delicatessen sprang from these fertile conditions. The term *delicatessen* is not unique to Jewish cuisine. Rather, it (like the food) is an adaptation, borrowing from the French and German words referring to the place where one bought *délicatesse*, "delicious things," such as cured meats and cheese. The first places that called themselves delicatessens sold non-kosher German food. It is probable that a German Jew first applied the label to an emporium selling the kosher foods familiar to the newly minted Jewish-Americans.

No one is quite sure exactly when the first New York City Jewish delicatessen opened, but there is no doubt the institution originated in New York. In all likelihood, the Jewish deli evolved from the efforts of Lower East Side residents who began selling homemade foods from their tiny tenement apartments and pushcarts. At some point, the first budding entrepreneur saw a business opportunity and moved the home or mobile operation into a storefront space.

Isaac Gellis is commonly associated with the development of the Jewish deli. He began selling kosher deli meats to Lower East Side residents in 1872. By the end of the century, many merchants were offering smoked and cured meats and meat products encompassing the specialties of their own distinct communities in Europe alongside those borrowed from other Ashkenazic population centers. German, Polish, Lithuanian, Ukrainian, Russian, and Romanian foodstuffs might all be purchased in the same store, many of which were kosher.

The early New York delis also served as community centers of sorts. As Gil Marks describes it, the delis "were a place where people could socialize and connect in a welcoming familiar atmosphere. Besides the synagogue, these stores offered a singular haven where one could feel a sense of community and connection."

As the flood of Jewish immigration into New York continued into the 1920s, the Jewish delicatessen evolved. Some of the delis began to look less like meat shops and more like restaurants. Others that began as reliable guardians of kosher doctrine, selling only meat and no dairy, slipped their dietary bonds and sold both. In so doing, they began to break down the dividing wall between delicatessens and the "appetizing stores" that had focused on selling dairy and the neutral pareve items, including lox and bagels. These evolutionary steps naturally led to revolutionary innovations, such as the Reuben sandwich, that would have been inconceivable a few decades earlier, but that modern diners recognize as a deli standard.

The most notable change between the two World Wars was the sheer number of establishments that opened. There were an estimated 500 Jewish delicatessens in Manhattan alone and as many as 2,000 in all of New York City during this time, among them the Hall of Fame names: Ratner's, Lindy's, Carnegie, and Katz's. Simultaneously, the deli began to spread across the United States and Canada as Jews discovered there was more to the New World than New York.

Of course the deli was popular with Jews, but that didn't fully explain its crossover appeal to others. Ted Merwin, a Judaic Studies professor at Dickinson College, cites several reasons. One leading factor is curiosity about Jewish culture. Jewish humor, exemplified by deli workers' well-rehearsed shtick and routinized verbal abuse of bewildered patrons, has always been a draw. Another cultural lure is an interest in the strange and unfamiliar foods of another people, much like modern Westerners seeking out Asian or Middle Eastern restaurants.

The "touristification" of the deli, to use Professor Merwin's phrase, also explains its popularity. Part of the standard itinerary for visitors to New York City and other cities with large Jewish populations is a visit to the local deli. There is no better example than Katz's, which still anchors the Lower East Side corner of Houston and Ludlow streets. Katz's opened its doors in 1888 and not only serves great deli specialties but also achieved mass notoriety for the celebrated orgasm scene portrayed there by Meg Ryan in the 1989 Hollywood hit *When Harry Met Sally*. (Following Ryan's explosive demonstration, one of the best straight lines ever uttered is deadpanned by a lady at the next table, played by director Rob Reiner's mother: "I'll have what she's having.")

But it has to be the hearty, heavy, fatty comfort and joy of deli cuisine itself that has always been the main allure of the Jewish deli: the enormous sandwiches, an emblem of prosperity and hospitality, and the long list of menu choices, all offered at wallet-friendly prices. For non-Jewish Americans of European descent, many of the dishes resemble their hereditary foods. "This sort of fusion cuisine rings familiar to other cultures," says Professor Merwin, adding that the deli's style of Jewish "soul food" has always struck a chord with and created a point of culinary kinship with African-Americans.

Just as the fortunes of the Jewish delicatessen skyrocketed in the early part of the twentieth century, they crashed in the latter half. The reasons are complex and are explained with unmatchable detail and readability in Sax's *Save the Deli*, which I recommend highly to anyone interested in a deeper exploration than I can offer here. The factors behind the deli's decline are:

1. Assimilation. Jews in America began as an insular community, or more precisely, a set of communities, keeping to themselves as they had become accustomed to doing in their European homelands. Jews married Jews, and they followed the ancestral traditions. But as new generations began to reap the blessings of liberty and many became learned and prosperous, they and their offspring increasingly joined the American mainstream, some consciously rebelling against the old ways. Intermarriage moved from scandalous rarity to commonplace practice. Those following kosher laws and other traditional ways diminished in substantial numbers. Jews live alongside non-Jews and join the same companies, country clubs, and organizations. Jewish-Americans have become Americans first.

2. Suburbanization. As American cities have expanded into the suburbs, their urban cores have languished. The densely packed central city Jewish populations that were the crucible of creation for the deli have dispersed. As Jews have achieved and assimilated, they have moved to the outlying areas to live in houses with yards and plenty of space just like other middle-class Americans. While suburban Jewish delis are not unheard of, the closely knit concentrated neighborhoods that gave birth to the Jewish delicatessen have either disappeared altogether or been repopulated with other, newer groups of immigrants.

3. Prosperity. Professor Merwin offers that the upward mobility of the North American Jewish population has also diminished the deli. The restaurant business—like other less prestigious businesses that Jews traditionally went into out of necessity—wasn't good enough for their children. Jewish parents who realized the American Dream in the 1950s or 1960s were adamant that their baby boom children go to good colleges and become doctors and lawyers.

4. Dietary Health. Just as the heartiness of a deli diet has traditionally been what people like about it, modern dietary trends favoring healthier, lighter foods have hit the deli hard. Everyone, it seems, is watching their fat, cholesterol, sodium, and carbohydrate intake. The traditional deli menu, full of pastrami, corned beef, salami, blintzes, and bread, has become an increasingly infrequent treat or something to be avoided altogether.

5. Economics. To put it simply, vegetables are cheap and meat is expensive. And the deli menu has always been heavy on the latter, lighter on the former. Compounding the problem is that everyone who walks in the door expects a sandwich the size of their head. Deli owners have been squeezed. On the one hand, they have to pay for all that pricey beef—brisket isn't nearly as cheap as it once was—while

customers still expect a bargain. What deli owner hasn't heard the kvetch, "What, you expect me to pay $15 . . . for a sandwich?" Just to get by, old-line deli owners have had to yield to the economic equation, buying instead of making their own products and often relying on inferior ingredients.

The Birth and Promise of the Artisan Deli

The factors behind the Jewish deli's decline inspired David Sax's battle cry *Save the Deli*. He believed that the institution was in mortal danger. By his count, New York City is down to a couple dozen Jewish delis, with another handful or two scattered around the rest of the country. But as Sax noted in his epilogue, the deli may be down, but it's not out. Indeed, I'm prepared to stand on the proposition that the deli isn't really dying at all. It is diminished and diluted. But in some ways, this is all as it should be.

Katz's isn't going anywhere; it is more popular than ever. And the same may be true of the remaining handful of famous old-school Jewish delicatessens. The 2nd Avenue Deli even reopened in 2007 after going out of business in 2006. Other classics, such as the Carnegie Deli, have created clones in Las Vegas. Though the demand will never be what it once was, there is sufficient love of deli food to sustain at least the kernel of the original Jewish delis as they existed during their salad days, so to speak.

But posterity will show that the real savior will be the handful of second-wave Jewish delis that have opened since the dawn of the new millennium. Those running these delicatessens could be the great-grandchildren of the early "deli men." They share with their forebears a pride of profession, a dedication to quality, and a love of the food. The delis' names include Wise Sons, Mile End, Caplansky's, Stopsky's, and Kenny & Zuke's, and their stories and recipes are scattered throughout this book.

Their formula for reviving a moribund institution draws on the owners' Jewish heritage and passion, and their focus on artisanship—the same wave that's cresting throughout the food service industry. Artisans are at work making great food of all sorts. They are using the best local and seasonal ingredients they can find to create bright and bold flavors. At the same time, they are eschewing cheaper, mass-produced, chemical-laden products. They are seeking to learn the traditional ways, some nearly forgotten. But they are neither naive nor enslaved by the past. As a result, the modern

Jewish deli artisans are updating and altering the traditional forms—and they are having fun with it in the process. Sandwiches do not need to be obscenely large to be popular. It is enough if they are made with the best pastrami or Montreal smoked meat you have ever tasted. These artisans know that it's a good idea to have salads and other vegetables on a well-balanced menu. And if a dish uses traditional ingredients in a nontraditional way, so much the better.

This cookbook is our attempt to capture the spirit of the modern artisan deli. Using these recipes, like the new generation of deli men and women, you can produce great deli dishes at home to feed your family and friends. There are the classic recipes, from pastrami to chopped liver to bagels to rye bread, but we also offer ideas our great-grandparents wouldn't recognize, such as the Shtetl Toast from our friends at Wise Sons, the Chinese broccoli dish from Mile End, and a couple of the big salads from Kenny & Zuke's. We also offer more than just recipes: Included here are the stories of the new generation of delis, the thoughts of those who remember the old ways, and the details of a few favorite dishes. This book serves as a repository that will always allow you to re-create the dishes—and the soul—of the Jewish delicatessen at home.

Deli

Made Fresh Daily!

FOOD BASICS

Homemade Chicken Broth ...
Chicken Schmaltz ...
Gribenes ...
Caramelized Onions ...
Pickled Red Onions ...
Zesty Zucchini Pickles ...
Kosher Dill Pickles ...
Pickled Green Tomatoes ...
Spicy Pickle Relish ...
Roasted Red Peppers ...
Ajvar and Bagel Chips ...
Russian Dressing ...
Kreplach and Varnishkes ...
Beef Filling ...
Mushroom Filling ...
Savory Cheese Filling ...

SOUP OF THE DAY

Matzo Ball
$4.95

Ask about Orders to Go!

NDWICHES

B

Chapter 1

You can't make a great chicken soup without a flavor-charged chicken broth. A Reuben wouldn't be true to its roots without a generous smear of creamy-tart Russian dressing. And so on it goes. The DIY spirit behind Jewish deli revivalism recognizes that there are basic building blocks for creating luscious deli dishes and that those basic components ought to be as lovingly constructed as the dishes they enhance.

To get the most out of your deli dishes, we provide a handful of important foundational recipes in this chapter—recipes for some of the ingredients that recur throughout the pages of this book. Besides the Russian Dressing (page 24) that's best in class and a chicken broth (page 4) that omits the excessive salt in the canned stuff, we have a recipe for schmaltz (rendered chicken fat, page 5), which adds incomparable flavor and richness to the dishes that rely on it. Our Dough for Kreplach and Varnishkes (page 18) is used in multiple recipes, as are our Roasted Red Peppers (page 15) and Zesty Zucchini Bread-and-Butter Pickles (page 10).

As much as we would love to see you make everything from scratch, it would be ridiculous to say that store-bought is always bad and that you should just skip making a dish if you aren't able to first prepare all of the basics behind it. We know firsthand that between work and kids and running around, it's hard enough just to get dinner on the table. Forget the style points. So, use these basics if you have time. But feel free to substitute if that's all that stands between you and a nice home-cooked deli-style meal. And we promise we won't tell your mother.

Talking Deli with . . . Joan Nathan

Joan Nathan is the most prolific writer and readily recognizable name today on the subject of Jewish food and cooking. In 2010, her seventh cookbook, *Quiches, Kugels, and Couscous*, was released, chronicling Jewish cooking in France. Her repository of recipes and wisdom naturally extends to deli dishes.

Did you grow up in a religious household? How did your upbringing affect what you ate?

Joan Nathan: My family wasn't very religious. We would go to synagogue on most Friday nights and for the High Holidays, but we didn't keep kosher. My parents were always interested in good food. I grew up initially in a town in Westchester County [New York] where there weren't any delicatessens. But my mom was from the Bronx, so we would go there once in a while to get bagels. I remember that my dad used to say that we could tell if our neighbors were Jewish by whether or not they ate bagels. Beyond that, we would sometimes eat dishes that reflected my parents' roots: Polish in the case of my mother and German for my father.

Honestly, though, my family's usual diet didn't reflect our religious heritage. My mother was a first-generation American and wanted to eat American food. And my father could have cared less about eating Jewish dishes.

Do you have any specific deli memories from growing up?

Joan Nathan: I remember one place, Behrman's in New Rochelle, the town over from ours. I don't know if it's still there. But I recall going there with my mother and I remember their huge sandwiches. They had great corned beef and my mother loved their Reuben.

How about any currentdeli favorites?

Joan Nathan: Well, I live in Washington, D.C., now and, I hate to say, there are no good Jewish delis here. I've heard that a couple kids are working to start one of the new-style Jewish delis, which would be wonderful. But if I want to eat deli, I still go to New York City. I've been to Mile End in Brooklyn and it's very good. I love their *kasha varnishkes*. I've spoken on a panel in San Francisco and it's great to see all these new delicatessens doing what the old places did: making their own meats from scratch, for example.

What is the future of the Jewish deli?

Joan Nathan: The Jewish deli has to be reinvented. I've already mentioned the idea of going back to the roots of Jewish deli food in America: making things from scratch instead of buying products from others. I also think the future of the deli means drawing from the whole Jewish culinary experience, not just one part. This is nontraditional, but the tradition needs to be reexamined. There are so many non–meat eaters these days, and there are lots of vegetarian dishes that can be pulled from the Sephardic tradition or even from Israeli cooking. I think of an Israeli dish called *shakshuka*, made from roasted red peppers, that I love. There's *matzo brei*, too.

Fundamentally, most people aren't interested in just eating giant sandwiches anymore. They want to know about the ingredients in the sandwiches. They are concerned about what they are putting in their mouths. The Jewish deli needs to respond to that concern. It's good to see that some of them are doing that.

Homemade Chicken Broth

Makes 16 cups

One of our favorite culinary reference works, *The Prentice Hall Dictionary of Culinary Arts*, defines broth as "a flavorful liquid obtained from the long simmering of meats and/or vegetables." That is an understated description of this deeply flavored, golden-colored extraction that results from a daylong stay on your stovetop. We like to use wings because they are not too fatty but still provide an intense chicken flavor for a soup base and a good yield of meat (roughly 4 cups) that can be reserved for another purpose. Why not put both to good use in our recipe for classic Matzo Ball Soup (page 64)?

4 large carrots, peeled and halved
1 large yellow onion, quartered
4 cloves garlic
2 bay leaves
½ teaspoon black peppercorns
4 to 5 pounds chicken wings

Put the carrots, onion, garlic, bay leaves, and peppercorns in the bottom of a large stockpot. Put the chicken wings on top of the vegetables. Add 4 quarts water, completely covering the chicken.

Place the stockpot over medium-high heat and bring just to a simmer, without letting the water boil. Decrease the heat to medium-low to maintain a simmer. Using a large spoon, skim away the foam and particulate matter that rises to the surface. Continue to simmer the broth for 1 hour, skimming the surface of the broth frequently.

Remove the stockpot from the heat. Using sturdy tongs, gently remove the wings from the broth, trying not to stir up anything that might cloud the broth. Place the wings on a rimmed baking sheet and set aside until cool enough to handle, about 30 minutes. Once cool, remove the chicken skin and bones from the meat, reserving the meat. Using tongs, gently return the bones and skin to the broth.

Place the stockpot over medium-high heat and bring just to a simmer. Decrease the heat to low and simmer the broth for 5 to 6 hours, skimming as needed and adding a little water to keep the bones covered, until the broth is flavorful and light golden in color.

Meanwhile, using your fingers or two forks, shred the meat. Transfer the meat to a covered container and refrigerate it for up to a week to use in chicken salad or soup.

To strain the broth, place a large fine-mesh sieve or colander lined with cheesecloth over a large heatproof bowl. Slowly and carefully strain the broth. Do not strain the very last of the broth that contains a high proportion of sediment. Discard the solids. Transfer the strained broth to a clean soup pot if using immediately. Otherwise, cool the broth slightly, cover, and refrigerate for up to 3 days or transfer to freezer containers and freeze for up to 6 months.

Chicken Schmaltz

(Rendered Chicken Fat) and Gribenes

Makes about 2 cups

Schmaltz is the key to great flavor in a wide variety of Jewish deli classics, such as Chopped Chicken Liver (page 54) and Matzo Ball Soup (page 64). Substitutions are often offered in the name of good health, but there is no adequate substitute for the real deal. Schmaltz is what our Slavic ancestors used as their foundational cooking fat, since butter was more expensive and tougher to obtain. Lard violated Jewish dietary laws, and the edible vegetable oils we take for granted today were all but nonexistent. Ask your butcher or grocer to set aside the quantity of chicken skin and trimmings needed for this recipe. Alternatively, purchase 10 pounds of chicken thighs and do the skinning and trimming yourself, using the skinned meat for another purpose. With its long storage life, you can afford to dole out your schmaltz stash judiciously, but by all means use it when the urge strikes to make a dish just the way your *bobe* did.

2 pounds chicken skin and fat trimmings
1 medium yellow onion, halved and thinly sliced

Place the chicken skin and fat trimmings, along with $\frac{1}{4}$ cup water, in a heavy-bottomed $2\frac{1}{2}$- to 3-quart saucepan, preferably nonstick. Bring to a simmer over medium heat, and then decrease the heat to low, allowing the fat to render slowly for 1 hour. Stir occasionally to make sure nothing sticks to the bottom of the saucepan.

Stir the onion into the simmering liquid. Continue to cook until the solids are a dark golden brown, 1 to 2 hours longer, stirring occasionally and making sure nothing sticks to the bottom of the pan. Turn off the heat and set aside to cool until lukewarm.

Pour the rendered fat (schmaltz) through a fine-mesh strainer into a container with a tight-fitting lid, retaining the solids (see Gribenes, right). Cover and refrigerate for up to 6 months, or freeze for up to 1 year.

Gribenes

The main by-product of the rendering process is *gribenes*, the delectable bits of deeply browned, crispy chicken skin. Think of *gribenes* as the Jewish analog to pork cracklings. After straining the schmaltz, lay out the *gribenes* on a paper towel and season them with salt and pepper. You'll end up with about 1 cup. Eat them out of hand as a snack or store in an airtight container in the refrigerator for up to a week, reserving them for other uses, such as adding them to Chopped Chicken Liver (page 54).

Wise Sons Deli: College Pals, Kitchen-Centered Harmonies

It's just past noon on a summer Saturday in 2011 and the line to enter Wise Sons' Saturday-only pop-up location in San Francisco's trés trendy Mission District is ten deep. Two gents in front of me—visitors from Montreal—chat about the Wise Sons story.

Fast forward a year and Wise Sons is ensconced full-time in a *heymish* (homey) 30-seat space in the Mission, and the five-day-a-week lines are even longer than in the pop-up days. A Tuesday booth at the Ferry Plaza farmers' market supplementing San Francisco's corned beef and pastrami sandwich supply is also a smashing success.

Wise Sons, the brainchild of college friends Leo Beckerman and Evan Bloom, offers a short menu of new-wave and traditional Jewish deli specialties prepared with an artisan attitude. Rye bread is made in-house. Pickles—and we're not just talking cucumbers—rotate seasonally. Pastrami is bathed in a sweet-salty brine before it's lightly smoked over hickory and hand-cut for service. Wise Sons' flair for tongue-in-cheek nods to the proprietors' Jewish heritage is noteworthy. Shtetl Toast, a name with a Yiddish reference to the crowded enclaves where Eastern European Jews once lived, uses traditional ingredients in a delightfully twisted way. Tempting for the name alone is their Shlubby Joe, a beer-braised brisket on sea salt–sprinkled challah. In a nod to Jewish dietary laws, the menu is pork-free.

Beckerman, dreadlocked and sporting a wraparound head scarf, is the order-taker on my first Wise Sons encounter. Bloom is in the kitchen sweating through an unrelenting rush of orders that may total as many as 300 over about 6 hours. Popular items on a concise menu include outrageously rich chocolate babka French toast, smoked trout salad, and locally made Montreal-style Beauty Bagels. Turns out that Bloom's two kitchen cohorts, Blake Joffe and Amy Ramsen, *are* Beauty Bagels, making them in small quantities for Wise Sons and a handful of other Bay Area outlets. In mid-2012, Beauty Bagels leased their own retail space, though Joffe, Ramsen (jokingly referred to as the token shiksa, a sometimes derogatory reference to a non-Jewish woman), Beckerman, and Bloom remain close.

When the rush finally subsides, Beckerman and Bloom are ready to chat, a new generation's kitchen-centered Simon & Garfunkel. That 1960s musical duo met and began singing in

Hebrew school. Beckerman and Bloom, both from Southern California, first joined forces in 2003, cooking at barbecues for a Jewish student group at the University of California, Berkeley. After graduation, Bloom and Beckerman worked separate jobs but stayed in touch. They drew up a business plan in 2009 and started Wise Sons the next year.

Of Wise Sons' rotating selection of Jewish specialties, Beckerman explains, "We wanted to be able to bring this food to a city that doesn't have it. And people are coming out of the woodwork." The Bay Area "has a large Jewish community, and we are trading on the culture." But Wise Sons' intended reach extends beyond the Jewish community. Beckerman adds, "We are reaching out to the younger, non-Jewish crowd. We want to expose them to Jewish food, too."

Judging by Wise Sons' broad popularity and the critical praise it has generated in a city spoiled by quality cuisine, Bloom and Beckerman are exceeding their most optimistic goals and proving themselves Wise Sons indeed.

Caramelized Onions

Makes 1 to 2 cups

Raw onions transform magically as they are slowly cooked and caramelized. Their cellular structure breaks down and, from a chemical standpoint, caramelization converts the simple sugar molecules to a broad range of flavor-rich compounds as they darken. Adding sugar and vinegar to the cooking onions makes for a more dynamic, rounded flavor, though these ingredients can be omitted for a more straight-ahead oniony taste. Adding a little water during the process will help ensure that the caramel color is evenly distributed, a tip Nick picked up years ago from Julie Sahni's seminal text, *Classic Indian Cooking*. The water content of onions can vary widely, which accounts for the variable yield for this recipe.

¼ cup vegetable oil

2½ pounds yellow or white onions (about 5 large), halved and thinly sliced

2 teaspoons kosher salt

1 tablespoon granulated sugar

1 tablespoon distilled white, cider, or white wine vinegar

In a large skillet, preferably nonstick, warm the oil over medium heat and then add the onions. Sprinkle the salt over the onions and stir until evenly distributed. Sauté the onions, stirring occasionally, until the edges of the onions begin to brown, 8 to 10 minutes. Stir in 2 tablespoons water and continue to cook until the browned edges are moistened and lightened, about 5 minutes longer. Decrease the heat to low if the onions are darkening excessively.

Continue to cook, stirring occasionally and adding up to 2 additional tablespoons water if the onions seem dry, until the onions reach a uniform deep caramel color, about 45 minutes. (A light brown or honey color is not dark enough.) Stir in the sugar and vinegar. Continue to cook until the sharp vinegar smell dissipates and the onions darken a bit further, about 5 minutes longer.

Remove the pan from the heat and allow the onions to cool to room temperature. Transfer to a container with a tight-fitting lid and refrigerate for up to 2 weeks or freeze for up to 6 months.

Pickled Red Onions

Makes 1½ to 2 cups

Our pickling brine moderates the sharpness of raw red onion and sends the flavor in multiple directions all at once: sweet, tangy, spicy, salty, and savory. No wonder these onions find their way into several of the recipes in this book. The pickled onions can be slipped into a sandwich or served as a condiment with grilled meats. Or in the "we can pickle that" tradition of our favorite television show, *Portlandia*, serve some of these as part of a multi-vegetable pickle platter. These pickled onions will keep safely in the refrigerator for a month, but be aware that the longer they are in the brine, the more potent they will become.

3 cups apple cider vinegar
1½ cups granulated sugar
2 bay leaves
1 (2- to 3-inch) cinnamon stick
1 teaspoon crushed red pepper (optional)
½ teaspoon black peppercorns
½ teaspoon whole cloves
¼ teaspoon kosher salt
1 large red onion (about 12 ounces), halved and thinly sliced

Combine the onion, vinegar, sugar, bay leaves, cinnamon stick, crushed red pepper, if using, peppercorns, cloves, and salt in a medium saucepan. Bring to a boil over high heat, stirring to dissolve the sugar. Boil for 1 minute. Add the onions and then remove the pan from the heat. Allow the onions and pickling brine to cool to room temperature, and then transfer to a nonreactive container with a tight-fitting lid. Refrigerate for 1 day to allow the flavors to meld. The pickled red onions will keep in the refrigerator for up to 1 month.

Zesty Zucchini Bread-and-Butter Pickles

Makes 3 to 4 pints

In North American parlance, a pickle is usually a small cucumber that has been preserved either in vinegar or brine flavored with an assortment of herbs, spices, and other flavorings. The world of pickles is far wider and more interesting than the humble cucumber, though. At craft-oriented restaurants in DIY-focused Portland, it seems that every restaurant has a pickle plate boasting a cornucopia of cured vegetables ranging in taste from sweet to downright puckery. When pickled in this particular brine, zucchini pickles are on the sweet side.

2 pounds zucchini, ends trimmed and cut into ⅛-inch-thick slices (about 6 cups)
1 large yellow onion, halved and cut crosswise into thin slices (about 2 cups)
2 teaspoons pickling salt
2 cups apple cider vinegar
1 ¼ cups granulated sugar
1 tablespoon mustard seeds
1 teaspoon ground turmeric
1 teaspoon celery seeds
1 teaspoon coriander seeds
1 teaspoon pickling spice
½ teaspoon crushed red pepper

In a salad spinner or large colander set over a bowl, toss the zucchini and onion with the pickling salt. Refrigerate, uncovered, for at least 4 hours or overnight. Dry in the salad spinner, or spread the vegetables out onto a work surface lined with a double thickness of paper towels and pat dry.

In a large saucepan, stir together the vinegar, sugar, mustard seeds, turmeric, celery seeds, coriander seeds, pickling spice, and crushed red pepper. Bring to a boil over high heat, stirring to dissolve the sugar. Add the zucchini and onion, and then remove from the heat. Set aside to cool to room temperature. Transfer to a nonreactive container with a tight-fitting lid. Refrigerate for 1 day to allow the flavors to meld. The zucchini pickles will keep in the refrigerator for up to 1 month.

Kosher Dill Pickles

Makes about 3 quarts

Kosher in name if not strictly in accordance with Jewish dietary laws, salty, sour, spicy, and juicy dill pickles are a Jewish deli staple. A lot of the old-line delis used to (and a few still do) have a dish of them sitting out on every table for customers to nosh on gratis while awaiting the arrival of steroidal sandwiches. Health codes and hard times have made the free pickle dish a relative rarity. The cultural legacy of the dill pickle is one of availability and economy. Dill is one of the few fresh herbs that grow in the harsh northerly climates of Eastern Europe. And pickling a bumper crop of cukes in summer and fall ensured that our forebears would have vegetables of some sort throughout the cold, harsh winters. Pickle recipes abound, so rather than try and reinvent the wheel, we are passing along an adaptation of one we really like: the Lower East Side Full-Sour Dills from Linda Ziedrich's authoritative *The Joy of Pickling*.

About 4 pounds pickling cucumbers, 3 to 5 inches long, blossom ends trimmed

8 cloves garlic, thinly sliced

2 tablespoons dill seeds or 4 to 6 fresh dill heads

2 small fresh or dried hot chiles, such as japonés or de árbol, slit lengthwise

2 tablespoons coriander seeds

1 tablespoon allspice berries

1 teaspoon black peppercorns

½ cup pickling salt

Layer the cucumbers in a wide-mouth, gallon-size ceramic or glass jar or food-grade plastic container. Sprinkle in the garlic, dill, chiles, coriander, allspice berries, and peppercorns.

Dissolve the pickling salt in 3 quarts water, and pour enough of the brine over the cucumbers to cover them. Push a gallon-size freezer bag into the jar, pour the remaining brine into the bag, and seal the bag. The brine bag should weight down the pickles to keep them submerged in the brine. (The bag is filled with brine instead of water so that in case there is a pinhole leak, the brine in the jar will not be diluted.) If needed, invert a plate or other heavy, flat object over the top of the brine bag for additional weight. It is essential that all of the pickles are completely submerged in the brine; even one pickle breaching the surface will ruin the entire batch. Cover the jar with a clean, dry kitchen towel and keep it at room temperature ranging anywhere from 55°F to 80°F (70°F to 75°F is optimal).

If scum or mold forms on top of the brine, skim it off daily and rinse off the brine bag. Within 3 days you should see the tiny bubbles in the brine, which will become cloudy as it ferments.

The pickles are ready when they are sour and olive green throughout, after about 2 weeks. At this point, remove the brine bag and any scum, cap the jar, and store it in the refrigerator, where the pickles will keep for several months.

Pickled Green Tomatoes

Makes 3 quarts

Compared to canning, pickling is a breeze since there is far less preparation involved. Local groceries do not usually stock pickled tomatoes, so home-pickled versions are a special treat. Traditionally, Jewish delis use green tomatoes, but if you can't find them, red ones are fine to use, too. Select the firmest, least ripe plum (Roma) tomatoes available. The optional crushed red pepper will add a moderate amount of spice for those who prefer their pickles perky.

3 pounds small green tomatoes or firm red plum (Roma) tomatoes
6 cups distilled white vinegar
3 tablespoons pickling salt
6 cloves garlic, minced or thinly sliced
4 large sprigs fresh dill
1 tablespoon pickling spice
1 tablespoon crushed red pepper (optional)
1 teaspoon yellow mustard seeds
1 teaspoon coriander seeds

Sterilize a wide-mouth, gallon-size, heat-resistant glass or food-safe plastic container by placing it in a clean sink and filling it with boiling water. Let stand for 5 minutes, and then carefully empty out the water. Set aside.

Meanwhile, halve the tomatoes lengthwise. Use a small spoon or your fingers to remove and discard the seeds without disturbing the flesh of the tomato. Rinse the tomatoes under hot tap water to clean them, shaking off any excess water.

Combine the vinegar, pickling salt, and 6 cups water in a large, nonreactive saucepan. Bring to a boil over high heat.

While the vinegar mixture is coming to a boil, put the garlic, dill, pickling spice, crushed red pepper, if using, and mustard and coriander seeds into the prepared jar. Place the tomatoes on top, filling the container no more than three-quarters full.

When the pickling liquid comes to a boil, turn off the heat, stir to dissolve the salt, and then let cool to room temperature. Pour the liquid over the tomatoes until they are covered by ½ to 1 inch of liquid, reserving at least 2 cups of the brine in the pot. Set aside to finish cooling.

Once the reserved brine has cooled, add 2 cups of it to a quart-size, freezer-strength, resealable plastic bag and seal the bag. Arrange it over the tomatoes to keep them submerged. (Alternatively, use a small plate to keep the tomatoes submerged.)

Cover the jar with a lid or a double layer of plastic wrap secured with a rubber band. Refrigerate the pickles for at least 1 week before eating. The pickled tomatoes will keep in the refrigerator for up to 1 month.

Spicy Pickle Relish

Makes 1½ cups

Relish is a basic condiment typically tossed on top of hamburgers and hot dogs served at summer barbecues. This versatile relish can do far more. It plays a strong supporting role in our Russian Dressing (page 24) and Deli Chopped Salad (page 91). We love the snap and sweet tang of the zucchini-based Bread-and-Butter Pickles (page 10) called for in this recipe, but if time is short, feel free to substitute a good-quality store-bought sweet pickle variety.

1 heaping cup chopped sour dill pickles
½ cup firmly packed Zesty Zucchini Bread-and-Butter Pickles (page 10)
½ cup firmly packed sliced pepperoncini
½ cup firmly packed Pickled Red Onions (page 9)
4 cloves garlic, peeled
1 teaspoon crushed red pepper

In the work bowl of a food processor fitted with the metal blade, combine both pickles, pepperoncini, onions, garlic, and crushed red pepper. Pulse, scraping down the sides as needed, until an evenly chopped relish forms. Transfer to a covered container, adding any excess pickle juices, and refrigerate for up to 1 month.

Roasted Red Peppers

Makes 4 to 8 roasted red peppers

There is no comparison between raw and roasted red bell peppers. The flavor and texture is completely different, so stark that they might as well be different vegetables. Roasting them takes an ordinary, even unpleasant, vegetable to a higher plane. With their bright color, slippery-soft texture, and mellow sweet-vegetal bite combined with just a touch of char, roasted red peppers make a welcome addition to a kaleidoscope of dishes, such as Ajvar (page 17) and Grandma's Goulash (page 168). Though there are plenty of excellent jarred varieties available at your local supermarket or Russian market (see Sources and Resources, page 242), resolute DIY types will definitely want to roast their own.

4 to 8 red bell peppers

Arrange an oven rack about 6 inches from the heating element and heat the broiler to high. Place the whole peppers on a broiler pan or sturdy baking sheet lined with aluminum foil. Broil the peppers, turning them with tongs as they blacken, until charred all over, 12 to 15 minutes. (Alternatively, the peppers can be charred directly over an open flame on a gas burner or on an outside grill. Using this method is the best way to prevent overcooking.) Be careful to blister the skin only, without cooking the flesh of the pepper any more than necessary.

Transfer the peppers to a shallow bowl, cover the bowl tightly with plastic wrap, and let stand for 15 minutes to steam and soften. Remove and discard the skins, stems, and seeds of the peppers under cool running water. Wipe gently with paper towels and cut and use as directed.

Ajvar

Makes about 4 cups

Throughout the Balkans, the versatile red pepper–based relish called ajvar (pronounced EYE-vahr) has been used for generations as a condiment, side dish, and spread. Nick likes it so much that he even uses it in place of salad dressing. According to Gil Marks in his *Encyclopedia of Jewish Food*, the name of this "wildly popular" preparation comes from the Turkish word for caviar, in reference to ajvar's traditionally lumpy (though fish-free) texture. For a spicier version, use a little more cayenne or swap in your favorite chiles for an equal quantity of the bell pepper. For those on a sodium-restricted diet, the quantity of salt may be halved.

- 1 medium eggplant (about 1 pound), trimmed, peeled, and cut crosswise into ½-inch-thick slices
- Olive oil, for brushing
- Kosher salt
- 8 Roasted Red Peppers (about 2 pounds; page 15)
- 4 cloves garlic, microwaved or boiled in water for 30 seconds
- 2 tablespoons distilled white vinegar
- 1 tablespoon granulated sugar
- ⅛ teaspoon cayenne pepper

Preheat the oven to 350°F. Line a large rimmed baking sheet with parchment paper.

Generously brush the eggplant slices on both sides with olive oil and arrange them in a single layer on the baking sheet. Sprinkle them with salt and roast in the oven until soft when pierced with a fork, about 1 hour. Set aside to cool for 10 minutes.

In the work bowl of a food processor fitted with the metal blade, combine the eggplant, roasted peppers, garlic, vinegar, sugar, cayenne, and 2 teaspoons salt. (If you prefer a smoother spread, use a blender.) Process until a spreadable paste forms, 30 to 60 seconds, scraping down the sides of the bowl once or twice. Transfer to a covered container and refrigerate for up to 1 week.

Dough for Kreplach and Varnishkes

Makes 1 pound

This basic egg dough does double duty—as the wrapper for the Jewish dumplings known as Kreplach (page 19) and as the bow-tie noodles, varnishkes in Yiddish, that go with Kasha (page 46). Whether you use a pasta machine or a rolling pin, be sure to roll out the dough to about 1⁄16 inch or thin enough to be able to see your hand through it. If the dough starts to pull back after hand-rolling, use an old baker's trick: Instead of fighting it, let the dough rest for a minute or two before rolling it out. Don't be discouraged if your pasta pockets or bow ties aren't perfect on your first try. It takes a little practice to be as good as your grandmother.

2 cups unbleached all-purpose flour, plus more for dusting
½ teaspoon kosher salt
3 large eggs, beaten

Combine the flour and salt in the work bowl of a food processor. Pulse three times to distribute the salt. Add the eggs and 1 tablespoon water and process until a ball forms, 15 to 30 seconds. If after 15 seconds the dough doesn't begin to form a ball (it will probably appear sandy or pebbly), add a little more water (just a teaspoon at a time) without stopping the machine until a ball forms.

Turn the dough out onto a lightly floured work surface and knead until the dough is smooth and supple, about 2 minutes. Form the dough into a ball, and then use a knife to divide it into 5 equal pieces. Shape each piece into a fat disk. Wrap each disk in plastic wrap and set aside at room temperature to rest for at least 20 minutes, and up to 3 hours, before using.

To roll out the dough: If using a pasta machine, set the roller to its widest setting. Remove the plastic from 1 disk of dough and shape the dough into a rectangular shape thin enough to pass through the pasta roller. Pass it through the pasta roller, and then fold it end to end and pass it through the rollers again. Repeat folding and passing the sheet of pasta through the rollers five more times, lightly dusting the pasta if it begins to stick to the rollers. Set your pasta roller to the next smallest width and pass the sheet of pasta through the rollers. Continue passing the pasta through the rollers, decreasing the width of the rollers each time, until the pasta is thin enough that you can see your hand through it, usually the thinnest or next-to-thinnest setting on the pasta rollers. Dust the pasta on both sides with flour and set on a clean dry work surface, Left uncut, the sheet of pasta should be about 32 inches long and 5½ inches wide. Cut it in half crosswise if it is too long to fit on the counter.

To cut the dough for kreplach: For triangular kreplach, use a sharp knife to cut the sheet of pasta lengthwise into 2 long even strips, each about 2½ inches wide. Cut the strips into 2½-inch squares, reserving any uneven edge pieces. For half-moon kreplach, use a 2½-inch biscuit cutter to cut pasta circles. The pieces of pasta can be dusted with flour, stacked, covered in plastic, and stored in the refrigerator for up to a day before using. The scraps can be re-rolled and cut to make additional pieces.

To cut the dough for *varnishkes* (bow-tie pasta): Using a sharp knife, cut the sheet of pasta lengthwise into 4 even strips, each about 1¼ inches wide. (Cutting the pasta will be easier if you cut the sheet of pasta into shorter segments first.) Cut each strip of pasta into rectangles twice as long as they are wide, creating individual pieces about 1¼ inches by 2½ inches. Place your index finger in the middle of one of the pieces, your thumb on the center of the bottom edge, and your middle finger on the center of the top edge of the piece of pasta. Delicately holding the piece of pasta in place with your index finger, draw your thumb and middle finger toward your index finger, dragging the edges of the pasta into your index finger and forming a bow-tie shape with a crease down the center of the piece of pasta. Lift your index finger from the pasta and squeeze your thumb and middle finger together, sealing the edges of the pasta together in the middle and securing the bow-tie shape.

Kreplach Fillings

The origins of the *krepl* (the singular in Yiddish; *kreplach* is plural) are uncertain. Different sources speculate that the idea of boiled or fried noodle pockets stuffed with a chopped filling came to the northern European Ashkenazis from Italy, the home of ravioli, or from Asia, brought by Tatar invaders. Regardless of origin, these dumplings represent a timeless method to efficiently use up too-expensive-to-waste leftover meat. Modern filling ideas encompass more than meat, such as our cheese or mushroom varieties. A little filling goes a long way, since only a small amount is needed for each *krepl*. Either freeze any unused filling for next time or call out the reinforcements to help make enough kreplach to serve everyone at extended family gatherings.

Mushroom Filling

Makes 1 cup (enough for about 100 kreplach)

This vegetarian-friendly filling is full of flavor and hearty enough to satisfy any appetite. If it's available, porcini powder (see Sources and Resources, page 240) adds a distinctive deep earthiness to the mix.

- 8 ounces cremini mushrooms, stem ends trimmed and sliced or coarsely chopped
- ¼ large yellow onion, coarsely chopped
- 1 clove garlic, peeled
- 1 tablespoon porcini mushroom powder (optional)
- ¾ teaspoon salt
- ½ teaspoon dried thyme
- ¼ teaspoon ground coriander
- ¼ teaspoon freshly ground black pepper
- 1 tablespoon vegetable oil

In the work bowl of a food processor, process the cremini mushrooms, onion, garlic, porcini mushroom powder, if using, salt, thyme, coriander, and pepper until the mixture is evenly and very finely chopped.

Place a medium skillet over medium-high heat and add the oil. When the pan is hot and the oil begins to shimmer, add the mushroom mixture.

Cook, stirring occasionally, until the mushrooms release their liquid and the liquid evaporates, leaving a moist paste, but no puddling in the pan, about 10 minutes. Use immediately; or cool, transfer to an airtight container, and refrigerate for up to 3 days or freeze for up to 1 month.

Beef Filling

Makes 2 cups (enough for about 200 kreplach)

This is an ideal use for leftover Seasonal Pot Roast (pages 153–161). Use the roast instead of fresh beef, skip the browning, and reduce the braising time to about 30 minutes.

1 tablespoon vegetable oil

1½ pounds beef brisket or boneless chuck, trimmed of fat and cut into 1-inch cubes

1 (3-inch) piece peeled carrot, coarsely chopped

½ medium yellow onion, coarsely chopped

2 cloves garlic, peeled

½ teaspoon dried thyme

½ teaspoon dried parsley

¼ teaspoon freshly ground black pepper

1 cup Homemade Chicken Broth (page 4), canned low-sodium chicken broth, or water

Kosher salt

Place a Dutch oven over medium-high heat and add the oil. When the oil begins to smoke, add the beef in one layer, without crowding the pan, and brown on all sides, about 10 minutes. (Brown the meat in batches, if necessary, adding more oil as needed.)

Meanwhile, in the work bowl of a food processor fitted with the metal blade, process the carrot, onion, and garlic until finely minced.

When the meat is browned, add the minced vegetables to the pan along with the thyme, parsley, and black pepper. Stir to combine, cooking until fragrant, about 1 minute. Add the chicken broth. Using a wooden spoon, stir to scrape up any browned bits that are stuck to the bottom of the pan. Bring to a boil, then decrease the heat to low and simmer, covered, until the beef is very soft and easily falls apart, about 2½ hours.

Remove the lid and raise the heat to medium. Using a fork or spatula, shred the beef. Continue to cook, stirring frequently, until nearly all of the liquid evaporates, leaving only moist shredded beef. Taste the meat, adding salt, if needed. Use immediately; or cool, transfer to an airtight container, and refrigerate for up to 5 days or freeze for up to 1 month.

Savory Cheese Filling

Makes ½ cup (enough for about 50 kreplach)

The simple combination of farmer cheese and seasonal fresh herbs completes our trio of filling favorites. Don't worry if most of the cheese absorbs into the kreplach skin. The flavor will remain intact.

½ cup farmer cheese

1 tablespoon finely chopped mixed fresh herbs (such as chives, flat-leaf parsley, and/or dill)

Kosher salt

In a medium bowl, whisk together the cheese and herbs. Most farmer cheese is salty enough on its own, but taste and add a pinch or two of salt, if desired. Use immediately, or transfer to a covered container and refrigerate for up to 3 days.

Russian Dressing

Makes 1 cup

Our not-so-secret Russian dressing recipe gets its zip from Worcestershire and hot sauces and our own Spicy Pickle Relish. If desired, substitute a sweetish store-bought relish to save some time. Mexican- or Louisiana-style hot sauces are fine to use, but for our money, the Asian-style sriracha is the best in class. This dressing can be used for salad, including our Deli Chopped Salad (page 91), but it is also a vital component in our Pastrami Reuben Sandwiches (page 149) and in Kenny & Zuke's popular Pastrami Burgers (page 151).

¾ cup mayonnaise

2 tablespoons ketchup

2 tablespoons Spicy Pickle Relish (page 14) or store-bought sweet pickle relish

1 teaspoon Worcestershire sauce

1 teaspoon hot sauce (Mexican, Louisiana, or sriracha variety)

1 teaspoon kosher salt

In a small bowl, combine the mayonnaise, ketchup, relish, Worcestershire sauce, hot sauce, and salt. Stir together until thoroughly combined. Transfer to a covered container and refrigerate for up to 1 week.

Bagel Chips

Makes 40 to 50 chips

Don't throw away those day-old or even two-day-old bagels! Make bagel chips instead. Lightly salted and baked with just a touch of oil, they are as addictive as potato or corn chips, but not nearly as greasy. These chips can also be used to accompany your favorite dip or, broken into pieces, as a salad topper in place of croutons. When slicing the bagels, ensure that the slices are of even thickness to avoid having some burn while others are not baked to complete crispness. Cooking spray ensures that these treats are all but oil-free; however, brushing the slices very lightly with vegetable oil works too.

2 bagels
Vegetable oil cooking spray
Kosher salt

Preheat the oven to 350°F. Line two baking sheets with silicone baking mats or parchment paper.

Place a bagel flat on a cutting board. Use a serrated bread knife or sharp chef's knife to slice the bagel as thinly as possible from top to bottom. Repeat with the other bagel.

Arrange the slices in a single layer on the prepared baking sheets. Evenly coat the bagel slices with the cooking spray, then turn them over and coat the other side. Lightly sprinkle the bagel slices with salt. Place in the oven and bake until lightly golden brown and beginning to crisp, 8 to 12 minutes. The bagel chips will crisp up more as they cool. Store in an airtight container for up to 1 week.

of the
MONTH

CH....$4.50
......$5.50
MI....$5.50
E.....$6.20
LL....$3.20
R.....$3.20
E.....$6.40
EL....$4.50
......$4.50

NCH

STARTERS AND SIDES
{Sold by the pound!

DELI SPECI

- Knishes
- Latkes
- Herbed Matzo Brei
- Noodle Keegal
- Shtetl Toast
- Chopped Chicken Liver
- Tzimmes
- Chinese Broccoli

Chapter 2

On a typical deli visit, the focus is invariably on the meats and breads—from pastrami and corned beef to rye bread and bagels. We love this stuff as much as anyone and devote entire chapters to each (Chapters 5 and 6). But that's barely scratching the surface of a century-long tradition of generous and wide-ranging Jewish deli hospitality.

Among a long list of favorites, there are dozens of items typically enjoyed before the jaw-challenging sandwiches are served or as an accompaniment to the main course. Many of the offerings center on the starches that helped keep shtetl-bound Ashkenazis full at minimal cost. The knish—a Jewish version of a savory turnover—is offered for your heat-and-eat pleasure in two versions: with mashed potato and onion (page 30) and with smoked meat (page 32), a recipe from our friends at Caplansky's in Toronto. The potatoey pleasure of the latke is another deli treat, and we have three recipes to try: classic Crispy Potato Latkes with Chunky Ginger Applesauce (page 36), simple Fluffy Potato Latkes (page 39), and lighter, modern-leaning Zucchini Latkes with Tomato Relish (page 41), which skip the potato altogether.

Not to ruin all the fun of poking around in this chapter (don't worry; it covers a lot of territory), but chopped-liver lovers will have to see how our version on page 54 stacks up against the kind their *bobe* (grandmother) used to make. And speaking of ancestral favorites, Michael's grandmother, Rose Fertig, who grew up in a Yiddish-speaking household, made a crispy-topped, buttery noodle keegal that we have lovingly re-created on page 44 from her original little-of-this-little-of-that instructions.

Wise Sons' Shtetl Toast

Serves 4 to 6

The Wise Sons supplied this recipe, which is a perfect example of old-line deli ingredients being used in a new and interesting way. Wise Sons co-proprietor Evan Bloom shared his thoughts: "Shmaltz is an ingredient that many wince at. We get a lot of empty stares when we tell people that it is rendered chicken fat and onions. I explain that it is the base of many delicious Jewish foods—from chopped liver to matzo balls to kasha varnishkes. We're not ashamed to say that we use it to build flavor in a lot of our cooking. Here it's spread on toast, the luxurious savory fat cut by a simple herb salad. Don't be scared—*bobe* lived to be 95!"

½ large clove garlic, minced
2 teaspoons white wine vinegar
2 tablespoons extra-virgin olive oil
Flaked sea salt and freshly ground black pepper
4 to 6 slices Classic Deli Sandwich Rye (page 190)
½ cup Chicken Schmaltz (page 5), at room temperature
Leaves from ½ bunch fresh flat-leaf parsley
Fronds from ½ bunch fresh dill
3 large radishes, thinly sliced into rounds (use red or French breakfast radishes)
⅓ cup coarsely chopped Gribenes (page 5)
Kosher salt

In a medium bowl, macerate the garlic in the vinegar for 15 minutes. Slowly whisk in the olive oil until completely combined (emulsified). Add sea salt and pepper to taste. Set aside.

Heat a griddle or large cast-iron pan over medium-high heat until hot. While the pan is heating, liberally brush both sides of the bread with schmaltz.

Arrange the slices on the griddle or in the pan and cook until crisp and golden brown, 2 to 3 minutes. Flip to crisp the other side, about 2 minutes longer.

Meanwhile, give the dressing a quick stir, add the herbs and radishes to the bowl, and toss until lightly dressed. Place a slice of the fried bread on a warm plate, mound a small portion of the salad in the center, and garnish with the *gribenes* and a sprinkling of kosher salt.

Open-Face Potato Knishes

Makes 16 knishes

With a heritage that stretches back to the pushcarts that plied the streets of New York City in the late nineteenth century, the knish is one of the defining Jewish delicatessen dishes. The open-face baked knish is a tradition that Yonah Schimmel's has carried on continuously for more than a century, first on Coney Island, then on the Lower East Side, where the shop that has been open since 1910 still remains. Our knish recipe, adapted from one by Canadian Jewish cookbook author and blogger Pam Reiss, follows the same luscious tradition. If desired, the potatoes can be mixed with cooked mushrooms, kasha, mashed sweet potatoes, other vegetables, or even meat (see page 32 for our Smoked Meat Knish recipe). These knishes make a fine side dish to roast chicken or one of our seasonal brisket preparations (pages 153–161). Or eat them as a snack with deli mustard on the side.

Dough

2 cups unbleached all-purpose flour

1 teaspoon baking powder

1 teaspoon kosher salt

1 large egg

½ cup vegetable oil

½ cup lukewarm water

1 teaspoon distilled white vinegar

Filling

3 pounds Russet potatoes, peeled and chopped

1 tablespoon kosher salt

½ teaspoon finely ground black pepper

1½ cups Caramelized Onions (page 8), plus ⅓ cup for topping the knishes

To make the dough, fit a stand mixer with the paddle attachment. In the mixer bowl, combine 1 cup of the flour, the baking powder, and salt. Mix the contents on medium speed for 15 seconds. Add the egg, oil, water, and vinegar to the center of the flour mixture. Mix on medium speed until fully combined and the mixture has the consistency of cake batter, about 2 minutes. Remove the paddle attachment, scraping any excess into the bowl. Fit the mixer with the dough hook attachment. Add the remaining 1 cup flour to the center of the bowl. With the mixer on low speed, knead the dough until it is smooth and glossy, 5 to 8 minutes. Use your hands to form the dough into a ball and wrap it tightly in plastic wrap. Set it aside to rest at room temperature for about 2 hours.

To make the filling, while the dough is resting, steam the potatoes in a pot fitted with a steamer basket until very soft, about 15 minutes. Drain the potatoes thoroughly, place them in a large bowl, and mash with the salt and pepper until most of the large lumps have been eliminated. Fold in the 1½ cups of caramelized onions until evenly distributed in the mashed potatoes. Allow the potato-onion mixture to cool to room temperature, about 30 minutes.

Preheat the oven to 375°F. Line a baking sheet with parchment paper or a silicone baking mat.

Unwrap the dough and place it on a large, smooth, unfloured work surface. Using a rolling pin, roll the dough out as thin as possible into a rectangle. Then begin stretching the dough by hand into a larger rectangle, approximately 16 by 32 inches, by lifting up the dough from the center and slowly and gently pulling it outward and laying it back down. Work around the dough in a circle, until it is stretched to the point of being very thin and translucent. Where it remains thicker in the middle of the sheet, lift up the dough so that it rests evenly on the backs of your hands, and gently stretch the dough before laying it back down on the work surface. It will tear in places, leaving holes. Since the dough will be rolled in a later step, creating layers, some tearing is acceptable. After the bulk of the dough is stretched into a rectangle, stretch any thick portions of the lip of the dough sheet as much as possible.

Along the full length of one long edge of the stretched dough and about 2 inches in from the edge, spoon the potato filling in a log shape, weaving around any holes. Slice off the outer lip of the dough, about ½ inch in from the edge, with a sharp knife or pizza cutter.

Pull and stretch the edge of the dough over and around the log of potato filling. Fold in the ends of the dough and, starting at one end of the log, slowly and carefully lift and roll the log of filling, one turn at a time, down the entire length, until all the dough has been rolled around the potato mixture. (Try not to compress the filling unnecessarily at any time while making the knishes or the potato filling will be more likely to expand and split the pastry shell when the knishes are baked.) Straighten the roll and cut it into 16 equal pieces with a sharp knife (wipe it clean between cuts). A serrated bread knife works best for this.

Take a piece of the log and lay the more cleanly cut end flat in your palm. Lightly press in on the potato filling, then pull the dough from the edge into the center of the knish, pinching it together until the dough fully encloses the potato mixture. Place the knish dough side down on the baking sheet. Lightly flatten the top of the knish and form it into a neat circle. Repeat with the remaining pieces of the knish log, evenly spacing the knishes on the baking sheet.

(At this stage, the unbaked knishes can be frozen and will keep for a month in the freezer. Thaw at room temperature before baking.)

Bake the knishes for 25 minutes or until the pastry is golden brown, rotating the baking sheet 180 degrees after 15 minutes. Top each knish with 1 teaspoon of caramelized onions and serve warm.

Baked knishes may be kept in the refrigerator, wrapped in plastic wrap, for up to 5 days. Reheat by placing them in a preheated 450°F oven until warm in the center, about 5 minutes.

Caplansky's Smoked Meat Knishes

Serves 8

"You must remember this, a knish is still a knish. . . ." We do not recommend belting out this lyric as you dish up the very same meat-party-on-a-plate served by zany-creative Zane Caplansky at his eponymous Toronto deli, Caplansky's. Watching *Casablanca* will never be quite the same, and besides, this modern twist on the humble Jewish savory pie is not just another knish. With its pastrami-rich gravy underlying the pastrami-and-potato-filled tart enveloped by a puff pastry rather than traditional piecrust, it bears little resemblance to what your *bobe* made your *zayde* back in the old country. We are pleased to share Caplansky's reinvented knish recipe, adapted for home cooks. Remember that "smoked meat" is a Canadian cured beef that's nearly identical to pastrami. Use whichever is most readily available in your area.

Gravy

1 tablespoon Chicken Schmaltz (page 5) or vegetable oil

½ medium white onion, diced

1 large clove garlic, minced

12 ounces pastrami, diced

3 tablespoons all-purpose flour

2 cups Homemade Chicken Broth (page 4) or canned low-sodium chicken broth, plus more as needed

1 teaspoon minced fresh rosemary

1 teaspoon minced fresh thyme

Kosher salt

Knishes

1 (12-ounce) box frozen puff pastry sheets (2 sheets)

1 pound Russet potatoes, cut into ½-inch dice

Kosher salt

1 tablespoon Chicken Schmaltz (page 5) or vegetable oil

1 medium white onion, diced

2 teaspoons minced fresh rosemary

1½ teaspoons ground coriander

1¼ pounds pastrami or smoked meat, finely diced

All-purpose flour, for dusting

1 large egg, beaten

3 teaspoons sesame seeds

To make the gravy, in a large saucepan, melt the schmaltz over medium heat. Add the onion and garlic and cook, stirring occasionally, until the onion is soft and translucent, 6 to 8 minutes. Add the pastrami and increase the heat to medium-high. Stirring almost constantly, cook the meat until it is evenly browned, 8 to 10 minutes. Decrease the heat to medium and stir in the flour. Continue stirring until the flour is light brown in color, 5 to 7 minutes. Stir in the chicken broth and bring the mixture to a boil over medium-high heat. Lower the heat to medium-low and add the rosemary and thyme. Simmer the gravy, stirring occasionally, until the flavors come together, about 5 minutes. Taste and add a pinch of salt, if needed. If the gravy is too thick, thin it with additional broth. If using the gravy immediately, keep it warm until the knishes are ready to serve. The gravy can be made in advance and then refrigerated, covered, for up to 3 days. Rewarm it over medium-low heat before serving.

To make the knishes, transfer the box of puff pastry to the refrigerator to partially thaw for about 40 minutes before it will be used. Preheat the oven to 400°F. Line a rimmed baking sheet with parchment paper.

Place the potatoes in a large saucepan. Fill the saucepan two-thirds full with cold water, add a pinch of salt, and bring to a boil over high heat. Decrease the heat to medium and simmer until the potatoes are tender when pierced with a fork, 8 to 10 minutes. Drain the potatoes well and transfer them back to the dry pan. Place the potatoes over low heat until the excess moisture has evaporated, about 1 minute. Remove the potatoes from the heat and mash them with a potato masher. Set them aside to cool.

In a medium skillet, melt the schmaltz over medium heat. Add the onion and cook, stirring occasionally, until it is soft and browned, 15 to 20 minutes. Add the rosemary and coriander and cook to release their aroma, about 30 seconds. Transfer the onion mixture to a large bowl. Add the mashed potatoes and pastrami, and stir to combine. Set aside.

Lightly dust a clean work surface with flour. Unwrap the puff pastry, and working with 1 sheet of puff pastry at a time, unfold the dough. Roll the dough out to an even 13-inch square, lightly flouring the top of the dough and the rolling pin as needed. Place half of the filling mixture in the center of the dough and use your hands to form the filling into a 5-inch square with straight edges and sharp corners that is about 1 inch high. Fold the top and bottom edges of the puff pastry over the top of the filling, and then fold over the sides to completely encase the filling in dough. If the dough is too short to meet in the middle, gently stretch it, or roll it a bit more with the rolling pin, until the edges will slightly overlap on top of the knish. Press the dough gently to secure it, making a tight, square-shaped knish. Transfer it to the prepared baking sheet. Repeat this process with the other sheet of dough and the remaining filling to form a second knish and place it on the other half of the baking sheet.

Lightly brush the tops of the knishes with the egg, and then sprinkle each with the sesame seeds. Bake the knishes until the crusts are golden brown and slightly puffy, about 30 minutes. Allow them to cool for about 5 minutes, and then cut each knish into 4 slices. Serve them on warmed plates atop a pool of the gravy.

Talking Deli with . . . Sharon Lebewohl

The 2nd Avenue Deli is on the short list of New York City classics. Sharon Lebewohl is the daughter of its founder, Abe Lebewohl, who was murdered in 1996 on his way from the deli to the bank. Sharon and Abe's brother, Jack Lebewohl, have carried on the family business ever since that sad day, with the exception of a one-year closure and relocation between 2006 and 2007.

What was it like growing up as a Jewish deli insider? Any special memories you can share?

Lebewohl: The deli, or "the store," as we referred to it, was my second home. After school, my sister and I went to the store to do our homework. On Sundays and holidays we both worked in the deli. We bused tables, socialized with customers, and hosted. I once filled in as the dishwasher. I felt very connected to the deli and my father. Even though my father worked 14 hours a day, which continued until the day he died, my sister and I saw him every day. During the summer, we would go to the deli at 10 PM and walk my father home. After I had children, they worked in the deli as well. We never took vacations, but I never felt deprived.

Thanksgiving to me was very special. We would deliver orders, work in the restaurant, and when we could no longer move, my whole family would sit down to Thanksgiving dinner together in the deli.

What are the most and least endearing qualities of the traditional Jewish deli?

Lebewohl: Jewish deli brings me back to my roots. It feels comfortable, soul-nourishing, and it fills me with a sense of belonging. But obviously deli food has some drawbacks.

My father was once on a panel with Mark Federman, third-generation owner of Russ and Daughters, the best appetizing store in the country. They were asked to speak on the topic, "Is deli dying in New York?" Mark had voluminous notes and spoke for a half hour about the health benefits of fish. My father, on the other hand, was not very prepared. When it was his turn to speak, he looked at the audience for a full minute without uttering a word. Finally he said, "What am I gonna tell you? My food will kill you." After the laughs died down and he gave his speech, all the health-conscious speakers and food writers made a beeline for the buffet. The first things to go were fatty mountains of *kishke*, pastrami, and corned beef.

You can't eat deli food every day, but when you eat it, it should be the best. Most customers eat a healthy diet most of the time, but it's OK to splurge every now and then.

Have you been to Mile End or any of the other modern Jewish delis?

Lebewohl: I have eaten at Mile End. I thought the food was amazing. I had smoked meat in Montreal, and Mile End's smoked meat was even better than I remember it.

Does the Jewish deli have a role in the advancement of Jewish culture? Do you have a prediction for the deli's future?

Lebewohl: Delis are definitely part of Jewish culture, and I often wonder what would happen to the cultural connection if the Jewish delis were to die out. There are "bagel and lox Jews" for whom the deli may be their only connection to Judaism, but they feel as connected as someone who goes to synagogue three times a day. There is definitely a future for the Jewish deli, but on certain conditions. Quality is the most important thing. The food needs to be homemade and not taste like it comes from a mix. The Jewish deli also needs to stay current with culinary trends. In his day, my father was always experimenting with new foods. To survive, today's delis need to do that, too.

Crispy Potato Latkes

with Chunky Ginger Applesauce

Makes 6 or 7 latkes

Latkes are a labor-intensive delicacy associated with the late fall or winter celebration of Hanukkah, the Jewish Festival of Lights. However, these traditional potato pancakes are delicious any time of year. It used to be that the sign of a dedicated latke maker was scraped knuckles from hand-grating potatoes and onions with a box grater, or even worse, the old standup grater that looked like a miniature washboard. For all but the most devout traditionalist, the food processor has taken the worst of the labor (and likelihood of injury) out of the equation. Use a coarse grating disk for the potatoes after slicing them in quarters lengthwise to fit into the feed tube. For the onions, grate them in the food processor using either the fine grating disk or by pulsing the onions into a fine mince using the metal blade. If you have Chicken Schmaltz (page 5) on hand, use it as a flavorful old-style frying medium in place of vegetable oil. But you didn't hear that from us.

1 pound Russet potatoes
1½ medium (8 ounces) yellow or white onions
1½ teaspoons kosher salt
½ teaspoon freshly ground black pepper
2 tablespoons all-purpose flour
1 large egg
1½ cups vegetable oil or Chicken Schmaltz (page 5)
1 cup Chunky Ginger Applesauce (optional; page 38)
1 cup sour cream (optional)

Fill a large bowl with ice water. Peel and grate the potatoes, placing the potatoes in the ice water to keep them from discoloring. Peel and grate the onions. Put the onions into a fine-mesh strainer and use your hand to press down until most of the liquid is drained. Drain the potatoes and dry them thoroughly using a salad spinner, paper towels, or a clean kitchen towel.

Place the potatoes, onions, salt, pepper, and flour in a large bowl and thoroughly mix the ingredients together. Add the egg and mix again until it is completely incorporated.

Preheat the oven to 200°F. Place a large skillet over medium heat. Add the oil and heat it until hot. Test the oil by dropping a small amount of the latke batter in the oil. If the batter bubbles and fries immediately, the oil is ready.

Measure ⅓ cup of the latke batter and place it between your hands, squeezing it, allowing most of the liquid to drain back into the bowl. In your hand, flatten the batter into a patty and place it gently in the hot oil. To minimize the risk of splattering, place the patty on a spatula and then use a fork or knife to slide the patty from the spatula into the oil. Repeat the process with as many patties as can fit into the skillet without crowding the pan. Cook until the underside is dark golden brown and crisp, about 5 minutes. To prevent uneven frying, the latkes can be rotated 180 degrees halfway through the cooking time.

Flip each latke, flattening it with the back of a spatula, and cook until dark golden brown and crisp on the second side, about 4 minutes, rotating them for even browning halfway through the cooking time.

Transfer to a heatproof platter or baking sheet lined with a double thickness of paper towels. Keep warm in the oven while you fry additional batches. Serve with applesauce or sour cream, if desired. The latkes can be held in a 200°F oven for up to 30 minutes.

Variations

Garlic Latkes

Add 2 tablespoons roasted puréed garlic to the ingredients when you add the onions. (Lightly roasted garlic is better than raw here, which can have an excessively sharp taste.)

Roasted Pepper Latkes

Add ⅔ cup of finely diced Roasted Red Peppers (page 15) to the ingredients when you add the onions. Or you can use the same quantity of Anaheim peppers roasted in a similar way, or buy canned or jarred red peppers. Add another 2 tablespoons finely diced peppers to ½ cup sour cream, if desired, and use as a topping for the latkes.

Chunky Ginger Applesauce

Makes about 2 cups

On its own or as a match-made-in-heaven accompaniment to potato latkes, this simple-to-prepare homemade applesauce beats the jarred varieties hands down. Our recipe refreshes the prosaic applesauce standard with assertive accents of ground ginger and cloves in addition to the more traditional cinnamon. Brown sugar replaces granulated white sugar for added depth, and using both tart-firm and sweet-soft apples as the foundation for the recipe lends a well-balanced flavor and texture to the finished applesauce. The bonus benefit from making this recipe is your heavenly smelling home.

For a milder, more classic-tasting applesauce, replace the brown sugar with ¼ cup granulated sugar and 2 tablespoons honey. Decrease the quantity of spices, using only ⅛ teaspoon cinnamon, ⅛ teaspoon ginger, and just a pinch of cloves. For a smooth-textured applesauce, cook the apples longer, until easily mashed with a fork or the back of a spoon. Instead of a potato masher, use an immersion blender, food processor, or full-size blender to make the sauce smooth rather than chunky.

2 Granny Smith or other firm, tart apples, peeled and diced
2 Golden Delicious or other soft, sweet apples, peeled and diced
1 cup lightly packed light brown sugar
1 teaspoon ground ginger
¼ teaspoon ground cinnamon
⅛ teaspoon ground cloves
Pinch of salt

In a medium saucepan, combine the apples, sugar, ginger, cinnamon, cloves, 2 tablespoons water, and the salt. Cover the pan and place over medium heat. Simmer the apple mixture until the apples release some liquid and the juices begin to simmer, 5 to 10 minutes. Uncover the pan and stir. Continue to cook, covered, until the apples have completely softened, 10 to 15 minutes longer. Remove from the heat and mash with a potato masher or the back of a fork until the sauce has a nice chunky texture. Transfer to a serving bowl. Serve immediately, or cover and refrigerate for up to 1 week.

Fluffy Potato Latkes

Makes 8 or 9 latkes

These latkes epitomize the trend in modern Jewish deli cooking to rethink and update classic dishes. Instead of the traditional shredded Russet potatoes, this recipe relies on the golden-colored, creamy-textured Yukon Gold variety, which is finely chopped in the food processor, not shredded. And for those trying to avoid excess calories, cooking oil is used sparingly—just enough to coat the skillet. Although we love our traditional latkes, one of our testers summarized her sentiments succinctly: "These latkes are less greasy, they're easier to make, and they taste better. And it was great not having to squeeze water out of the potatoes." Give them a try and see what you think.

1 pound Yukon Gold potatoes

1½ medium (8 ounces) yellow or white onions, coarsely chopped

1½ teaspoons kosher salt

⅛ teaspoon freshly ground black pepper

¼ teaspoon baking powder

¼ teaspoon baking soda

1 cup all-purpose flour

2 large eggs, lightly beaten

¼ cup vegetable oil, plus more for frying

Chunky Ginger Applesauce, for serving (optional; page 38)

Sour cream, for serving (optional)

Fill a large bowl with ice water. Peel and dice the potatoes, placing them in the ice water to keep them from discoloring. Place the onions in a food processor and pulse until finely minced. Transfer the onions to a fine-mesh strainer and press to remove as much liquid as possible. Set aside, over a bowl to allow further draining. Thoroughly drain the potatoes and place them in the food processor. Use long pulses to finely chop the potatoes, scraping down the sides of the work bowl as needed. The potatoes should be finely minced but not pureed.

Transfer the potatoes and onions to a large bowl. Add the salt, pepper, baking powder, and baking soda. Thoroughly mix the ingredients together. Add the flour and thoroughly incorporate it. Fold in the eggs, and then stir in the ¼ cup oil. Place the bowl of latke batter, covered, in the refrigerator until ready to use, up to 1 hour.

Preheat the oven to 200°F. Lightly coat a large nonstick skillet with 1 tablespoon oil. Heat the pan over medium-low heat. Pour ⅓ cup of the batter into the pan, leaving room for 2 more latkes. Using the bottom of a spoon or flat measuring cup, spread the batter to create a circular pancake about 4 inches in diameter. Repeat to form 2 more latkes.

Fry the latkes on one side until mottled golden brown on the bottom and around the edges and bubbles rise and pop in the middle of the latke, 4 to 5 minutes. To prevent uneven cooking, the latkes can be rotated 180 degrees halfway through the cooking time. Flip the latkes and cook on the other side until crisp and golden brown, 3 to 4 minutes. (The second side takes less time than the first.) Again, the latkes can be rotated halfway through the cooking time to ensure even browning. Transfer to a warm platter lined with paper towels to absorb excess oil. Keep warm in the oven. Continue to fry latkes, adding more oil, as needed.

Serve warm, topped with applesauce or sour cream, if desired. The latkes can be made up to 30 minutes in advance and kept warm in the oven, but they will be much better if eaten fresh from the frying pan.

Zucchini Latkes

with Tomato Relish

Makes 8 latkes

We know that latkes are supposed to be made with potatoes. But in the manner of the modern Jewish deli, tradition is sometimes better off giving way to lighter eating. Traditionalists can claim heresy, but one taste of this delicious, less starchy version of the classic latke should put any flavor-based concerns to rest. The bonus benefit to this recipe is that it adds another alternative to combat the bounty of home gardens overflowing with the fruit of prolific zucchini vines. And if your garden is also teeming with ripe red tomatoes, we recommend our simple tomato relish accompaniment instead of the usual applesauce or sour cream.

1 medium white or yellow onion, coarsely chopped

1 clove garlic, peeled

1 ½ pounds zucchini

1 tablespoon kosher salt

½ teaspoon dried marjoram

½ teaspoon dried thyme

2 large eggs

1 ½ cups matzo meal

Vegetable oil, for frying

Sour cream, for serving (optional)

Tomato Relish, for serving (optional; page 42)

Process the onion and garlic in a food processor until they are finely pureed. Place the puree in a fine-mesh strainer set over a bowl; set aside to allow the liquid to drain away.

Coarsely grate the zucchini using a box grater, mandoline, or food processor. Place in a wide-mesh strainer or the insert of a salad spinner. Add 2 teaspoons of the salt and toss to combine. Set aside for 30 minutes to drain. If you used a salad spinner, spin it as you would salad greens to strain away any liquid from the zucchini. Otherwise, use your hands or a flexible spatula to press as much of the liquid as possible out of the zucchini in the strainer.

Place the zucchini in a large bowl and add the marjoram, thyme, onion-garlic puree, and the remaining 1 teaspoon salt. Mix well. Thoroughly mix in the eggs. Finally, stir in the matzo meal.

Preheat the oven to 200°F. Place a large heavy skillet over medium-high heat. Add ⅜ inch of oil and heat until it shimmers; do not allow the oil to reach the smoking point. Using your hands, press ½ cup of the zucchini batter into a ½-inch-thick patty and carefully slip it into the pan, letting the patty fall away from you to avoid being splattered with the hot oil. Add 2 more latkes to the skillet and fry for 3 minutes per side, rotating the latkes 180 degrees after 2 minutes on each side to evenly brown them. Transfer the latkes to a baking sheet lined with paper towels to absorb excess oil. Keep warm in the oven while frying the rest of the latkes. Serve warm, topped with sour cream or tomato relish, if desired.

Tomato Relish

12 ounces cherry tomatoes, halved

6 tablespoons extra-virgin olive oil

⅓ cup finely chopped red onion or shallot

2 tablespoons chopped fresh flat-leaf parsley

2 tablespoons freshly squeezed lemon juice or red wine vinegar

½ teaspoon minced garlic

Kosher salt

In a medium bowl, combine the tomatoes, oil, onion, parsley, lemon juice, and garlic. Stir until the tomatoes are evenly coated. Add salt to taste. Transfer to a serving bowl and set aside until ready to serve. The tomato relish can be made up to 2 days in advance. Cover and refrigerate. Remove from the refrigerator 1 hour before serving.

Herbed Matzo Brei

Serves 4

Matzo brei is Yiddish for "matzo pulp." Introduced to North America by Ashkenazic émigrés, it takes its name from the process of soaking matzo in water, which results in a coarse mash that is first squeezed to remove excess water, then mixed with egg and seasonings and panfried in the manner of either scrambled eggs (the method we use) or an omelet. Matzo brei is a breakfast treat traditionally associated with Passover, when most other grain products are prohibited, but it has evolved to become a morning-time Jewish deli favorite year round. Though sweet versions, topped with butter and maple syrup, are most common, we suggest this savory approach, which picks up the flavor of sautéed onions and fresh herbs from your kitchen garden.

3 tablespoons unsalted butter or Chicken Schmaltz (page 5)
½ large yellow onion, thinly sliced
Kosher salt and freshly ground black pepper
4 whole matzos, broken into approximately 1½-inch pieces
10 large eggs
2 tablespoons chopped mixed fresh herbs (such as flat-leaf parsley, dill, chives, and/or tarragon)
¼ cup sour cream

Melt the butter in a large skillet over medium heat. Add the onion and a pinch of salt and pepper and cook, stirring occasionally, until it is evenly browned and the butter turns nut brown, 12 to 15 minutes.

While the onion is cooking, soak the matzo pieces in a large bowl of warm water until they are soft on the outside but still a little crisp inside, about 2 minutes. Drain in a colander, gently pressing them to squeeze out excess water. Beat the eggs in a large bowl with a pinch or two of salt and pepper.

When the onion is cooked and the butter is browned, stir the matzo into the egg mixture. Decrease the heat to medium-low and add the egg mixture to the pan with the onion, spreading it out into an even layer. Allow it to set on the bottom, about 1 minute, and then use a heatproof spatula to begin turning the mixture, breaking it up into large curds as you would with scrambled eggs. Cook, stirring in this manner, until the eggs are just set but still moist, 3 to 5 minutes. Just before the eggs are set, turn off the heat and stir in the herbs. Taste and adjust the seasoning with salt and pepper. Portion the *matzo brei* onto warmed plates, and serve topped with a dollop of sour cream.

Mammy's Savory Noodle Keegal

Serves 12 to 16

Michael got a little misty-eyed the first time he tasted our spot-on version of his family's heritage baked noodle, egg, and dairy casserole. Previously, the "recipe" existed only in vague text fragments and the taste memories handed down to Michael's mother and aunt from his beloved (and long-departed) maternal grandmother, Rose Fertig (whom Michael nicknamed "Mammy" when he was a toddler) . Michael recounts: "Mammy grew up in a Yiddish-speaking home in Portland before she married my grandfather, a lawyer. To be honest, she wasn't a great cook, but all us grandkids and now our kids adore this dish. My mom or aunt still makes it, by popular demand, for every family gathering, which is good since it serves a small army." Keegal and kugel are variant names for the same range of sweet or savory dishes made with a noodle or other starch base. The different pronunciations relate back to the different regions of Eastern Europe where the dish was made.

Cooking spray
3½ tablespoons kosher salt
18 ounces wide egg noodles (about 1½ packages)
½ cup (1 stick) plus 2 tablespoons unsalted butter, cubed
3 cups small-curd cottage cheese
3 cups sour cream
6 large eggs, beaten
½ teaspoon freshly ground white pepper

Preheat the oven to 350°F. Spray a 9 by 13-inch glass baking dish with cooking spray and set aside.

Fill a large pot with about 5 quarts water, add 2 tablespoons of the salt, and bring it to a boil. Add the egg noodles and cook until they are nearly tender but still undercooked, about 5 minutes. Drain the noodles in a colander, shaking out the excess water. Transfer them back to the dry pot. Add ½ cup of the butter and stir to melt. Allow the noodles to cool slightly, about 5 minutes.

Stir in the cottage cheese and sour cream. Add the eggs, pepper, and the remaining 1½ tablespoons of salt and stir to thoroughly combine. Pour the noodle mixture into the baking dish and spread it out into an even layer. Dot the top of the keegal with the remaining 2 tablespoons butter. Bake until the keegal is set in the center and lightly browned on top and around the edges, 45 to 55 minutes. Allow the keegal to cool for about 10 minutes before cutting and serving.

Store any leftover keegal, covered, in the refrigerator for up to 3 days. To reheat, add a drizzle of milk or a few dots of butter to the top of the keegal and bake it at 350°F, covered, until heated through. (The cooking time will depend on the quantity being reheated.)

Kasha Varnishkes

with Wild Mushroom Sauce

Serves 4 to 6

Kasha is made with hulled kernels of buckwheat (also called buckwheat groats). The kernels are sautéed, then steamed to tenderness like rice, yielding a nutty, earthy flavor for a standout side dish. With a complementary mushroom sauce, kasha could even be offered as a red meat-free main. Add schmaltz to the sauté pan and the sauce intensifies the flavor, though you may substitute vegetable oil. Traditionally no herbs are added to kasha, but this modern adaptation with fresh thyme in the sauce and parsley in the kasha itself is more colorful and brighter tasting than its historic inspiration. If served with a meat entrée that has a sauce of its own, the mushroom sauce may be omitted.

Sauce

- 3 tablespoons Chicken Schmaltz (page 5) or 2 tablespoons vegetable oil
- 1 pound mushrooms, such as cremini, chanterelle, and porcini, trimmed and thinly sliced
- 1 large yellow onion, thinly sliced
- 2 tablespoons all-purpose flour
- ½ cup dry white wine
- 2 cups Homemade Chicken Broth (page 4) or canned low-sodium chicken broth
- 2 teaspoons chopped fresh thyme
- 1½ teaspoons kosher salt
- ⅛ teaspoon freshly ground black pepper
- ¼ teaspoon sweet or smoked paprika

Kasha varnishkes

- ¼ cup Chicken Schmaltz (page 5) or 2 tablespoons vegetable oil
- 2 medium yellow onions, thinly sliced
- 2 cups Homemade Chicken Broth (page 4) or canned low-sodium chicken broth
- 1 cup medium or coarse kasha
- 1 large egg, lightly beaten
- 2 tablespoons plus 1 teaspoon kosher salt
- ¼ teaspoon freshly ground black pepper
- 8 ounces fresh varnishkes (page 46)
- 5 tablespoons chopped fresh flat-leaf parsley

To make the sauce, melt the schmaltz in a medium saucepan over medium-high heat. Add the mushrooms and onion and cook, stirring occasionally, until the mushrooms have released their liquid and it has evaporated and the onion is very tender and golden brown, 10 to 12 minutes. Stir in the flour until it is dissolved, about 1 minute. Add the wine and stir to release any browned bits on the bottom of the pan. Cook until the wine has reduced by half, about 3 minutes. Stir in the chicken broth, thyme, salt, pepper, and paprika. Bring the mixture to a boil. Decrease the heat to medium-low and simmer to allow the sauce to thicken and the flavors to meld, about 20 minutes. Adjust the seasoning with salt and pepper to taste. Cover and keep the sauce hot over low heat.

To make the *kasha varnishkes*, melt the schmaltz in a large saucepan or skillet with a lid over medium-high heat. Add the onions and cook, uncovered, stirring frequently, until golden brown, about 15 minutes. Pour in the chicken broth, stir the bottom of the pot to release any browned bits, and bring it to a simmer.

Meanwhile, place a dry sauté pan over medium-high heat. Mix together the kasha and egg in a small bowl, then pour the mixture into the hot pan. Using a fork or wooden spoon, spread out the egg-coated kasha, and then stir, breaking it up into individual grains as the egg dries and the kasha becomes lightly toasted and aromatic, 2 to 3 minutes. Immediately add the kasha to the simmering chicken broth. Add 1 teaspoon of the salt and the pepper. Cover the pan, decrease the heat to medium-low, and cook until the kasha is tender, 12 to 15 minutes. Lower the heat to low to keep it hot.

Fill a large pot with 3 quarts water, add the remaining 2 tablespoons salt, and bring it to a boil over high heat. Add the *varnishkes* and stir briefly to prevent the pasta from sticking together. Boil until the pasta is just tender, about 1 minute. Drain well and add the *varnishkes* to the pan with the kasha. Sprinkle in 3 tablespoons of the parsley and gently stir to thoroughly combine the ingredients. Serve immediately in warmed bowls with the mushroom sauce spooned over the top. Garnish with the remaining 2 tablespoons parsley.

Both the *kasha varnishkes* and the sauce can be made up to 3 days in advance and refrigerated, separately, in covered containers. Reheat both on the stovetop over medium heat. Add about ¼ cup more chicken broth to the *kasha varnishkes* if it is dry. If you plan to prepare it in advance, it is best to wait to add the parsley until after it is reheated and just before serving.

Ginger- and Orange-Glazed Carrot and Fruit Tzimmes

Serves 4

This slow-cooked root vegetable stew echoes the common Ashkenazic theme of turning cheap and abundant ingredients into a flavor-charged, rib-sticking meal in a pot. In this case, the common foundation is the humble carrot. Over the generations, tzimmes has become a staple dish served on Rosh Hashanah, the Jewish New Year. The understandable rap on tzimmes is that it's too often sickly sweet. We have put that problem to rest by using fresh orange juice and just a touch of honey for a complex tart sweetness, along with adding a generous dose of fresh ginger, pepper, and dried cherries or cranberries along with the more traditional prunes. Serve as a side dish with meat or poultry.

1 pound carrots, trimmed, peeled, and diagonally cut into ¼-inch-thick slices

½ cup freshly squeezed orange juice

2 teaspoons honey

3 slices peeled fresh ginger

1 (2-inch) cinnamon stick, broken in half

½ teaspoon black peppercorns

½ teaspoon kosher salt

½ cup pitted prunes

⅓ cup dried cherries or cranberries

Place a heavy 2½- to 3-quart saucepan over medium heat and add the carrots, orange juice, honey, ginger, cinnamon, peppercorns, and salt. Stir in ½ cup water. Cover, bring to a boil, and then decrease the heat to low. Simmer until the carrots are tender, about 15 minutes.

Using a slotted spoon, scoop the carrots into a bowl. Remove and discard the peppercorns, ginger slices, and cinnamon stick. Leave the liquid in the pan. Cover the carrots and keep warm.

Increase the heat to medium and add the prunes and cherries to the saucepan. Cook until the liquid thickens to a thin syrup, 5 to 10 minutes. Add the carrots back to the pot, stirring to coat them and evenly distribute the fruit. Serve warm.

Mile End Delicatessen: The New Deli in New York City

Jewish deli culture has flourished in New York City for more than a century. The names famously associated with deli food are all here: Katz's, Carnegie, and 2nd Avenue Deli. The new kid on the block, literally and figuratively, is Mile End Deli, with its beginnings in Brooklyn and a second, sandwich shop location in Manhattan.

The original is a tiny place on a side street in the Boerum Hill neighborhood, where young, upper-middle-class families mix with an even younger hipster crowd, and galleries, pubs, and restaurants abound. Mile End's setup is comprised of three communal tables, each optimistically seating six, and a counter adjacent to the narrow open kitchen that hosts five more. Tables and counter were crafted from a repurposed bowling alley, the thud of balls and clatter of pins having given way to the cluck and chatter of satisfied diners. The Manhattan venue is everything the original is not: sleek, modern, and angular. Plus, you eat your sandwiches standing. The setup may not make everyone happy, but it's probably good for digestion—and no one's complaining about the food.

The husband and wife proprietors are Noah Bernamoff and Rae Cohen, though manager Zack Fishman holds forth happily on the quirks of brisket. He explains that Mile End uses all the parts, including the fattier deckle, to create Bernamoff's signature Montreal smoked meat. A kissing cousin to pastrami, Mile End's smoked meat is dry-cured with one rub, soaked in water, then generously rubbed with a spice mixture heavy on cloves. It's served in sandwiches and, optionally, as part of a crazy Montreal specialty called poutine that combines French fries, cheese curds, and gravy.

Discussion yields to my dinner: "schmaltzed" corn on the cob, with chile, lime, and dill dominating the palate, a new-wave idea for sure. Like a good Jewish mother, the kitchen insists on sending out a flurry of additional tastes from the menu: smoked turkey rillettes tempered with sweet-tart apricot jam; pickled belly lox with onion and dill, an adaptation of traditional pickled herring; fried baby artichokes, a classic Mediterranean-Jewish preparation; and a hot dog, crafted in-house using ground brisket and a touch of maple syrup, enclosed in a snappy beef casing.

Bernamoff and Cohen are a handsome young couple who met as students at McGill University. She's a dark-haired New Yorker with glasses and an easy smile. He's a Montreal native, tall and voluble. Bernamoff decided to move beyond

cooking as a hobby and become a deli owner after disillusionment with law school and the prospect of a typecast career and lifestyle. Cohen didn't see herself joining the business, but that changed when the recession of 2008 dealt a hammer blow to her museum job.

Once Bernamoff got his smoked meat recipe down and was able to rent "the cheapest location I could find," Mile End opened in 2010 with no thought about Jewish deli revivalism. The philosophical piece has come in hindsight. He explains that he wants to "expose Jewish cooking and demonstrate Jewish culture in a non-nostalgic way." Cohen is even more succinct. The goal at Mile End, she says, is to "honor the craft of Jewish cookery."

Chinese Broccoli

Serves 3 or 4

Secular American Jews have long had an affinity for Chinese food, perhaps because Chinese restaurants tended historically to be the only ones open on Sundays and major Christian holidays. In a tongue-in-cheek nod to the longstanding Jewish-Chinese culinary association, our friends from Mile End Deli in New York City created this recipe and passed it along to us. It combines a multitude of ingredients most easily sourced from an Asian grocery store. The beef salami adds a bit of protein and an unmistakable Jewish deli attitude to the sturdy stalks of Chinese broccoli. As an alternative, substitute pastrami for the salami. As unfamiliar as it might be, we think our forebears would approve.

1 pound Chinese broccoli (kai-lan or gai-lan), trimmed and cut into 2-inch pieces

2 tablespoons plus 2 teaspoons canola or other neutral oil

1 teaspoon minced fresh ginger

1 teaspoon minced fresh garlic

1 teaspoon minced shallots

¼ cup finely chopped beef salami

Kosher salt

½ cup Homemade Chicken Broth (page 4) or canned low-sodium chicken broth

2 tablespoons hoisin sauce

1 tablespoon rice wine vinegar

1 teaspoon chili sauce (preferably sriracha)

2 large eggs

1 cup fresh croutons, preferably from challah

Korean chili flakes or crushed red pepper (optional)

Store-bought pickled carrot rounds (optional)

Bring a large pot of salted water to a boil over high heat. Have ready a large bowl of ice water, along with tongs or a slotted spoon. Cook the broccoli until it turns bright green but is still very crisp, about 1½ minutes. Immediately transfer the broccoli to the ice water to stop the cooking. As soon as it is cool, transfer to a plate lined with a double thickness of paper towels and blot completely dry.

Heat a wok or large sauté pan over high heat. When the pan is hot, add 2 tablespoons of the oil. Quickly add the ginger, garlic, and shallots. Using a wok spatula or large wooden spoon, stir-fry the aromatics just until fragrant, 10 seconds. Immediately add the salami and stir-fry until the salami begins to crisp, about 20 seconds. Carefully add the broccoli to the pan along with a pinch of salt. Stir-fry for 30 seconds. Add the chicken broth, hoisin sauce, vinegar, and chili sauce. Stir-fry to evenly coat the broccoli. Continue to cook until the sauce is reduced and thickened, about 1 minute. Taste the sauce and add another pinch of salt, if desired. Remove from the heat and keep warm.

Place a small frying pan over medium-high heat and add the remaining 2 teaspoons oil. Fry the eggs until the whites have just coagulated and the yolks are warm and runny.

Scatter the croutons evenly on the bottom of a warm bowl or deep platter. Using a slotted spoon, arrange the broccoli over the top. Spoon the sauce evenly over the top. Carefully place the fried eggs on top of the broccoli. Garnish with chili flakes, if desired. Serve warm along with pickled carrots, if desired.

Chopped Chicken Liver

Serves 6

In the Slavic shtetls of Eastern Europe, 150 years before "nose-to-tail eating" became a mantra among big-name chefs, full utilization of animals was driven by dietary necessity rather than political economy. Chopped chicken livers—chopped liver for short—have been part of the Ashkenazic diet going back to the sixteenth century. Traditionally enriched with schmaltz, chopped liver has been a stalwart on Jewish delicatessen menus and American Passover tables since the late 1800s. You may substitute oil, shortening, or butter for the schmaltz, though the taste won't be nearly as luxurious or authentic. Use as a spread on crackers, matzo, or bread, or serve on its own with fresh or pickled vegetables.

⅓ cup plus 1 tablespoon Chicken Schmaltz (page 5)
1 pound chicken livers, trimmed of connective tissue
2 teaspoons kosher salt
1 teaspoon freshly ground black pepper
1 cup Caramelized Onions (page 8)
1 tablespoon red wine vinegar
4 large hard-boiled eggs
1 cup chopped Gribenes (page 5; optional)

Place 1 tablespoon of the schmaltz in a medium to large skillet set over medium heat. (Allow the remaining schmaltz to come to room temperature.) Add the livers, salt, and pepper to the skillet. Sauté the livers, flipping after 5 minutes, until they are just browned, about 10 minutes altogether.

Remove the pan from the heat and add the onions and vinegar, mixing thoroughly. Let cool to room temperature.

Place the eggs in the work bowl of a food processor fitted with the metal blade. Add the *gribenes*, if desired. Use three short pulses (each pulse taking about the time it takes to say "chopped liver") to coarsely chop the eggs. Transfer the chopped eggs to a large bowl.

Add the liver and onion mixture to the food processor along with the remaining ⅓ cup schmaltz. Use four to five one second pulses to coarsely chop the liver. The liver should be chopped a bit more finely than the eggs, but not pureed, so the end result is not too dense.

Transfer the liver-onion mixture to the bowl with the eggs and fold the liver into the eggs until thoroughly combined. Season with salt to taste. Transfer to a covered container and refrigerate for up to 3 days.

Triple-Cooked French Fries

Serves 4 to 6

Yes, we know that French fries are not Jewish food. They are so popular, though, that they have found their way into modern deli culture. At Kenny & Zuke's, they are available with nearly any sandwich and are the foundation for one of the deli's most popular guilty pleasure foods: Kenny & Zuke's Pastrami Cheese Fries (page 56). For this recipe, we rely on an axiom that every French fry expert worth his or her salt endorses: precooking the cut-up potatoes before immersing them in their finishing hot oil bath results in a superior French fry. These fries are cooked first in boiling water to leach away excess starch and are then fried twice. The result is crispy and nearly greaseless on the outside and creamy and fluffy inside. If you enjoy them as much as we do (with or without pastrami and cheese), consider making extra-large batches and storing some or all by following the recipe through the first frying, then freezing the potato slices on a baking sheet and storing them frozen in serving-size portions until needed.

2 pounds Russet potatoes (3 large or 4 medium)
2 tablespoons kosher salt, plus more for sprinkling
2 tablespoons distilled white vinegar
Canola or peanut oil, for frying

Peel the potatoes and place them in a large bowl of ice water to keep them from discoloring while you cut individual potatoes into fries. Cut the potatoes into ¼- to ⅜-inch-thick fries, discarding any smaller pieces. (The smaller pieces can be used, but they may burn or become overly soft.) Place the fries in the ice water until ready to use.

In a 3- to 4-quart pot, bring the salt, vinegar, and 8 cups water to a boil over high heat. Add the potatoes and simmer until tender but still sturdy, 10 to 15 minutes. Using tongs or a larger skimmer, transfer the potatoes to baking sheets lined with a double thickness of paper towels; arrange in a single layer and allow them to dry.

Meanwhile, fill a heavy, 4-quart (or larger) pot with 3 inches of oil and heat the oil to 390°F over high heat. (For safety's sake, it is important that the oil be no more than halfway up the pot so that when the potatoes are frying, the oil does not spill over the edge of the pot and catch on fire.) Use a large slotted spoon or wide-mesh skimmer (also known as a spider) to lower a small batch of potatoes into the oil. Do not crowd the pot. Fry for 1 minute, stirring as necessary to prevent the potatoes from sticking together. Transfer to a baking sheet lined with a double thickness of paper towels. Repeat until all the potatoes are fried. (Decrease the heat to low or turn the heat off if not immediately frying the potatoes again. Once the potatoes are cool, they can be refrigerated or frozen until ready to use.)

When ready to serve, bring the oil back to 390°F, if necessary. Fry the potatoes in small batches until crisp and golden, about 4 minutes. Using a large slotted spoon or spider, lift the potatoes from the oil, letting as much excess oil as possible drain off the potatoes and back into the pot. Transfer the fries to a large bowl and toss with a generous pinch of salt. Serve immediately, or keep warm in a low oven for no more than 10 minutes.

Kenny & Zuke's Pastrami Cheese Fries

Serves 4 to 6

When Nick used to work the late shift soon after Kenny & Zuke's opened, he and the cooks sometimes had a few minutes to indulge their deli food fantasies. This decadent combination of French fries, smoky pastrami, and oozy melted cheese was at first shared with envious customers who happened to notice the insider feeding frenzies, then added to the menu by popular demand. This is a great dude dish for TV sports get-togethers and other occasions when calorie counting and restraint give way to bonhomie and shameless noshing. We prefer to use Swiss cheese because it and the pastrami (with the Russian dressing dip) mimic the key components of a Reuben sandwich. Good-quality pastrami from your favorite deli or grocery store can be used in place of homemade. You may also substitute store-bought French fries; if using them, look for those that include rice flour in the ingredients, as they tend to be crispier than those without.

2 pounds freshly cooked Triple-Cooked French Fries (page 55)
12 ounces Home-Oven Pastrami (page 142), cut into bite-size pieces
4 ounces Swiss cheese, grated (about 2 cups)
Russian Dressing (page 24), for dipping

Preheat the oven to 450°F.

Place half the cooked fries in a single, dense layer on a rimmed baking sheet. Top with half the pastrami and then half the cheese. Place another layer of fries on top of the first layer and top with the remaining pastrami followed by the remaining cheese.

Bake until both layers of cheese are fully melted, about 5 minutes. Transfer to a warmed serving bowl or platter and serve hot with a side of Russian dressing.

Delicates

$11.50 LB.

2.95 LB.

MI $6.50 LB.

I $8.99 LB.

$5.99 LB.

Soup and Salad

Wild Mushroom and Kreplach Soup

Matzo Ball Soup

Green Sorrel Spring Borscht

Cold Beet and Raspberry Summer Bo

Autumn Cabbage and Smoked Meat B

Caplansky's Beet and Braised Beef W

Curried Lentil and Sweet Potato Soup

Mushroom-Barley Soup

Hungarian Mushroom Soup

Tangy Potato Salad

Caper and Red Onion Potato Salad

Latke Salad

Hungarian Casino Egg Salad

Russian Egg Salad

Seasonal Chicken Salad

Spring Chicken Salad with Peas, F

Chapter 3

The rap on Jewish deli food is that it is heavy and fatty. Some dishes fit that description, but plenty of others suit lighter, more health-conscious diets, especially the offerings we have adapted from modern Jewish deli menus that favor quality over mass quantities.

Many of the soups and salads in this chapter have been around for generations, with origins in the Slavic countries where Ashkenazic Jews once lived in large numbers. Often impoverished, the Ashkenazis who opened the original Jewish delicatessens in North America preferred filling dishes—including soups and salads—that relied on abundant, inexpensive ingredients. The Deli Health Salad (page 97) is a typical Eastern European salat that would be welcome on any self-respecting New York deli table. The Russian Egg Salad (page 79) returns boring picnic fare to its flavorful origins. Borscht is a prime example of Ashkenazic traditions recovered and reenvisioned. We have updated the traditional basic beet broth to reflect today's popular and sensible seasonal eating patterns. So when the summer sun is high, our Cold Beet and Raspberry Borscht (page 69) is a terrific sweet-tart treat, and at the opposite end of the seasonal spectrum, a beefy hearty winter borscht (page 72) is sure to instill a warm inner glow as it fills up the fortunate diners at your table. Our Classic Chicken Salad on page 82 also gets the seasonal treatment with four variations (pages 84–87) perfect for any time of the year.

Some popular deli dishes will never need updating. We offer two chicken soup alternatives: traditional (and filling) Matzo Ball Soup (page 64) and Wild Mushroom and Kreplach Soup (page 61), each of which relies on our rich and intense Homemade Chicken Broth (page 4) as a foundation. On the other hand, innovation is a calling card for today's deli dining—and for our selection of recipes. For fun and great flavor, don't pass on the Latke Salad (page 78). Whatever you choose, rest assured that every recipe from this chapter will keep well in the refrigerator for at least a day or two after it's made—that is, in the unlikely event there are leftovers.

Wild Mushroom and Kreplach Soup

Serves 4

For a heartier, updated version of a basic chicken soup recipe, use this red meat–free adaptation of the more common meat-filled kreplach (page 22). Our rich chicken broth gets an umami bump from earthy dried mushrooms in the broth and chopped fresh button or cremini mushrooms in the ravioli-like kreplach.

8 cups Homemade Chicken Broth (page 4) or canned low-sodium chicken broth

Kosher salt

All-purpose flour, for dusting

4 ounces Dough for Kreplach (page 18), cut into 24 (2½-inch) squares

¼ cup Mushroom kreplach filling (page 20)

1 ounce dried wild mushrooms (porcini, morel, chanterelle, or a mix)

1 carrot, thinly sliced

4 small tender sprigs fresh thyme

Bring the chicken broth to a simmer in a covered saucepan over medium heat. Add salt to taste and keep warm over low heat.

Bring a large pot of salted water to a boil over high heat. Lower the heat so the water just simmers.

Meanwhile, make the kreplach. Set a small bowl of water near your work space and lightly flour a baking sheet. Working with 6 to 8 squares of kreplach dough at a time, orient them on an angle into diamond-shape squares. Place ½ teaspoon of the mushroom filling in the center of each square. Dip an index finger into the water, quickly shaking off the excess. Run your finger along the outer edges on the top half of the square of dough, wetting it. Fold over the dough to make a triangle. Press the dough edges together, removing any air pockets from around the filling and sealing the edges by pressing down firmly against the work surface. Press the tines of a fork down into the edge of the pasta dough until the entire edge has been sealed with the fork. As you finish each kreplach, set it aside on the baking sheet. Repeat to fill and seal the remaining kreplach.

To cook the kreplach, gently drop the kreplach into the simmering water along with the dried mushrooms, increasing the heat to maintain a low boil. Cook for 5 minutes, stirring occasionally to prevent the kreplach from sticking to each other. Add the sliced carrot, return to a low boil, and cook for 10 more minutes.

For each serving, ladle 2 cups chicken broth into a warmed soup bowl. Add 6 kreplach and a portion of the mushrooms and carrot slices to each bowl. Garnish with a sprig of thyme.

What Are . . . Matzo Balls?

When my teenage daughter was little, she asked a lot of questions. Mostly it was about life's small wonders, such as magnets and sports teams' jersey colors. With a food-obsessed father, her inquiries soon turned to culinary matters, including the strange range of breadless wonders served at our family's annual Passover dinner.

For the uninitiated, Passover is the Jewish holiday that primarily celebrates the Israelites' successful—and biblical rumor has it, miraculous, escape from Egypt through a divided Red Sea, eluding their unhappy Egyptian slave masters. As the story goes according to the Passover Haggadah, the Israelites were in such a big hurry that they didn't even have time to let their bread rise, leading to the invention of matzo, cakes comprised of nothing more than flour and water, quickly baked under the glare of the desert sun.

To commemorate the occasion, observant Jews have for centuries eaten no leavened products during Passover. And at the traditional Passover seder—a ritualized meal and reading of the Haggadah—families eat foods that follow this dietary rule as they read the holiday story, sing, and pray. In my family, it's always been mainly about the meal. Which brings us to matzo balls, also known as knaidlach, the Yiddish diminutive for "dumpling."

The ever-resourceful Ashkenazis—frequently impoverished and living in climates that offered little in the way of easy sustenance—always found ways to stay full and content. The doughy dumpling filled the bill, as an accompaniment to bits of inexpensive protein and an extender of soups—a way to stretch limited food resources. Passover time was an obstacle to consuming the usual dumplings, and the matzo ball was the logical answer to the Ashkenazis' holiday dilemma.

According to Gil Marks's exhaustive *Encyclopedia of Jewish Food*, the first recorded English recipe for matzo balls was published in 1846. The ingredients were ground matzo, eggs, fat, and seasonings, plus a little onion—not all that different from current versions. Beef suet was the fat of choice in that early recipe, though schmaltz, or rendered chicken fat, is truer to the Ashkenazic tradition (and socioeconomic status), in which chickens were far more common and easier to look after than cows. As mass production of matzo meal became possible with mechanization, matzo balls in chicken soup have moved from the Passover table to become a quintessential Jewish deli dish.

This leads to the ultimate question: Which are better, matzo balls that bob buoy-like atop the chicken broth ("floaters") or denser versions that promptly drop to the bottom of the bowl on introduction to the soup ("sinkers"). This is an endless multigenerational, interfamilial debate with no clear winner. Each type is easily enough accomplished: floaters by including more fat in the mix and using a lighter hand in forming the ball, sinkers with less fat and greater compression. Neither is objectively better—or more authentic, for that matter—than the other. As Marks sagely observes, "preference is almost always based on childhood memories" of what your mother or grandmother made. Those who lack any hereditary bias are encouraged to experiment, then join the fray.

—MCZ

Matzo Ball Soup

Serves 4

With its claimed restorative powers, this timeless deli classic is frequently referred to—only half in jest—as "Jewish penicillin." These matzo balls avoid the "sinkers versus floaters" debate and steer a safe middle course, benefiting from a little schmaltz, egg whites, and baking soda for a texture everyone can embrace.

1 cup matzo meal

¼ teaspoon baking powder

¼ teaspoon freshly ground black pepper

Kosher or sea salt

4 large eggs, separated

8¼ cups Homemade Chicken Broth (page 4) or canned low-sodium chicken broth

¼ cup Chicken Schmaltz (page 5)

1 tablespoon finely chopped fresh flat-leaf parsley

2 medium carrots, thinly sliced (about 1 cup)

2 cups shredded poached or roasted chicken (about 8 ounces)

4 teaspoons chopped fresh dill

To make the matzo balls, in a small bowl, stir together the matzo meal, baking powder, pepper, and 1 teaspoon salt. In a medium bowl, whisk the egg whites until stiff peaks form. Gently fold the matzo meal mixture into the egg whites. In another small bowl, whisk together the egg yolks, ¼ cup of the chicken broth, the schmaltz, and parsley. Gently fold the egg yolk mixture into the egg white mixture until thoroughly combined. Cover the matzo ball dough tightly with plastic wrap and refrigerate until the dough is firm enough to shape into balls, at least 1 hour or overnight.

Fill a large, wide pot with at least 3 inches of water and bring to a boil over high heat. Add ½ teaspoon salt for every 1 cup water. Adjust the heat so the water just simmers.

Meanwhile, remove the matzo ball dough from the refrigerator. Fill a small bowl half full of cool water and have ready for dipping your hands while making the matzo balls. (Wet hands will keep the dough from sticking to your fingers and palms.) To form the matzo balls, use a soupspoon to scoop up about 2 tablespoons of the dough. With wet hands, form the dough into a golf ball–size dumpling. Using a slotted spoon, gently place the ball into the simmering water. Continue to form additional balls with the remaining dough. There should be enough dough to form about 12 matzo balls total. Add the matzo balls to the simmering water as you form them. Cover the pot and simmer for 1 hour. The matzo balls can be served immediately. Alternatively, drain the matzo balls and place them on a rimmed baking sheet. Cover tightly with plastic wrap and refrigerate for up to 2 days. Reheat the matzo balls by cooking them in a pot of simmering water until heated through, about 10 minutes.

While the matzo balls are cooking, make the soup. Bring the remaining 8 cups chicken broth to a simmer and add salt to taste. Add the carrots and cook until tender, about 10 minutes. Add the shredded chicken to the broth, heat through, and then remove from the heat. To serve, arrange 3 matzo balls in each warmed soup bowl. Ladle about 2 cups of hot broth over the top, and divide the carrots and chicken evenly among the bowls. Garnish each with 1 teaspoon dill and serve immediately.

Curried Lentil and Sweet Potato Soup

Serves 4

It's nearly impossible to find a Jewish foods cookbook—or respectable deli—that doesn't showcase a lentil soup. This version adds lemon juice for a bright note, and sweet potato for body and sweetness, plus curry powder for an extra kick. Though you might think of curry as an oddball addition to a Jewish dish, it is a recurring component in Jewish cooking, documented back at least to the mid-twentieth century. This recipe also echoes the legume-based soups from the Indian subcontinent, where curries are basic to the culinary culture.

- 2 tablespoons extra-virgin olive oil
- ½ large yellow onion, finely chopped
- 2 tablespoons curry powder
- 1 bay leaf
- 1¼ cups brown lentils, picked through, rinsed, and drained
- 2 cloves garlic, peeled and minced
- 2 dark-orange-fleshed sweet potatoes, peeled and finely chopped (4 cups)
- 1 tablespoon granulated sugar
- 2 teaspoons kosher salt
- Juice of 1 lemon

Place a large Dutch oven or soup pot over medium heat and add the oil. When the oil begins to shimmer, add the onion and cook, stirring occasionally, until soft and translucent, about 10 minutes. Stir in the curry powder and bay leaf, coating the onion evenly, and sauté until fragrant, about 1 minute. Add the lentils and garlic, stirring to coat the lentils with the curry, about 30 seconds, and then add 5 cups water. Increase the heat to high and bring the mixture to a boil. Cover the pot, decrease the heat to low, and simmer for 25 minutes.

Add the sweet potatoes, sugar, and salt, stirring to combine, and then bring the soup back to a boil over medium-high heat. Decrease the heat to low, cover, and simmer until the sweet potatoes are tender but not falling apart, about 20 minutes. Stir in the lemon juice. Taste and adjust the seasoning. Serve immediately.

Seasonal Borschts

With origins in the Ukraine and deep roots throughout Central and Eastern Europe, traditional borscht is readily identified as a tangy, deep purple-red beet soup that can be served hot or cold. Impoverished Ashkenazic Jews naturally adopted borscht as part of their basic diet since beets tended to be cheap and abundant. Variations on the basic beet-based broth typically picked up tartness from different souring agents—*zoyers* in Yiddish—and depth from whatever meat and bones might be available to enrich the soup. The four borscht versions included here find their respective directions from ingredients commonly available with the cycle of the seasons.

Green Sorrel Spring Borscht

Serves 6

Borscht and beets may seem inseparable, but that has not always been the case. In early medieval times, even before beets were common in the more northerly climes of Eastern and Central Europe, the family soup pot would be filled with any root vegetables and greens that could be foraged close to home. The traditional Ukrainian green borscht evolved to rely on parsnips, potato, and sorrel, an herb that adds a delicate lemony flavor and greenish hue to the soup.

- 2 tablespoons extra-virgin olive oil
- 1 large leek (white and light green parts), halved lengthwise and thinly sliced
- 1 medium yellow onion, finely diced
- 2 large cloves garlic, minced
- 2 large Yukon Gold potatoes, peeled and cut into ½-inch dice
- 2 small carrots, halved lengthwise and thinly sliced into half-moons
- 1 medium parsnip, peeled, halved lengthwise, and thinly sliced into half-moons
- 4 cups Homemade Chicken Broth (page 4) or canned low-sodium chicken broth
- 1½ teaspoons kosher salt
- 1 teaspoon minced fresh thyme
- ¼ teaspoons freshly ground black pepper
- 2 tablespoons chopped fresh flat-leaf parsley
- 2 tablespoons chopped fresh dill
- 2 tablespoon minced fresh chives
- 8 ounces sorrel, trimmed, stems discarded, and leaves coarsely chopped (about 8 cups)
- 3 to 6 soft-boiled eggs (optional)

In a large soup pot, heat the oil over medium-low. Add the leek and onion and cook, stirring occasionally, until they are very sweet and extremely soft but not brown, about 20 minutes. Decrease the heat to low after about 10 minutes of cooking to prevent browning. Stir in the garlic and cook for 1 minute longer. Add the potatoes, carrots, parsnip, chicken broth, salt, thyme, and pepper. Raise the heat to medium-high and bring the broth to a boil, and then lower the heat to medium-low and simmer, stirring occasionally, until the vegetables are just tender, 10 to 12 minutes.

Meanwhile, in a small bowl, mix together the parsley, dill, and chives. Stir half of the herb mixture into the soup and all of the sorrel; the sorrel should wilt into the soup within a few seconds. Adjust the seasoning with salt and pepper to taste.

Cut the soft-boiled eggs, if using, in half lengthwise, and season each half with salt. Portion the soup into warmed bowls and add 1 or 2 egg halves to each bowl. Garnish with the remaining herb mixture and serve immediately.

Cold Beet and Raspberry Summer Borscht

Serves 4

This borscht variation exemplifies the melding of tradition and seasonality. The raspberries add a fruity roundness to the soup's usual sweet-tart flavor. When they are available—typically peak summer in the Pacific Northwest—substitute supersized loganberries, tayberries, or any red cane berry in place of the raspberries.

- 6 medium beets, trimmed
- 1 pound fresh or frozen raspberries, plus 2 cups pristine fresh raspberries
- 4 allspice berries
- 2 whole cloves
- 2 tablespoons sugar
- 2 teaspoons kosher salt
- Juice and finely grated zest of 2 lemons
- 1 large cucumber, ends trimmed, halved lengthwise, seeds removed, and finely chopped
- ½ cup sour cream
- 4 fresh baby dill fronds, torn into small pieces

Peel and coarsely grate 2 of the beets. Add them, along with 8 cups water and ½ pound of the fresh or frozen raspberries, to a large pot set over medium-high heat. Bring to a boil, and then stir in the allspice, cloves, sugar, and salt. Decrease the heat to low, and simmer, covered, for 30 minutes. Remove from the heat and set aside, uncovered, to cool until still warm to the touch, about 30 minutes.

Add the remaining ½ pound fresh or frozen raspberries to the pot. Working in batches, puree the soup in a blender, being sure to include some of the solids along with plenty of liquid in each batch. Pour through a fine-mesh strainer set over a bowl. Discard the solids and transfer the soup to a container with a tight-fitting lid. Stir in the lemon juice. Refrigerate until cold, about 4 hours. (The soup can be made up to this point and refrigerated up to 2 days.)

While the soup is chilling, place the 4 remaining beets in a medium saucepan and add enough water to cover the beets by 2 inches. Put the pot over medium heat and slowly bring to a boil. Turn the heat to low and simmer until the point of a knife easily pierces the beets, about 1 hour. Drain off the hot water and run cold water over the beets until they are cool enough to handle. Peel the beets, and then thinly slice and chop them into bite-size pieces. Transfer to a covered container and refrigerate until ready to serve.

When ready to serve, ladle the soup into 4 chilled soup bowls. Evenly distribute the chopped beets, cucumber, and pristine whole raspberries over the top. Garnish each bowl with a large dollop of sour cream, a little lemon zest, and the fresh dill. Serve immediately.

Autumn Cabbage and Smoked Meat Borscht

Serves 10 to 12

That wild and crazy Zane Caplansky loves his Montreal smoked meat (even though his deli, Caplansky's, is in Toronto—go figure). We have adapted one of his updated Jewish deli classics to suit our cycle of seasonal borschts. This beet-free version captures the spirit of autumn, since that's when those giant heads of cabbage overflow the local markets. The smoked meat (or, outside Canada, nearly identical pastrami) is yummy and available anytime, of course. The quantities of vinegar and sugar called for in the recipe are not typos—don't be alarmed. This is supposed to be a knock-your-socks-off sweet-and-sour stew that's a party-size meal in a bowl.

1 small green cabbage (about 1½ pounds)
2 tablespoons canola or other neutral oil
1 large white onion, thinly sliced
4 large cloves garlic, minced
2 teaspoons kosher salt
1 pound pastrami (or smoked meat), diced
1 (28-ounce) can diced tomatoes, drained
1 cup distilled white vinegar
⅔ cup firmly packed light brown sugar

Cut the cabbage into quarters lengthwise through the core. Trim out and discard the core from each quarter. Cut the cabbage crosswise into thin slices.

Heat the oil in a large pot over medium-high heat. Add the cabbage, onion, garlic, and salt and stir to coat the vegetables in the oil. Pour in ½ cup water and cook, covered, stirring occasionally, until the cabbage and onion are tender, 12 to 15 minutes.

Stir in the pastrami, tomatoes, vinegar, and sugar. Pour in enough additional water to cover the mixture by about 1 inch and bring it to a boil over high heat. Decrease the heat to maintain a low simmer. Skim the foam that rises to the top of the borscht. Cook, uncovered, until the cabbage is very tender and the flavors come together, about 1 hour. Serve immediately, or refrigerate, covered, for up to 5 days.

Beet and Braised Beef Winter Borscht

Serves 6

When the days are short and cold, this winter elixir really hits the spot. The broth is bolstered by a bounty of shredded beef and red cabbage. A tart note comes from the addition of red wine vinegar. Try it as a "souper" starter or on its own as a light meal.

Broth

1 (2½- to 3-pound) 7-blade chuck roast

1 tablespoon vegetable oil

½ large yellow onion, chopped

4 cloves garlic, peeled

1 teaspoon dried thyme

1 teaspoon dried dill

1 teaspoon kosher salt

¼ cup red wine vinegar

12 ounces beets (about 2 large), trimmed, peeled, and grated

Soup

1½ pounds beets (about 4 large), trimmed

1 tablespoon vegetable oil

½ large yellow onion, chopped

½ head red cabbage (about 1 pound), shredded

2 teaspoons kosher salt

1 medium Russet potato (about 8 ounces), peeled, grated, and soaked in cold water to prevent browning

2 cloves garlic, finely chopped

2 carrots, coarsely grated

¾ cup red wine vinegar

1 small handful fresh baby dill (3 or 4 sprigs), plus more for garnish

Sour cream, for garnish (optional)

To make the broth, rinse and pat the chuck roast dry with paper towels. Place a 6-quart Dutch oven over medium-high heat, add the oil, and swirl to coat the bottom of the pan. When the oil begins to smoke, add the chuck roast to the pan and brown on both sides, about 5 minutes per side. Transfer the chuck roast to a large plate. Decrease the heat to medium, and then add the onion, garlic, thyme, dill, and salt. Sauté, stirring constantly, until the garlic is fragrant, about 30 seconds. Immediately pour the vinegar into the pan, and use a wooden spoon to scrape up any browned bits clinging to the bottom of the pan. Add the chuck roast back to the pan along with 6 cups water and the grated beets. Bring to a boil, cover, decrease the heat to low, and simmer until the meat is tender but not falling apart, about 2 hours.

Transfer the meat to a cutting board. Pour the broth through a fine-mesh strainer set over a large, clean saucepan, and then set aside. Shred the beef, discarding any bones and gristle, and set aside for use in the soup. Discard any remaining vegetable pieces. Wipe out the Dutch oven to use for the soup.

To make the soup, put the beets in a medium saucepan, add enough water to cover the beets by 2 inches, and bring to a boil over high heat. Lower the heat so the water just simmers, and cook the beets until tender when pierced with the tip of a knife, about 30 minutes. Drain off the water and set the beets aside until cool enough to handle, about 20 minutes. Slip the skins off the beets and grate them using the large holes on a box grater. Set aside.

Bring the strained broth to a low simmer over medium-low heat. Place the Dutch oven over medium heat and add the oil. When the oil begins to shimmer, add the onion. Sauté until it begins to soften, about 5 minutes. Add the cabbage and salt. Sauté the cabbage, stirring occasionally, until it begins to wilt, about 5 minutes. Meanwhile, drain the water from the grated potato and squeeze dry.

Add the garlic to the pan with the cabbage and sauté, stirring constantly, until fragrant, about 30 seconds. Add the potato, along with the grated carrots, grated beets, and shredded meat. Pour the simmering broth over the top and bring to a boil. Cover, decrease the heat to low, and simmer for 20 minutes. Stir in the vinegar and dill. Turn off the heat and leave covered for 5 minutes before serving to allow all the flavors to meld. Garnish each bowl with sour cream, if desired, and a small sprig of dill.

Mushroom-Barley Soup

Serves 8

Modern science teaches that in addition to salty, sour, sweet, and bitter, there is a fifth taste: umami. That's a Japanese term for a flavor that is sometimes described as "savory" or "meaty." But meats aren't the only food packed with umami savor. Mushrooms top the list of umami-intensive vegetables. This soup, richly textured with barley, will have carnivores swearing there's meat in the pot, while vegans will celebrate that there isn't.

2 tablespoons canola or other neutral oil

1½ pounds cremini or button mushrooms, stem ends trimmed and sliced

Kosher salt

1 medium white onion, finely diced

1 tablespoon dried thyme

1 bay leaf

3 tablespoons porcini mushroom powder (see Sources and Resources, page 240)

1 tablespoon minced garlic

1 cup pearl barley

4 medium carrots, diced (about 3 cups)

½ cup chopped fresh flat-leaf parsley

¼ cup chopped fresh dill

Set a large Dutch oven or large, heavy pot over medium-high heat and add 1 tablespoon of the oil. When the oil begins to shimmer and smoke, add the mushrooms and ½ teaspoon salt. Cook, stirring occasionally, until the mushrooms are tender and lightly browned, about 10 minutes. Transfer the mushrooms to a plate and set aside.

Add the remaining 1 tablespoon oil to the pan and stir in the onion. Lower the heat to medium and cook, stirring occasionally, until the onion is translucent and soft, about 10 minutes. Add the thyme and bay leaf, sautéing until fragrant, about 30 seconds. Add the porcini powder, stirring to coat the onion. Add the garlic and the reserved mushrooms and sauté, stirring frequently, for 2 minutes. Stir in the barley and 8 cups water. Bring the mixture to a boil, decrease the heat to low, cover, and simmer for 30 minutes.

Stir in the carrots and cook, covered, until the barley is tender, about 30 minutes longer. Add the parsley and dill. Taste and adjust the seasoning. Serve immediately.

Hungarian Mushroom Soup

Serves 4 to 6

No, the mushrooms aren't from Hungary, but paprika is a traditional Hungarian flavoring. Though in Hungary the word refers broadly to all peppers, paprika here in the United States is a dried and powdered form of red chile peppers. Dark, earthy, and pungent smoked paprika lends depth and complexity, while bright red cayenne adds heat to this soup's creamy base. Sliced mushrooms and bits of chopped red pepper complete a rich and delicious presentation that differs little from what Hungarians have been enjoying for generations.

- 4 tablespoons (½ stick) unsalted butter
- 1 large yellow onion, finely chopped
- 2 large red bell peppers, cored, seeds and ribs removed, and finely chopped
- 2 pounds button or cremini mushrooms, stem ends trimmed and sliced
- 1 tablespoon kosher salt
- 3 tablespoons tomato paste
- 2 tablespoons Hungarian sweet paprika
- 1 tablespoon Hungarian smoked paprika
- 2 teaspoons dried dill
- 1 teaspoon dried thyme
- ¼ teaspoon cayenne pepper
- 4 cloves garlic, very finely chopped
- 8 cups half-and-half
- 3 tablespoons all-purpose flour
- ½ cup sour cream, plus more for garnish
- 6 sprigs fresh dill, for garnish

In a large Dutch oven or other heavy-bottomed pot set over medium heat, melt 2 tablespoons of the butter. Add the onion and bell peppers and sauté, stirring occasionally, until the onion is translucent and soft, about 10 minutes. Increase the heat to medium-high, and then stir in the mushrooms along with 1 teaspoon of the salt. Cook the mushrooms, stirring every few minutes, until they are tender and brown and have given up their liquid, 10 to 15 minutes.

Stir in the tomato paste, and then both paprikas, along with the dried dill, thyme, and cayenne. Stir until the mushrooms are evenly coated with the dark red paste. Continue to cook for another 3 minutes, stirring often to release the flavors and aromas of the herbs and spices. Stir in the garlic and cook until fragrant, about 30 seconds longer.

Pour all but ¼ cup of the half-and-half into the pot, stirring to dissolve any clumps of spices. Bring the soup to a simmer, but do not let it boil, continuing to stir as needed to keep any solids from sticking to the bottom of the pot.

Meanwhile, put the flour in a small bowl and slowly whisk in the remaining ¼ cup half-and-half. Whisk until smooth.

When the soup begins to simmer, slowly stir in the half-and-half mixture. Continue to stir to prevent any lumps from forming. Decrease the heat to low, cover the pot, and simmer, stirring every 5 minutes to prevent the soup from sticking to the bottom of the pot, until the flavors meld and the soup thickens, 30 minutes longer. Stir in the sour cream until smooth, and then add the remaining 2 teaspoons salt.

To serve, ladle the soup into warmed soup bowls and garnish with a dollop of sour cream and fresh dill.

Note: If you can't find smoked paprika, use additional sweet paprika as a substitute.

Tangy Potato Salad

Serves 6 to 8

Most modern American delis make a bland potato salad heavily dressed in mayonnaise. This picnic-quantity recipe borrows from the German tradition of dressing potatoes with vinegar for a tangier result, adding just a bit of the traditional mayonnaise and egg. Sour pickles and their juice add just a touch more puckery punch. The end result is a zesty but still creamy potato salad.

2 pounds red potatoes, cut into ¾-inch cubes
1 tablespoon plus ½ teaspoon kosher salt
¼ cup red wine vinegar
2 large hard-boiled eggs, finely diced
¼ medium red onion, finely diced
⅓ cup finely chopped sour dill pickles
2 teaspoons sour pickle juice from the pickle jar
⅓ cup mayonnaise
2 tablespoons whole-grain mustard
1 tablespoon freshly squeezed lemon juice
¼ cup finely chopped fresh flat-leaf parsley
2 tablespoons chopped fresh baby dill
Freshly ground black pepper

Place the potatoes in a large saucepan and cover with cold water by at least 3 inches. Stir in 1 tablespoon of the salt. Bring to a boil over high heat and cook until the potatoes are tender, about 10 minutes.

Drain the potatoes and transfer them to a large bowl. Add the vinegar and the remaining 1 teaspoon salt, stirring to evenly coat the potatoes. Set aside to cool for 10 minutes.

Add the eggs, onion, pickles, pickle juice, mayonnaise, mustard, lemon juice, parsley, and dill. Gently mix everything together, taking care not to smash the potatoes. Season to taste with salt and pepper.

Transfer the potato salad to a serving bowl or covered container. Serve warm, or refrigerate until cold. The potato salad will keep in the refrigerator for up to 3 days.

Caper and Red Onion Potato Salad

Serves 4 to 6

One taste of this super-tangy potato salad and you'll think twice about going back to your old mayonnaise-based version. The capers add a sharp-salty note. Pickled onions add their own special bite. And the herbs round out this full-flavored dish. Best of all, it's simple to make and a satisfying side dish for home or sharing at a summer potluck.

2 pounds new red or yellow potatoes

1 tablespoon plus ½ teaspoon kosher salt

¼ cup capers, drained

¾ cup Pickled Red Onions (page 9), drained, plus 1 tablespoon of the pickling liquid

1 tablespoon whole-grain or stone-ground mustard

2 tablespoons extra-virgin olive oil

2 tablespoons chopped fresh flat-leaf parsley

2 tablespoons chopped fresh dill

Cut the potatoes into ⅛- to ¼-inch-thick slices. Put in a large bowl filled with ice water to keep them from discoloring.

Fill a medium pot half full of water and bring to a boil over high heat. Add the 1 tablespoon of salt. Drain the potatoes and transfer them to the boiling water. Cook until tender but not falling apart when pierced with a fork, 7 to 10 minutes. Drain the potatoes thoroughly.

In a large bowl, combine the capers, pickled onions plus pickling liquid, the remaining ½ teaspoon salt, the mustard, olive oil, parsley, and dill. Add the potatoes and toss to evenly distribute, being careful to avoid breaking up the potatoes. Cover and refrigerate for at least 2 hours to chill and allow the flavors to meld. The potato salad will keep in the refrigerator for up to 3 days.

Latke Salad

Serves 4

Have leftovers from your Hanukkah celebration? Looking for an excuse to eat our Crispy Potato Latkes and call it a "salad?" Do we have the dish for you. It's a combination of chopped-up latkes and your favorite variety of crunchy-sweet apple, diced up and bound together with sour cream and accented with fresh dill. The end result is a modern classic to share with family and friends.

6 Crispy Potato Latkes (page 36)

1 large full-flavored apple (such as Jonagold, McIntosh, or Honeycrisp), chopped (about 2 cups)

1 tablespoon minced fresh dill

½ teaspoon kosher salt

⅛ teaspoon freshly ground black pepper

¼ cup sour cream

1 tablespoon milk

Coarsely chop the latkes and put them in a large bowl with any crispy crumbs that result from the chopping. Add the apple, dill, salt, and pepper.

In a small bowl, whisk together the sour cream and milk until smooth. Using a rubber spatula, gently fold the sour cream dressing into the latke-apple mixture until thoroughly combined.

Serve immediately, or cover and refrigerate until chilled.

Russian Egg Salad

Serves 4 to 6

This traditional egg salad—a variation of a dish common in Russia—is as much a breeze to make as it is a pleasure to eat. It is similar to, but has a different flavor profile than, the Hungarian Casino Egg Salad on page 81, which emphasizes the umami in the anchovies and capers. This salad balances the rich eggs with piquant and aromatic horseradish and dill. The simple list of ingredients is readily found at any neighborhood grocery store. For punch, use the hottest horseradish you can find. And if the eaters in your household prefer a less chunky salad, the whites of the hard-boiled eggs can be chopped to whatever consistency they prefer. Serve with lettuce and fresh vegetables as a salad, or make a terrific sandwich with lettuce and tomato on toast.

6 hard-boiled eggs, halved
¼ cup mayonnaise
2 teaspoons distilled white vinegar
¼ teaspoon salt
¼ teaspoon freshly ground black pepper
2 teaspoons finely chopped fresh dill
⅛ teaspoon prepared horseradish

Scoop the yolks from the halved eggs and put them in a medium bowl. Add the mayonnaise, vinegar, salt, and pepper. Whisk together until a creamy, smooth paste forms.

Coarsely chop the egg whites and add them to the bowl, along with the dill and horseradish. Fold the ingredients until thoroughly mixed.

Serve immediately, or cover and refrigerate until ready to serve. The egg salad can be made up to 3 days in advance.

Hungarian Casino Egg Salad

Serves 4 to 6

This egg salad supposedly originated with a chef who cooked for European royalty before a stint at the National Casino in Budapest, Hungary. Odds are you won't find this delicious dish on any Las Vegas or Atlantic City menu, but it is a sure bet for lunch or at the dinner hour. Butter and sour cream lend a rich foundation, but it's still lighter than a typical mayonnaise-based egg salad. And the anchovies add a hint of salt and briny depth. This is terrific served with lettuce and fresh vegetables as a salad, or with lettuce and tomato on toast as a sandwich.

- 6 hard-boiled eggs, halved
- 3 tablespoons unsalted butter, melted and cooled slightly
- 3 tablespoons sour cream
- 2 teaspoons distilled white vinegar
- ¼ teaspoon freshly ground black pepper
- 3 anchovy fillets packed in oil, drained and minced
- 1 tablespoon chopped capers
- 1 tablespoon snipped fresh chives
- 1 tablespoon finely chopped red onion or shallot

Scoop the yolks from the halved eggs and put them in a medium bowl. Add the butter, sour cream, vinegar, and pepper. Whisk together until a creamy, smooth paste forms.

Coarsely chop the egg whites and add them to the egg yolk mixture, along with the anchovies, capers, chives, and red onion. Gently fold the ingredients until fully mixed.

Serve immediately, or cover and refrigerate until ready to serve. The egg salad can be made up to 3 days in advance.

Classic Chicken Salad

Serves 4

For this updated traditional deli dish, shredding the chicken once it is cooked and cooled gives the best texture to the finished salad. A lighter hand with the mayonnaise means that dieters shouldn't be afraid to try at least a little. Be judicious with the horseradish, or leave it out altogether if you prefer. A little goes a long way.

1 pound boneless, skinless chicken breasts, trimmed of fat

2 tablespoons plus ½ teaspoon kosher salt

¼ medium yellow or white onion, minced

2 celery stalks with leaves, leaves chopped and ribs cut into ¼-inch dice

3 tablespoons mayonnaise

½ to 1 teaspoon prepared horseradish (optional)

⅛ teaspoon freshly ground black pepper

Juice of 1 small lemon

Place the chicken breasts in a medium saucepan and add enough cold water to cover the chicken by 2 inches. Add 2 tablespoons of the salt. Measure 2 tablespoons of the onion and set aside. Add the remaining minced onion to the pan with the chicken. Bring to a boil over high heat. Decrease the heat to medium-low and simmer the chicken until it reaches an internal temperature of 160°F on an instant-read thermometer and is no longer pink inside, about 10 minutes. Drain and rinse the cooked chicken breasts under cold water until cool to the touch, then pat dry with paper towels.

Shred the chicken and place it in a large bowl. Add the reserved minced onion along with the celery and celery leaves. Toss to combine.

In a small bowl, whisk together the mayonnaise, horseradish, if using, the remaining ½ teaspoon salt, the pepper, and lemon juice. Using a rubber spatula, gently fold the mayonnaise mixture into the chicken until thoroughly mixed.

Serve immediately, or cover and refrigerate until ready to serve. The chicken salad can be made up to 3 days in advance.

Seasonal Chicken Salad

With chicken the meat of choice among old-country Ashkenazis, it came to be used in innumerable traditional recipes, providing sustenance in a diverse range of dishes. Chicken salad is one that emerged to become a standard in New World delicatessens. It is equally amenable to further variation by being adapted to modern seasonal eating habits. In the recipes that follow, we provide both a "classic" take along with variations for spring, summer, fall, and winter.

Spring Chicken Salad

with Peas, Radish, and Mint

Serves 4

In our hometown of Portland, Oregon, seasonal eating is practically a religion. This chicken salad variety is at its very best with the emergence of succulent early spring produce: peas, mint, and radishes. Of course, all these ingredients can be found fresh or frozen year-round, so if you like this dish as much as we do and can't wait for spring to roll around, you can manage to make it any time.

1 pound boneless, skinless chicken breasts, trimmed of fat
2 tablespoons plus ½ teaspoon kosher salt
¾ cup fresh or frozen shelled peas (about 12 ounces in pods)
4 to 6 radishes, trimmed and diced
3 tablespoons finely chopped fresh mint
¼ cup mayonnaise

Place the chicken breasts in a medium saucepan and add enough cold water to cover the chicken by 2 inches. Add 2 tablespoons of the salt. Bring to a boil over high heat. Decrease the heat to medium-low and simmer the chicken until it reaches an internal temperature of 160°F on an instant-read thermometer and is no longer pink inside, about 10 minutes. Drain and rinse the cooked chicken breasts under cold water until cool to the touch, then pat dry with paper towels.

Shred or dice the chicken and place it in a large bowl.

If using fresh peas, steam them for 3 minutes and then rinse them under cold water for 1 minute. Pat dry with paper towels. If using frozen peas, cook the peas in boiling water just until fully thawed and slightly warm to the touch, 1 to 2 minutes. Rinse in cold water until cold, and pat dry with paper towels. Add the peas, radishes, mint, and the remaining ½ teaspoon salt to the bowl with the chicken. Toss until evenly distributed. Using a rubber spatula, gently fold in the mayonnaise until well combined.

Serve immediately, or cover and refrigerate until ready to serve. The chicken salad can be made up to 3 days in advance.

Summer Chicken Salad

with Tomatoes, Cucumber, and Cracklings

Serves 4

Bright red tomatoes, heavy on the vine, are a sure sign of high summer. The sun and heat also bring cucumbers along to their plump-to-bursting peak. Our summer chicken salad highlights these flavors of the warm months. For a crunchy counterpoint, the baked chicken skins, or cracklings—an alternative to more traditional Gribenes (page 5)—are mixed into the salad just before serving.

- 1 pound boneless, skin-on chicken breasts
- 2 tablespoons plus 1 teaspoon kosher salt
- 2 ripe plum (Roma) tomatoes or 8 ounces cherry tomatoes
- 1 medium cucumber, ends trimmed, halved lengthwise, seeds removed, and diced
- ¼ cup finely chopped fresh flat-leaf parsley
- 1 tablespoon finely chopped fresh thyme
- ⅛ teaspoon freshly ground black pepper
- ¼ cup mayonnaise
- 1 teaspoon freshly squeezed lemon juice

Preheat the oven to 375°F.

Remove and set aside the skin from the chicken breasts. Place the chicken breasts in a medium saucepan and add enough cold water to cover the chicken by 2 inches. Add 2 tablespoons of the salt. Bring to a boil over high heat. Decrease the heat to medium-low and simmer the chicken until it reaches an internal temperature of 160°F on an instant-read thermometer and is no longer pink inside, about 10 minutes. Drain and rinse the cooked chicken breasts under cold water until cool to the touch, then pat dry with paper towels.

Place the chicken skins, stretched as much as possible without tearing, in a nonstick rimmed baking pan. Alternatively, line a baking sheet with aluminum foil and lightly coat the foil with cooking spray. Lightly sprinkle the chicken skins with ½ teaspoon of the remaining salt. Roast the chicken skins until golden brown, 15 to 20 minutes. Transfer the chicken skins to a plate lined with a double thickness of paper towels to absorb the excess fat. (They will be somewhat flexible when first removed from the oven, but will crisp up fully as they cool. Any rendered chicken fat left on the baking sheet can be poured into a container and reserved in the refrigerator for uses requiring schmaltz.)

Shred or dice the chicken and place it in a large bowl.

If using plum tomatoes, cut them in half lengthwise, remove the core and seeds, and then cut into ½-inch dice. If using cherry tomatoes, cut them in half, leaving the seeds intact. Add the tomatoes, along with the cucumber, parsley, thyme, pepper, and the remaining ½ teaspoon salt, to the bowl with the chicken. Using a rubber spatula, mix until thoroughly combined. Add the mayonnaise and lemon juice and mix again to thoroughly combine.

Coarsely chop the cracklings. Just before serving, mix the cracklings into the salad, or reserve them and garnish each portion with about 2 tablespoons of the cracklings.

Serve the chicken salad immediately, or cover and refrigerate until ready to serve. The chicken salad can be made up to 3 days in advance.

Autumn Chicken Salad

with Roasted Red Peppers

Serves 4

Like the turning leaves on autumn trees, this seasonal chicken salad variation takes on a brilliant reddish hue from an infusion of Ajvar, the Balkan roasted red pepper and eggplant puree. Color also comes from cayenne and more red pepper. The recipe calls for roasted peppers, but finely chopped raw red bell peppers will work, too, especially for those who prefer more crunch. For a milder flavor, omit the cayenne.

1 pound boneless, skinless chicken breasts, trimmed of fat

2 tablespoons plus ½ teaspoon kosher salt

2 Roasted Red Peppers (page 15), coarsely chopped

1 clove garlic, minced

¼ teaspoon freshly ground black pepper

¼ teaspoon cayenne pepper (optional)

2 tablespoons mayonnaise

2 tablespoons Ajvar (page 17)

Place the chicken breasts in a medium saucepan and add enough cold water to cover the chicken by 2 inches. Add 2 tablespoons of the salt. Bring to a boil over high heat. Decrease the heat to medium-low and simmer the chicken until it reaches an internal temperature of 160°F on an instant-read thermometer and is no longer pink inside, about 10 minutes. Drain and rinse the cooked chicken breasts under cold water until cool to the touch, then pat dry with paper towels.

Shred or dice the chicken and place it in a large bowl. Add the peppers, garlic, the remaining ½ teaspoon salt, the black pepper, and cayenne, if using, along with the mayonnaise and *ajvar*. Using a rubber spatula, mix thoroughly to combine.

Serve immediately, or cover and refrigerate until ready to serve. The chicken salad can be made up to 3 days in advance.

Winter Chicken Salad

with Apple, Cranberry, and Preserved Walnuts

Serves 4

Preserved walnuts, jarred and packed in sweet syrup, are the magic ingredient here. They can often be found in Russian markets along with the jams and jellies. You can substitute candied walnuts, and the syrup used for candying, if you strike out. Tart, chewy dried cranberries, aromatic caraway seeds, and chopped apple are the other keys to this unusual seasonal dish.

1 pound boneless, skinless chicken breasts, trimmed of fat
2 tablespoons plus ½ teaspoon kosher salt
1 medium-firm apple (such as Jonagold, Honeycrisp, or McIntosh)
Finely grated zest and juice of 1 small lemon
½ cup dried cranberries
6 preserved walnuts, finely chopped
3 tablespoons mayonnaise
1 tablespoon preserved walnut syrup
1 teaspoon caraway seeds
⅛ teaspoon freshly ground black pepper

Place the chicken breasts in a medium saucepan and add enough cold water to cover the chicken by 2 inches. Add 2 tablespoons of the salt. Bring to a boil over high heat. Decrease the heat to medium-low and simmer the chicken until it reaches an internal temperature of 160°F on an instant-read thermometer and is no longer pink inside, about 10 minutes. Drain and rinse the cooked chicken breasts under cold water until cool to the touch, then pat dry with paper towels.

Shred or dice the chicken and place it in a large bowl.

Cut the apple in half, remove the core, and cut the apple into ¼-inch dice. Immediately toss the apple with the lemon juice and zest to keep it from browning. Add the apple, along with the juice and zest, to the chicken in the bowl. Add the dried cranberries and walnuts.

In a small bowl, combine the mayonnaise, walnut syrup, the remaining ½ teaspoon salt, the caraway seeds, and pepper. Using a rubber spatula, fold the mayonnaise dressing into the chicken mixture and mix thoroughly to combine.

Serve immediately, or cover and refrigerate until ready to serve. The chicken salad can be made up to 3 days in advance.

Cucumber Salad

with Sour Cream-Dill Dressing or Zuke's Ranch Dressing

Serves 6

The trick to keeping a cucumber salad from becoming too watery is to use salt to extract excess liquid from the cucumbers. That's why this recipe calls for combining salt with the sliced cukes and letting the mixture sit for at least an hour before making the salad. Pickling salt is preferred because it contains no additives. You may substitute kosher salt, but double the quantity because it is much lighter by volume. There's a choice of dressings for this salad, each with its own charms: a sour cream–dill version balanced with vinegar and the Zukin family's home-style ranch dressing—laden with fresh herbs—that Nick grew up with.

2 large cucumbers, trimmed, peeled, and cut into ⅛-inch-thick slices (about 4 cups)

1 teaspoon pickling salt

Sour Cream–Dill Dressing or Zuke's Ranch Dressing (recipes follow)

Toss the cucumbers with the pickling salt in a salad spinner or colander set over a large bowl. Refrigerate for at least 1 hour or overnight. Dry the cucumbers in the salad spinner or turn them out onto a work surface lined with paper towels and pat dry. Place the cucumbers in a large bowl and toss with the dressing of your choice. Cover and refrigerate for at least 1 hour before serving.

Sour Cream-Dill Dressing

½ large white onion, cut crosswise into thin slices (about 1 ¼ cups)

1 cup white vinegar

1 cup granulated sugar

½ cup sour cream

1 tablespoon whole milk

1 tablespoon finely chopped fresh dill

Combine the onion, vinegar, sugar, and 1 cup water in a small saucepan. Place over high heat and bring to a boil. Boil for 1 minute, stirring constantly. Remove from the heat and let cool to room temperature. Drain the onion, reserving the boiled vinegar mixture.

In a large bowl, whisk together the sour cream, milk, and dill, along with 1 tablespoon of the boiled vinegar mixture. Fold in the onion. Taste and add more salt, if desired. Cover and refrigerate until ready to toss with the cucumbers.

Zuke's Ranch Dressing

½ cup mayonnaise

½ cup buttermilk

1 clove garlic, very finely chopped

½ teaspoon very finely chopped serrano chile (optional)

2 tablespoons finely chopped fresh dill

1 tablespoon finely chopped fresh flat-leaf parsley

1 tablespoon snipped fresh chives

1 tablespoon fresh thyme leaves (optional)

¼ teaspoon kosher salt

⅛ teaspoon freshly ground black pepper

In a medium bowl, whisk together the mayonnaise, buttermilk, garlic, chile, if using, dill, parsley, chives, thyme, if using, salt, and pepper. Cover and refrigerate for at least 1 hour to allow the flavors to meld, then toss with the cucumbers. Taste and add more salt, if desired.

Deli Chopped Salad

with Russian Dressing

Serves 4

The "chef's salad" is a mainstream lunch-hour throwback in which the salad greens play a secondary role to the smorgasbord of meats, cheese, hard-boiled egg, and dressing piled on top. This family-size recipe revamps the classic, relying on ingredients typically associated with Jewish delicatessen dining: pastrami, kosher salami, Russian dressing, and bagel chips that stand in for croutons. For an attractive presentation, chop up the toppings and artfully arrange them over the lettuce in each individual salad bowl. If appearance is less important, everything can be tossed together before serving.

4 hearts of romaine lettuce, coarsely chopped
1 cup Russian Dressing (page 24)
1 cup Spicy Pickle Relish (page 14)
1 cup chopped Home-Oven Pastrami (page 142) or Backyard Barbecue Pastrami (page 144)
1 cup chopped kosher salami
1 cup chopped roast turkey
1 cup chopped Swiss cheese
4 hard-boiled eggs, chopped
40 Bagel Chips (page 25)

Combine the romaine, Russian dressing, and pickle relish in a very large bowl. Using tongs, toss the romaine with the dressing until the lettuce is evenly coated. Divide the salad among large salad bowls. Add ¼ cup each of the pastrami, salami, turkey, and Swiss cheese to each bowl, arranging it in an attractive semicircle along the inside rim of the bowl. Dividing it evenly, arrange a portion of the chopped eggs along the inside rim. Scatter 10 bagel chips over the top of each salad. Serve immediately.

Alternatively, you can combine all of the ingredients in one large bowl and toss with the dressing, but if you are not serving the salad immediately, reserve the bagel chips until serving time.

Creamy Cabbage Slaw

Serves 4

Nick just can't keep himself from tinkering with the recipes for traditional deli favorites—typically improving them in the process. To the standard cabbage-carrot-mayonnaise coleslaw trinity, this updated version adds cornichons, olives, pickled pepper, parsley, and black pepper. Once you taste it, the only question is whether you can ever go back to your old school slaw.

½ head green cabbage, cored and shredded (about 6 cups)
2 teaspoons kosher salt
1 carrot, coarsely grated
3 cornichons, finely chopped
2 garlic-stuffed green olives, finely chopped
1 small pickled pepper (such as banana wax pepper, sport pepper, or pepperoncini), stem removed and finely chopped
2 tablespoons chopped fresh flat-leaf parsley
3 tablespoons mayonnaise
⅛ teaspoon freshly ground black pepper

Place the cabbage in a salad spinner or a colander set over a large bowl. Toss the cabbage with the salt. Refrigerate for at least 1 hour or overnight. Rinse the cabbage under cool running water and then dry in a salad spinner or by turning out the cabbage onto a work surface lined with paper towels and patting the cabbage dry.

In a large bowl, toss together the cabbage, carrot, cornichons, olives, pickled pepper, parsley, mayonnaise, and black pepper until thoroughly combined. Taste and adjust the seasoning, adding more salt if desired. Cover and refrigerate for at least 30 minutes before serving to allow the flavors to meld.

Honey-Sweet Apple-Cabbage Slaw

Serves 4

Though slaw is an adaptation of the Dutch word for "salad," the cabbage that is the foundation for most slaws was as cheap and plentiful in the Jewish shtetls of nineteenth-century Slavic Europe as it is in American backyard gardens today. This crunchy cabbage salad is enhanced by the addition of Granny Smith apples, though you can use any super-crispy seasonal apple variety. The honey-vinegar dressing adds a pleasantly sweet tang to the slaw.

- ½ head green or red cabbage, cored and shredded (about 6 cups)
- 2 teaspoons kosher salt
- 2 Granny Smith apples, halved and cut into matchsticks about ¼ inch thick
- Juice of 1 lemon
- ¼ cup honey
- 4 teaspoons cider vinegar
- ½ teaspoon prepared horseradish
- ¼ cup mayonnaise, or as needed

Place the cabbage in a salad spinner or a colander set over a large bowl. Toss the cabbage with the salt. Refrigerate for at least 1 hour or overnight. Rinse the cabbage under cool running water and then dry in a salad spinner or by turning out the cabbage onto a work surface lined with paper towels and patting the cabbage dry.

In a large bowl, toss together the cabbage, apples, and lemon juice.

In a small bowl, whisk together the honey, vinegar, and horseradish and pour over the slaw. Mix until the slaw is evenly coated with the dressing. Add half the mayonnaise and mix it into the slaw. If not sufficiently dressed, add more of the mayonnaise, 1 tablespoon at a time, mixing after each addition. Taste and adjust the seasoning, adding more salt if desired. Cover and refrigerate for at least 1 hour to allow the flavors to meld. The cabbage slaw can be made up to 2 days in advance.

Zuke's "Diet" Salad

Serves 4

In the "Big Salad" episode of Seinfeld, Elaine describes "a salad, only bigger, with lots of stuff in it" as a popular staple at diners and chain restaurants. In tribute to the Big Salad, Kenny & Zuke's serves artisan-quality versions of these upsized lettuce-plus assemblages using freshly made dressings, house-cured meats, and anything else in the deli pantry that tastes good. Zuke's "Diet" started as an inside joke that referred to a salad that may have been slightly less caloric than a Reuben sandwich but that was still unlikely to win approval from any organized weight-loss program. Nick created it for his own consumption at the deli. Customers asked about it, so Zuke's "Diet" Salad was added to the Kenny & Zuke's menu. Now anyone can make one.

Dressing

4 cloves garlic, peeled

½ cup whole milk

¼ cup sour cream

¼ cup mayonnaise

1 teaspoon white vinegar

2 teaspoons freshly squeezed lemon juice

Pinch of cayenne pepper

4 ounces blue cheese, crumbled

Kosher salt

Salad

4 hearts of romaine lettuce, coarsely chopped

2 cups Classic Chicken Salad (page 82)

1 large cucumber, trimmed and thinly sliced (about 60 slices)

1 cup Pickled Red Onions (page 9)

4 hard-boiled eggs, thinly sliced

40 Bagel Chips (page 25)

To make the dressing, cook the garlic in a small pan of boiling water, or in a microwave-safe bowl half filled with water on medium power, for 30 seconds to mute the harsh garlic flavor. Drain the garlic and place it in a blender along with the milk, sour cream, mayonnaise, vinegar, lemon juice, and cayenne. Blend until smooth, about 30 seconds. Transfer the dressing to a small bowl, and then stir in the crumbled blue cheese. Taste and adjust the seasoning, adding salt if desired. Cover and refrigerate for at least 1 hour to allow the flavors to meld. The dressing can be made up to 3 days in advance.

To make the salad, put the romaine in a very large bowl. Pour the dressing over the top, and use tongs to toss the salad until the lettuce is evenly coated. Divide the salad evenly among large bowls. Arrange ½ cup chicken salad, about 15 cucumber slices, ¼ cup pickled red onions, 1 sliced egg, and 10 bagel chips in an attractive semicircle around the inside rim of each bowl. Serve immediately.

29
21
22
14
28
2

Deli Health Salad

Serves 4

It's not your typical salad and, even with its foundation of shredded cabbage, it's not quite a slaw either. But it definitely makes a light and nourishing first course that's filled with crunchy garden vegetables. The low-fat dressing is a simple combination of dill, cider vinegar, sugar, vegetable oil, and mustard. It's a breeze to make and, according to one of our testers, a "go-to dish" for healthy eating.

½ head green cabbage, cored and shredded (about 6 cups)

3 teaspoons kosher salt

1 carrot, coarsely grated (about 1 cup)

½ English cucumber, halved lengthwise and thinly sliced (about 1 cup)

4 celery stalks with leaves, stalks cut crosswise into thin slices (about 1 cup) and leaves coarsely chopped

1 tablespoon finely chopped fresh dill

½ cup cider vinegar

¼ cup granulated sugar

¼ cup vegetable oil

1 tablespoon whole-grain or stone-ground mustard

Place the cabbage in a salad spinner or a colander set over a large bowl. Toss the cabbage with 2 teaspoons of the salt. Refrigerate for at least 1 hour or overnight. Rinse the cabbage under cool running water and then dry in a salad spinner or by turning out the cabbage onto a work surface lined with paper towels and patting the cabbage dry.

In a large bowl, toss together the cabbage, carrot, cucumber, sliced celery and leaves, dill, and the remaining 1 teaspoon salt.

In a small saucepan, combine the vinegar and sugar. Bring to a boil over high heat, whisking until the sugar is dissolved. Remove from the heat, and whisk in the oil and mustard. Pour the dressing over the salad and mix until thoroughly combined. Cover and refrigerate for at least 30 minutes to allow the flavors to meld.

Eggs Fish and Dairy

easonal Schmears

Smoked Salmon
Garlic and Herb $1.75
Summer-Perfect Berry

SUNDAY BR
SPECIAL

Challah French To
Chocolate Babka
Cheese Blintzes
Savory Buckwhea
Smoked Salmon P
Corned Beef Hash
Pastrami Benedic
Frittata-Style Sala
Gravlax
Kippered Salmon
Lox, Eggs, and On
Pickled Herring in
Smoked Whitefis
Loxter Roll
Garlic and Herb S
Bagels and Lox

Chapter 4

Breakfast is the favorite meal of the day for many deli fanatics. It's the ideal time to consume the sort of hearty dishes that offer the energy to jump-start an ambitious afternoon of yard chores—or the caloric shock to send you back home for a lazy day on the couch. The foundation of most morning meals: eggs, dairy, and, in the long-standing Jewish deli tradition, smoked and other types of cured fish.

At Kenny & Zuke's and the other modern artisan delis we have visited, eager guests descend in droves and wait in line for a weekend brunch that routinely stretches from midmorning to late afternoon. Instead of braving the wait to eat brunch at a city deli, why not make your morning meal at home? A deli brunch is easily within reach of home cooks of all experience levels.

To spread on your morning bagel (preferably one of ours, pages 180–183), there are an infinite number of schmears that are all a snap to make. We offer several cream cheese–based varieties, ranging from a typical smoked salmon spread on page 132 to our summer-perfect berry version on page 128.

Make sure to try your hand at a classic Jewish deli breakfast food: the lightly sweet, fresh cheese–filled, crepe-like pancake known as a blintz. Reflecting the modern deli ideal of adapting traditional dishes to seasonal eating, follow our lead to re-create topping variations that evoke your favorite time of the year, such as spiced pumpkin for fall (page 109) or strawberry balsamic for spring (page 108).

Boker tov (Hebrew for "good morning")!

Chocolate Babka French Toast

Serves 6

Babka French toast started as a special that Wise Sons made on a whim, and it turned into one of their most popular menu choices. While it makes for a very sweet breakfast, it is also a great dessert that brings out the kid in everyone. The babka is made with plenty of chocolate that melts and creates a gooey, rich center in this dish. The sour cream provides a cold, tangy contrast. Use any fruit that looks good—yellow peaches in the summer are our personal favorite.

6 large eggs, beaten

1 cup whole milk

1 tablespoon granulated sugar

¼ teaspoon kosher salt

6 (1-inch-thick) slices Chocolate Babka (page 224)

2 tablespoons unsalted butter

½ cup sour cream

2 cups sliced fresh seasonal fruit, such as peaches, strawberries, or blood oranges

In a large bowl, whisk together the eggs, milk, sugar, and salt. Transfer to a high-sides baking dish for soaking the babka. Submerge each slice in the batter for 2 to 3 minutes, flipping the slices after 1½ to 2 minutes.

Meanwhile, heat a griddle or large cast-iron skillet over medium-high heat. Add the butter, letting it melt just until it begins to foam. Lift the soaked babka from the batter, allowing the excess to drip back into the baking dish. Place the babka on the griddle and cook until browned on one side, 3 to 4 minutes. Use a wide spatula to flip the slices and cook on the other side until browned, 2 to 3 minutes longer. Transfer the French toast to warmed plates. Top each slice with a dollop of sour cream and a large spoonful of fruit. Serve immediately.

Challah French Toast

Serves 4

With its generous measure of honey and eggy richness, our challah dough makes great braided bread (page 199) that, in turn, serves as a fantastic foundation for this morning classic. If there is no time to bake the bread yourself, a store- or bakery-bought challah (or brioche loaf) can be used. The challah should be at least a couple of days old because dry, stale challah does a much better job of soaking up the egg mixture, yielding a custardy-soft breakfast confection. We prefer grade B maple syrup because of its deep maple flavor; however, feel free to use any of the lighter grades of pure maple syrup based on availability and your preference.

8 large eggs
2 cups half-and-half
¼ cup honey
½ teaspoon ground cinnamon
½ teaspoon ground ginger
1 teaspoon pure vanilla extract
2 teaspoons finely grated orange zest
¼ cup all-purpose flour
⅛ teaspoon kosher salt
8 (1-inch-thick) slices challah, preferably stale or nearly stale
Vegetable oil cooking spray or 2 tablespoons unsalted butter, melted
Unsalted butter, at room temperature, for serving
Pure maple syrup or orange-honey sauce, for serving (see Note)

Preheat the oven to 200°F.

Combine the eggs, half-and-half, honey, cinnamon, ginger, vanilla, orange zest, flour, and salt in a blender and blend on high speed for 30 seconds. Pour the custard into a glass baking dish just large enough to snugly fit no more than 4 of the slices of challah laid flat. Place the first 4 slices of challah in the dish and soak on one side for 5 seconds, just enough to wet it, and then flip the slices over and soak for 5 to 10 minutes. Flip the slices over again and allow the slices to soak for another 5 to 10 minutes. Repeat with the remaining 4 slices in the baking dish, as you cook the first 4 slices.

Heat a large nonstick skillet over medium-low heat. Lightly coat the skillet with cooking spray or use a silicone brush to lightly coat the pan with 1 tablespoon of the melted butter. Lift a slice of soaked challah and allow the excess custard to drain back into the dish. Place the challah in the skillet. Repeat with the remaining 3 slices. Cook until dark golden brown on one side, 4 to 5 minutes. (Rotate the slices 180 degrees halfway through the cooking time to ensure that they are evenly browned.) Use a wide spatula to flip the slices and cook on the other side until dark golden brown, 4 to 5 minutes longer. Transfer the French toast to a baking sheet and keep warm in the oven while the second batch is cooking. Serve immediately along with butter and maple syrup.

Note: As an alternative to maple syrup, you can make an orange-honey sauce as a topping. To serve 4, combine 6 tablespoons freshly squeezed orange juice with ¼ cup honey and ¼ teaspoon ground ginger.

What Are . . . Blintzes?

In the never-the-twain-shall-meet world of traditional kosher cooking, dairy foods must not be paired with meat; it's the culinary version of the Capulets and Montagues or the Hatfields and McCoys. For lovers of lactose, the practical problem presented by this edict was that most of the early New York Jewish delicatessens kept kosher and served meat. Pastrami, corned beef, chicken soup, and chopped liver got all the press. Meanwhile, the best of the dairy dishes languished in relative obscurity. So it was with blintzes, even now an underappreciated luminary among old-time deli lights.

At the greatest of the all-dairy (*milchig* in Yiddish) kosher restaurants in New York, the much loved and now-lamented Ratner's (1905–2002), sarcastic, surly servers dealt blintzes by the score. The most popular were cheese blintzes, which remain the most common variety, when you can find blintzes at all. Unfortunately for deli diners, making blintzes is a labor-intensive endeavor best reserved for the home cook who doesn't have to worry about 50 other menu items. We included the recipe in this book in part for that reason.

As with so many Jewish foods, the blintz traces a labyrinthine path to the deli table. Its antecedents date back to the Turks fourteenth-century conquest of the Balkans. Then it was on to Romania, the Ukraine, and finally to Poland and Lithuania. Initially, the Slavic blintz—thicker than a crepe, thinner than a modern pancake—was usually made with buckwheat flour. As such, it shares a heritage (and linguistic root, *blin*, the Slavic word for any type of pancake) with blini, the buckwheat cakes that have famously shared the stage with the finest Russian caviar.

The more plebian blintz jumped the Atlantic with the late-nineteenth-century Ashkenazic immigrants. In America, it underwent its modern makeover, taking advantage of America's plentiful supply of inexpensive white wheat flour. Cheese continued to be the most common blintz filling, though what cheese to use has always been a source of vexation. Many references are made to "farmer" (or "farmers") or "pot" cheese or even ricotta, the selections encompassing a range of dry curd, sometimes tangy or salty; and fresh cheeses, often lightly sweetened and occasionally mixed with other dairy products, such as sour cream, cream cheese, or even mascarpone or crème fraîche, to lend a smoother texture and more nuanced flavor.

Cheese fillings aren't the only possibility, however. Non-kosher delis sometimes made blintzes with chopped beef or chopped liver. And there was nothing wrong with a little starch filling either, such as potato or kasha. Fruit fillings of all sorts are traditional, too. My mom even made a blintz casserole when I was growing up in the 1970s. The details elude me, but I think it was eggy, sweet, and delicious.

Tradition be damned. I fully expect one of today's modern artisan delis to bust out of the mold and plumb the limits of blintz craft. Just as the passage of time has rendered the dairy-only Jewish restaurant a dietary artifact, it is time to throw off any remaining historical shackles.

Bring on the chocolate blintz.

—MCZ

Cheese Blintzes

with Seasonal Toppings

Makes 12 blintzes

Most blintz recipes use a filling that begins with ricotta cheese, but we found that ricotta produced an inferior, runny blintz. Our preference is farmer cheese, which is tangier and much drier than ricotta, resembling cottage cheese that has had nearly all the moisture pressed out of it. It is also closer in taste and texture to the European fresh cheese fillings used by Ashkenazis in the nineteenth century (or even earlier) to make their blintzes. If farmer cheese is unavailable at any nearby markets (see Sources and Resources, page 239), small-curd cottage cheese, processed in a food processor until smooth, then wrapped and pressed in cheesecloth for at least 1 hour, is an adequate substitute.

Crepes

4 large eggs
1 cup whole milk
2 cups all-purpose flour
4 tablespoons (½ stick) unsalted butter, melted
1 tablespoon granulated sugar
1 teaspoon kosher salt

Filling

3 cups farmer cheese, at room temperature
¼ cup confectioners' sugar
⅛ teaspoon kosher salt
Finely minced zest of 1 large lemon
1 large egg, beaten

Unsalted butter, melted, for making the crepes
Seasonal fruit topping, for garnish (recipes follow)
Sour cream, for garnish

To make the crepe batter, combine the eggs, milk, 1 cup water, flour, melted butter, sugar, and salt in a blender and blend for 30 seconds. Using a rubber spatula, scrape down the sides of the blender container, and then continue blending for another 15 seconds. Pour the batter into a bowl, and lightly press plastic wrap directly on top of the batter so that air can't get to it and form a skin. Refrigerate for at least 1 hour before using.

To make the filling, in a medium bowl mix together the farmer cheese, confectioners' sugar, salt, lemon zest, and egg until thoroughly combined. Cover and refrigerate until ready to use.

To make the crepes, place a 6- to 7-inch nonstick omelet pan over medium heat. Using a silicone brush, lightly coat the bottom and sides of the pan with melted butter. (You may need to coat the pan with butter before you cook each crepe to avoid sticking.) When the butter is warm and the bubbles subside, pour ¼ cup crepe batter into the center of the pan and quickly turn the pan at a steep angle in order to evenly coat the entire inside of the pan with batter. It should be done in one smooth motion, taking no more than a few seconds to coat the pan, creating one thin disk of batter. Cook until the bottom of the crepe is speckled and golden brown, 1 to 1½ minutes. Using a small, thin spatula, gently lift one edge of the crepe and, using your fingertips,

continued on next page

grab the edge of the crepe and quickly but carefully turn it over. Cook the other side for 30 seconds or until it is mottled with brown spots. Tilt the pan and slide the crepe onto a plate, adjusting it with your fingers so it lays flat. Repeat with the remaining batter to make the rest of the crepes. As the crepes cool, layer them between pieces of parchment paper or plastic wrap, creating a stack. The stack of crepes can be wrapped on the plate in plastic wrap and kept in the refrigerator for up to 1 day before using.

To assemble and make the blintzes, lay a crepe, dark side down, on a flat surface. Put ¼ cup of the cheese filling into the lower third of the crepe, spreading the cheese mixture into a long rectangle about 1½ inches wide and 4½ inches long. Fold the bottom edge away from you over the filling. Fold the two outside edges of the crepe into the center and roll the crepe away from you until the crepe fully wraps around the filling, like an envelope. Place the blintz seam side down on a baking sheet. Repeat to fill all the blintzes. Cover and refrigerate until ready to cook.

In a large nonstick skillet over medium heat, use about 1 tablespoon melted butter to generously grease the pan. Arrange 3 or more blintzes seam side down in the pan, without crowding, and cook on one side until browned and crisped on the bottom, about 5 minutes. Turn and cook on the other side until browned, crisped, and heated through, about 5 minutes longer. (If the blintzes are not fully warm throughout, lower the heat slightly and cook for another minute or two.)

Serve with a heaping ¼ cup seasonal compote of your choice and garnish with a rounded tablespoon of sour cream.

Spring: Strawberry-Balsamic Compote

1 pound fresh strawberries (about 4 cups), trimmed and thinly sliced

¼ cup granulated sugar

1 tablespoon plus 1 teaspoon balsamic vinegar

Pinch of kosher salt

½ teaspoon cornstarch

In a large bowl, toss the berries with the sugar and set aside for 30 minutes or until the strawberries begin to give off their juice. Place half the berries and all of their exuded liquid, along with 1 tablespoon of the balsamic vinegar and a pinch of salt, in a small saucepan over medium heat. Cover the saucepan and bring the mixture to a gentle boil. Decrease the heat to low and simmer until the strawberries are very soft, about 5 minutes. Remove the saucepan from the heat and, using the back of a fork or a potato masher, crush the strawberries.

Combine the cornstarch with ½ teaspoon water in a small cup, stirring to remove all lumps. Pour the slurry into the saucepan and mix with the mashed strawberries and juice until thoroughly combined. Place the saucepan over medium heat and bring the berry mixture to a simmer. Continue to cook, stirring constantly to prevent lumps or scorching, until the strawberry sauce thickens to a light gravy consistency, about 1 minute. Pour the hot strawberry mixture over the remaining sliced strawberries in the bowl and add the remaining 1 teaspoon balsamic vinegar. Gently mix the sliced strawberries with the sauce. Cool to room temperature. Cover and refrigerate until ready to serve or for up to 1 week.

Summer: Blackberry-Lavender Compote

1½ pounds fresh blackberries (about 6 cups)

6 tablespoons granulated sugar

1 tablespoon fresh lavender flowers (about 2 buds)

Pinch of kosher salt

½ teaspoon cornstarch

In a large bowl, toss the berries with the sugar and set aside for 30 minutes or until the blackberries begin to give off their juice. Place half the berries and all of the exuded liquid, along with the lavender and pinch of salt, in a small saucepan over medium heat. Cover the saucepan and bring the mixture to a gentle boil. Decrease the heat to low and simmer until the berries are very soft, about 5 minutes. Remove the saucepan from the heat and, using the back of a fork or a potato masher, crush the blackberries. Cover the saucepan and set aside for 10 minutes to allow the lavender to steep in the berry juice. Strain the mixture through a fine-mesh sieve, pressing on the solids with a rubber spatula to strain out and capture as much liquid as possible. Pour the strained liquid back into the saucepan. Discard the solids.

Combine the cornstarch and ½ teaspoon water in a small cup, stirring to remove all lumps. Pour the slurry into the saucepan and mix with the berry juice until thoroughly combined. Place the saucepan over medium heat and bring the berry mixture to a simmer. Continue to cook, stirring constantly to prevent lumps or scorching, until the sauce thickens to a light gravy consistency, about 1 minute. Pour the sauce over the remaining berries in the bowl, gently mixing the berries with the sauce. Cool to room temperature. Cover and refrigerate until ready to serve or for up to 1 week.

Fall: Spiced Pumpkin Compote

3 cups granulated sugar

4 cups coarsely chopped sugar pumpkin or butternut squash

2 teaspoons ground nutmeg

¼ teaspoon ground ginger

⅛ teaspoon ground cloves

Pinch of kosher salt

Combine the sugar and 3 cups water in a medium saucepan over medium-high heat. Bring to a simmer and cook without stirring until the sugar dissolves, about 10 minutes. Add the pumpkin, nutmeg, ginger, and cloves. Stir to mix in the spices, and bring back to a boil. Decrease the heat to medium-low and simmer until the pumpkin is soft but still holds its shape, about 15 minutes.

Gently drain the pumpkin, reserving the syrup. Return half of the pumpkin to the saucepan along with 1 cup of the syrup and add a pinch of salt. Bring to a boil, cover, decrease the heat to low, and simmer the pumpkin until very soft, about 10 minutes. Transfer the mixture to a blender and puree until smooth. The puree should be thinner than gravy but thicker than heavy cream. Add more of the reserved syrup if the puree is too thick. Combine the remaining cooked pumpkin with the puree. Cool to room temperature, and then cover and refrigerate until ready to serve or for up to 1 week.

Winter: Blood Orange Compote

4 medium to large blood oranges, plus the juice of 2 blood oranges

2 thin slices peeled fresh ginger

4 cardamom pods

¼ cup granulated sugar

Pinch of kosher salt

¼ teaspoon cornstarch

Using a paring knife, trim the ends and then remove the peel from 4 of the blood oranges, cutting away any of the remaining white pith. Separate the orange segments over a small saucepan to collect any juices and set aside the segments. Squeeze into the saucepan the juice from any remaining pieces of orange flesh that cannot be separated into segments. Add the blood orange juice, ginger, cardamom, sugar, and salt. Cover the saucepan and bring the liquid to a gentle boil. Decrease the heat to low and simmer for 15 minutes. Remove the saucepan from the heat. Strain the liquid through a fine-mesh sieve into a small bowl. Return the liquid to the saucepan. Reserve the orange segments.

Combine the cornstarch and ¼ teaspoon water in a small bowl, stirring to dissolve all lumps. Pour the cornstarch slurry into the saucepan and mix with the liquid until thoroughly combined. Place the saucepan over medium heat and bring to a simmer. Continue to cook, stirring constantly in order to prevent lumps or scorching, until the sauce thickens to a thin gravy consistency, about 1 minute. Add the orange segments, stir gently to combine, and then remove from the heat. Cool to room temperature, and then cover and refrigerate until ready to serve or for up to 1 week.

Savory Buckwheat Blintzes

Makes 16 to 20 blintzes

The blintzes common on Jewish deli menus have a lightly sweet cheese filling and crepe-like shell made with white flour. Until the late 1800s, when wheat flour became more accessible, the standard blintz was made with a grayish, nutty-tasting buckwheat wrapper. Buckwheat was relatively cheap and abundant in northern Europe, and it happens to make a heaven-made match for a savory filling. It may take a few tries to get the hang of swirling the buckwheat crepes to a thin, even layer, and they should be quite thin. Keep at it until you've mastered the swirling and flipping, even if the first few have to be discarded. Our primary filling is made with potato, but we also offer an alternative in which smoked salmon takes center stage.

Crepes

2 cups milk

¾ cup all-purpose flour

½ cup buckwheat flour

3 large eggs

4 tablespoons (½ stick) unsalted butter, melted

1 teaspoon granulated sugar

½ teaspoon kosher salt

Potato filling

1 pound (2 medium) Russet potatoes

1 tablespoon extra-virgin olive oil

½ large yellow onion, finely diced

Kosher salt

1 cup farmer cheese

½ cup sour cream, plus more for topping the blintzes

2 tablespoons chopped fresh flat-leaf parsley

¼ teaspoon freshly ground black pepper

Unsalted butter, for frying

16 to 20 sprigs fresh dill

To make the crepes, combine the milk, all-purpose flour, buckwheat flour, eggs, melted butter, sugar, and salt in a blender. Blend until the mixture is very smooth and frothy, about 20 seconds, stopping once to scrape down the sides with a rubber spatula. The batter should be the consistency of heavy cream; if it is too thick, add 1 to 2 tablespoons water. Refrigerate the batter, covered, for at least 1 hour and up to 2 days before cooking the crepes.

To cook the crepes, heat an 8- to 10-inch nonstick omelet pan over medium heat. Swirl a small pat of butter around the pan to lightly coat, and then pour off the excess. (This only needs to be done before cooking the first crepe and should be enough for the entire batch.) With the handle of the pan in one hand, quickly pour a scant ¼ cup of the batter into the center of the pan, and then immediately tilt the pan in a circular motion, swirling the batter around the pan to coat it with a very thin, even layer. Once the crepe is formed, cook until it is set on one side and the edges easily pull away from the pan, 1 to 2 minutes. Using a combination of a heatproof rubber spatula and your fingertips, delicately lift and flip the crepe over in the pan. Cook until the second side is just set, 20 to 30 seconds. Be sure to pull the crepe from the pan while it is still tender and pliable; if it is crisp, it will crack and tear when it's filled.

Repeat with the remaining batter. (If you found that the first crepe was too thick, decrease the amount of batter for subsequent crepes accordingly.) Stack the finished crepes between sheets of waxed paper to avoid sticking. Cool them to room temperature. The crepes can sit out at room temperature, covered, for up to 1 day before they are filled. They can also be stored in the refrigerator for several days or in the freezer for up to 1 month.

To make the potato filling, preheat the oven to 400°F. Pierce the potatoes in several places with the tines of a fork. Bake the potatoes directly on the oven rack until they are tender, 35 to 45 minutes.

While the potatoes are baking, heat the oil in a medium skillet over medium-high heat. Add the onion and a pinch of salt and cook, stirring occasionally, until it is tender and lightly browned, 6 to 8 minutes. Transfer the cooked onion to a large bowl and set aside.

When the potatoes are baked and cool to the touch, cut them in half lengthwise and scoop out the flesh. Using a food mill or ricer, puree the potatoes into the bowl with the onion. Let the mixture cool to room temperature, and then stir in the farmer cheese, sour cream, parsley, pepper, and 2 teaspoons salt. Taste and adjust the seasoning, if desired.

To assemble the blintzes, work with a single crepe at a time. Spread about ¼ cup of the filling (a little less if you are using the Smoked Salmon Filling) just below the center of the crepe, leaving about a 1½-inch border on the bottom and either side. Fold the bottom of the crepe over the filling, and then fold in the sides. Roll the blintz up as you would a burrito or other type of filled crepe. Place it on a large platter or baking sheet with the seam side down. Repeat until all of the crepes are filled. The blintzes can be wrapped tightly in plastic wrap and refrigerated for up to 2 days before frying, or frozen for a few months.

To fry the blintzes, melt 2 tablespoons butter in a large skillet over medium-high heat. When the butter is bubbling, add 4 to 6 of the blintzes, seam side down, and fry until they are golden brown and warmed through, about 2 minutes. Carefully turn the blintzes over and fry them on the other side. Transfer the fried blintzes to a large platter. Repeat with the remaining blintzes, adding more butter to the pan as needed. Serve the blintzes topped with a dollop of sour cream and a small sprig of fresh dill.

Smoked Salmon Filling

For smoked fish lovers and those who prefer a more assertively flavored savory blintz, this filling variation is a keeper. We know our smoked salmon, but any flaky smoked fish should be fine. Use a fork to flake 1 pound of smoked salmon into a small bowl. Add 3 cups farmer cheese, 1 cup sour cream, 3 tablespoons thinly sliced scallions, the finely grated zest of 1 lemon, 2 teaspoons freshly squeezed lemon juice, 1 teaspoon kosher salt (or less to taste), and ¼ teaspoon freshly ground black pepper. Stir to combine. Use as instructed in the main recipe for the potato filling.

Wise Sons' Corned Beef Hash

Serves 4

The word corned refers to the grains of salt used to cure beef. In former English usage, any grain (though most commonly cereal grain) was referred to as "corn." Corning and other methods of salt-curing meat have ancient origins. Inexpensive, long-lasting corned beef brisket became a staple protein among Ashkenazic Jews living in late nineteenth-century New York City. Making hash from corned beef was the last-ditch way to avoid waste by mixing the last scraps of meat with potato, vegetables, and seasonings, then frying it all together. The owners of Wise Sons Deli in San Francisco supplied us with their take on corned beef hash that doesn't stray too far from tradition. In Evan and Leo's version, however, the potatoes are first boiled, then deep fried, so they stay super crispy on the outside and soft in the middle. Grilled peppers make a nice addition to the mix.

- 1 ½ pounds (3 medium) Russet potatoes
- Kosher salt
- Vegetable oil, for deep frying
- 2 tablespoons Schmaltz (page 5) or unsalted butter
- ½ large yellow onion, diced
- 1 cup chopped green bell pepper
- Freshly ground black pepper
- 12 ounces cooked corned beef, cut into ¼-inch cubes
- 2 tablespoons chopped fresh flat-leaf parsley
- 4 to 8 over-easy eggs, for serving
- Rye toast, for serving

Peel the potatoes and cut them into ¼-inch cubes. Place the potatoes in a large pot and fill it with water to cover them by 1 inch. Season the water generously with salt and bring it to a boil over high heat. Decrease the heat to medium-high and simmer until the potatoes are softened but still hold their shape, about 5 minutes. Drain the potatoes thoroughly, and spread them out on a rimmed baking sheet to cool and allow the remaining moisture to evaporate. (The potatoes can be boiled, drained, and cooled a day in advance and stored, covered, in the refrigerator.)

Fill a large, heavy-bottomed pot with 2 inches of oil. Heat the oil over high heat until it registers 360°F on a deep-fat thermometer. Adjust the heat as necessary to maintain the oil temperature. Working in two batches, deep-fry the potatoes until they are crisp and golden brown on the edges, 6 to 8 minutes per batch. Use a large slotted spoon or medium-mesh strainer to remove the potatoes from the oil, allowing the excess to drain over the pot, and transfer them to a large bowl. Season the potatoes with a generous pinch of salt while they are still hot.

In a large skillet, melt the schmaltz over medium-low heat. Add the onion and cook, stirring occasionally, until it is translucent, about 5 minutes. Add the green pepper and season with salt and black pepper. Continue cooking, stirring occasionally, until the onion and pepper are browned on the edges, about 10 minutes more. Increase the heat to medium-high and add the corned beef. Cook until heated through and beginning to crisp on the edges, about 3 minutes. Stir in the fried potatoes and parsley and cook until the mixture is heated through, about 1 minute. Taste and adjust the seasoning. Turn off the heat and cover to keep warm until ready to serve. Serve the hash with the over-easy eggs on top and rye toast on the side.

Stopsky's Delicatessen: Homemade Deli Food Away From Home

The Seattle bedroom community of Mercer Island has long been the center of the Jewish community and culture in the Pacific Northwest's biggest city. It's far from the trendy neighborhoods popular with many of Seattle's budding entrepreneurs, but it's where Stopsky's Delicatessen owner Jeff Sanderson lives and where, in 2011, he chose to open his living tribute to a struggling but resilient culinary tradition. There's no doubt when you walk into the small, 35-seat space that Stopsky's was created to intertwine with the local Jewish community. It's named for Sanderson's grandfather, who emigrated here and changed his name "to something less ethnic." Along one wall is a large and growing collection of photos showcasing generations of the Stopsky/Sanderson family and other Mercer Island locals.

The restaurant is otherwise decorated in muted earth tones with plenty of natural wood. Repurposed church pews share seating duty with a scattering of tables and chairs. An open kitchen is adjacent to the take-out counter. Above the counter, a blackboard announces Stopsky's sandwich, starter, and beverage offerings. Next to the counter is the obligatory cold case full of deli specialties.

Of course it's the range of house-made offerings that draws in the locals and distinguishes Stopsky's from the degraded national deli standard. Breads are one source of pride: challah, plain and seeded; hearty rye; and an array of traditional bagel varieties, plus an updated chewy onion option that incorporates bits of caramelized onion right into the dough. The bagels are hand-rolled, boiled, and baked. There are sweets, too, including seasonal raspberry rugelach with a crispy pastry; hamantaschen in poppy, prune, and apricot flavors; and an impossible-to-resist chocolate babka. Overall, the baking program at Stopsky's may be the most ambitious among all the revivalist Jewish delis in North America.

That's not to downplay the other made-in-house offerings. Meats include pastrami, both standard and Wagyu beef versions along with a turkey variation, each long-smoked over alder and encrusted with a coriander and black pepper rub. Also on the house-prepared protein list: corned beef, salami, tongue, and steak'n—boneless beef short rib cured and smoked like bacon. Pork should be so lucky.

Sanderson's priority is to use local products first, so he eschews the usual Great Lakes whitefish, instead smoking local firm-fleshed fish, such as cod, halibut, or sturgeon, to create a whitefish salad that combines the best of the modern and traditional. Likewise, Pacific salmon is simply smoked or becomes gravlax. And so it goes. Even the mustard is made on-site.

Sanderson has hired a young and eager staff to help build his deli dream as a long-term community contributor. The head baker brings years of experience to the job. The chef, who doubles as the general manager, is dedicated and confident. And the twentysomething floor manager, who's also the main waitress, exhibits a youth-defying deftness at building rapport with customers young and old.

Stopsky's, along with Kenny & Zuke's in Portland, is a mandatory Pacific Northwest stop on any revivalist Jewish deli tour. And it's true to its motto encapsulating the revivalist ethic: "Tradition, Updated."

Pastrami Benedict

Serves 4

Eggs Benedict is a luxurious breakfast dish rumored to have originated in New York City as a luncheon offering at the legendary Delmonico's restaurant. This twisted modern Jewish deli version was adopted at Stopsky's in Seattle. While the hollandaise and poached eggs are the same as in the original, latkes substitute for bread and pastrami for Canadian bacon. This recipe takes a little extra effort to put together. However, if you have made ahead and frozen some of our Crispy Potato Latkes (page 36), the preparation time can be cut in half. Any premium-quality pastrami will suffice in this dish, though naturally we think our Home-Oven Pastrami (page 142) works best.

Hollandaise sauce

5 large egg yolks

1 tablespoon Dijon mustard

Juice of 1 lemon

½ teaspoon kosher salt

⅛ teaspoon cayenne pepper

½ cup (1 stick) unsalted butter, melted and kept hot

8 Crispy Potato Latkes (page 36)

1¼ pounds pastrami, sliced or coarsely chopped

8 large eggs

2 teaspoons distilled white vinegar or freshly squeezed lemon juice

2 tablespoons chopped fresh flat-leaf parsley

Preheat the oven to 200°F. Line two large rimmed baking sheets with paper towels.

To make the sauce, place the egg yolks, mustard, lemon juice, salt, and cayenne in a blender and blend on medium speed until frothy. With the blender running, pour in the hot melted butter in a slow, steady stream. Be sure not to add the butter too fast or the sauce will break. If needed, add warm water, 1 tablespoon at a time, to thin the sauce to a consistency that will coat the back of a spoon. Taste and adjust the seasoning. Cover the sauce to keep warm.

Place the latkes on one of the lined baking sheets and put them in the oven to warm up.

In a large skillet over medium heat, and working in two batches, fry the pastrami, turning once or twice, until it is hot, about 5 minutes. Transfer the pastrami to the other lined baking sheet and put it in the oven to stay warm.

To poach the eggs, bring about 2 inches of water to a boil in a large skillet. When the water boils, add the white vinegar. Decrease the heat so the water is just below a simmer. One at a time, crack the eggs into a small bowl and slip them into the water. After about 3 minutes, use a slotted spoon to lift the first egg to see whether the white has completely set. When the whites are set, remove the eggs with a slotted spoon and gently blot the excess water with a clean kitchen towel. Transfer the eggs to a large plate and, if desired, use a paring knife to trim any ragged edges from the whites. Cover the eggs to keep them warm.

To serve, warm the serving plates. With the sauce nearby, remove the latkes and pastrami from the oven. Place 2 latkes on each plate. Pile some of the pastrami on top of each latke. Place a poached egg on top of each stack, and then spoon a generous amount of hollandaise sauce over the top. Garnish with the parsley and serve immediately.

Frittata-Style Salami and Eggs

Makes 4 to 8 servings

In this deli breakfast standard, premium-quality beef salami is the star and coarse mustard adds a complementary but not too powerful kick. Though the recipe calls for kosher salami, you may substitute other good-quality all-beef varieties, such as summer sausage. Or search out a local Russian market for evreyskaya, which is a dry, all-beef salami sometimes sold as "Jewish salami," with an intense, sharp flavor. Accompaniments might include latkes, rye toast, or even corned beef hash. For ketchup lovers, try our Ajvar (page 17) as a condiment instead.

2 tablespoons vegetable oil
½ medium yellow onion, finely chopped
8 ounces kosher salami, thinly sliced and quartered
8 large eggs
2 tablespoons whole-grain or stone-ground mustard
1 teaspoon kosher salt
¼ teaspoon freshly ground black pepper

Place a large skillet over medium heat and add the oil. When the oil is hot and begins to shimmer, add the onion. Cook the onion, stirring occasionally, until just beginning to soften, 2 minutes. Add the salami and cook until the onion is translucent and the salami begins to brown, about 8 minutes.

While the onion and salami are cooking, in a large bowl whisk together the eggs, mustard, salt, and pepper. Pour the mixture into the pan along with the onion and salami. Continually stir the mixture until the eggs are opaque throughout and beginning to solidify. Decrease the heat to low and cover the pan. Cook for 3 minutes. Remove the pan from the heat and let sit for another 3 to 5 minutes, covered, until the eggs are fully set. Using a thin spatula, loosen the frittata from the bottom of the pan. Place a plate face down over the pan and, holding the bottom of the plate, securely flip the skillet and plate over, turning out the salami and eggs onto the plate in one piece. Cut the frittata in quarters or eighths and serve immediately.

Gravlax

Makes 2 pounds

Cured salmon has long been associated with the Jewish delicatessen. Everyone knows about lox, but for a simple-to-make home-cured salmon, gravlax is the way to go. For many, this mild dill-flavored cure is preferable to the saltier, smokier flavor of lox. Gravlax means "buried salmon," from the ancient Scandinavian practice of burying salmon in dry sand to preserve it. Fortunately, this method has been refined over the centuries, and making gravlax now is a single-step process requiring only a few inexpensive, readily available ingredients and a few days' time. We recommend sushi-grade salmon for its premium quality. Serve on bagels, bagel chips, or squares of rye bread with cream cheese, crudités, and pickled veggies.

1 (2-pound) sushi-grade salmon fillet, ½ to ¾ inch thick, pinbones removed

⅔ cup granulated sugar

½ cup kosher salt

4 teaspoons freshly ground black pepper

2 cups chopped fresh dill

1 lemon, cut crosswise into ⅛-inch-thick slices

Rinse the salmon fillet under cold water and pat dry. In a small bowl, mix together the sugar, salt, and pepper. Set the fillet in a nonreactive dish, such as a glass or porcelain baking dish, skin side down and rub the salt and sugar mixture into the flesh side of the salmon until it forms an even, thick coating over the entire fillet. Repeat with the dill, creating a second thick layer. Finally, place the lemon slices in one layer over the dill.

Cover the fish with plastic wrap, pressing down so that the plastic directly contacts and covers the entire fillet. Place a smooth-bottomed dish at least the size of the fillet onto the salmon and weight it with something heavy, such as cans of food or pie weights. The weighting isn't necessary to cure the fish, but it does make for a denser texture. Refrigerate for 3 to 5 days. More time will intensify the brine's flavor in the fish.

Remove the salmon from the refrigerator, rinse the fillet clean, and pat dry. Slice across the grain into thin strips and serve as desired. The gravlax may be stored, wrapped tightly in plastic, in the refrigerator for up to 3 days.

Kippered Salmon

Makes 2 pounds

To "kipper" means to cure fish by rubbing it with salt or spices and smoking it. The verb comes from the age-old preservation treatment accorded herring that, when split, dressed, and cured, are called kippers. From the Middle Ages onward, kippers were popular with Ashkenazic Jews who lived near the Baltic Sea, where herring was abundant. When the New York Jewish delis were booming in the 1920s and 1930s, kippering was adapted for use with cheap and plentiful North American salmon. The kippering method in this recipe is simplified for home-oven preparation and incorporates aquavit, a caraway-flavored spirit, for a little tang. But if a smoker is accessible, by all means use it. Smoking the salmon (typically with apple or cherry wood) will produce a more complex, traditional flavor. Serve in a salad, hash, blintz, or omelet or simply on crackers or bagels with cream cheese and pickles.

1 (2-pound) sushi-grade salmon fillet, ½ to ¾ inch thick, pinbones removed
⅔ cup granulated sugar
½ cup kosher salt
1 tablespoon freshly ground black pepper
6 tablespoons aquavit
½ cup light brown sugar

Rinse the salmon fillet under cold water and pat dry. In a small bowl, combine the granulated sugar, salt, and pepper. Set the fillet in a nonreactive dish, such as a glass or porcelain baking dish, skin side down. Brush or sprinkle 2 tablespoons of the aquavit onto the fish. Next, rub the salt and sugar mixture into the flesh side of the salmon until it forms an even, thick coating over the entire fillet.

Place a smooth-bottomed dish at least the size of the fillet onto the salmon and weight it with something heavy, such as cans of food or pie weights. Refrigerate for 4 to 12 hours or overnight. If cured for longer than 12 hours, the fish may become unpalatably salty for some. Remove the salmon from the refrigerator, rinse the fillet clean, and pat dry.

Combine the brown sugar and the remaining 4 tablespoons aquavit in a small saucepan set over medium-high heat. Dissolve the brown sugar in the liquor and boil for about 5 minutes or until the liquid has reduced by half to a syrup that coats the back of a spoon.

Preheat the oven to 250°F.

Use a pastry brush or back of a spoon to glaze the salmon with some of the syrup. Allow the fish to rest uncovered until the glaze has set, about 15 minutes. Glaze again and let rest, and repeat the process two or three more times, until a thin layer of the glaze has formed. Place the salmon in the oven and cook until the salmon reaches an internal temperature of 130°F, 20 to 25 minutes. The salmon will exude a white liquid and will be firm, flaky, and opaque in the center. It's important not to overcook the fish or it will become dry and mushy.

The salmon may be stored, wrapped tightly in plastic, in the refrigerator for up to 3 days.

Lox, Eggs, and Onions

Serves 4 to 6

For a simple, savory breakfast meal, give this a try. Lox and eggs have an affinity for one another, and the onions add another complementary angle. Accents from the fresh chopped dill and freshly ground black pepper round out an attractive presentation. If you like, substitute Gravlax (page 119) or Kippered Salmon (page 120) for the lox. Though it lacks the traditional Jewish deli stamp, it still offers a subtle cured salmon-dill flavor on par with its piscine relative.

2 tablespoons unsalted butter
½ large yellow onion, thinly sliced
10 large eggs
2 tablespoons milk
1 teaspoon kosher salt
4 ounces sliced lox, cut into 1-inch pieces
2 tablespoons plus 2 teaspoons fresh chopped dill
Freshly ground black pepper

In a large, nonstick skillet, melt the butter over medium heat. When it is bubbly, add the onion and cook, stirring occasionally, until it is tender and translucent but not browned, about 5 minutes.

While the onion is cooking, in a large bowl thoroughly beat the eggs with the milk and salt. Stir in the lox and 2 tablespoons of the dill. When the onion is done, pour the egg mixture into the pan and let it set on the bottom for about 30 seconds. Using a heatproof rubber spatula or a wooden spoon, begin to push the cooked eggs from the bottom of the pan into the center, allowing the uncooked eggs to come into contact with the pan. Continue to cook the eggs in this manner, forming large curds, until they are just set but still moist. Immediately divide into portions and serve on warm plates. Sprinkle each serving with a little of the remaining 2 teaspoons of dill and the black pepper, and serve immediately.

Pickled Herring in Cream Sauce

Serves 8 to 10

Herring is a variety of small, oily fish abundant in cold northerly waters. As a readily available source of cheap protein, herring have been a cross-cultural staple in northern European diets for centuries. Ashkenazic Jews have traditionally enjoyed pickled herring prepared several ways. This sour cream sauce–based version begins with pickled herring packed in oil. You can substitute vinegar- or white wine–packed pickled herring, but if you do, reduce the amount of apple cider vinegar to 3 tablespoons, or to taste.

1 cup sour cream
¼ cup cider vinegar, plus more as needed
1½ tablespoons granulated sugar, plus more as needed
1 pound pickled herring in oil, well drained
1 large Golden Delicious apple, peeled, cored, and thinly sliced
1 small white onion, thinly sliced
3 tablespoons snipped fresh chives
Crackers or Pumpernickel Rye (page 195), for serving

Mix together the sour cream, vinegar, and sugar in a large bowl. Add the herring, apple, and onion and toss to combine. Cover the bowl with plastic wrap and place it in the refrigerator for at least 24 hours and up to 5 days to allow the flavors to develop.

Before serving, taste and adjust the flavor as desired by adding more vinegar for acidity or more sugar for sweetness. Transfer the herring mixture to a serving dish and garnish it with the chives. Serve with crackers or with thinly sliced pumpernickel bread (toasted, if you like).

Smoked Whitefish Salad

Serves 8

Smoked whitefish, golden hued and sourced from the Great Lakes, can be hard to track down in many parts of the country. Although it is available by mail-order (see Sources and Resources, page 240), you can often find it (or its relative, smoked chubs) for a fraction of the price in European, international, and gourmet food markets. This salad makes a superlative spread for toasted bagels or matzo. For a twist, scoop it over endive or romaine lettuce leaves for an alluring presentation, or serve it as a substantial salad on its own, paired simply with cherry tomatoes and sliced cucumbers.

- 1½ pounds whole smoked whitefish, or 1 pound smoked whitefish, boned and skinned
- 1 celery stalk, finely diced
- ¼ red onion, finely diced
- 1 tablespoon finely chopped fresh flat-leaf parsley
- 2 teaspoons finely chopped fresh dill
- ½ cup sour cream
- ¼ cup mayonnaise
- Juice of 1 small lemon
- Kosher salt and freshly ground black pepper

Place the fish in a medium bowl and break it up into flakes with a fork. Add the celery, onion, parsley, and dill and mix until thoroughly combined. Stir in the sour cream, mayonnaise, and lemon juice. Add salt and pepper to taste. Serve immediately, or cover and refrigerate until ready to serve. The salad can be made up to 3 days in advance.

Left Coast Gefilte Fish

Makes 22 to 24 pieces

Gefilte fish has had a place on Ashkenazic festival tables for nearly 500 years. Fish fillets, classically carp, pike, and other inexpensive whitefish, are ground, seasoned, shaped into ovals or spheres, then poached in fish stock and chilled before serving. Though New Yorkers may argue the point, the best gefilte fish has long been made on the Pacific Coast. For a hundred years, from the mid-nineteenth to the mid-twentieth century, salmon in the streams of the Columbia River Basin were so abundant that superior-tasting pink-tinged, gefilte fish became the gold standard. Our "Left Coast" version is adapted from a recipe made by Michael's paternal grandmother, Edith Zusman. To prepare your fish the traditional way that she did, instead of using a food processor, mince it by hand in a wooden bowl with a crescent-shaped blade. It's fine to substitute less expensive rockfish (or traditional whitefish varieties) for halibut. The perfect condiment for gefilte fish is creamy horseradish, as hot as you can stand it.

1½ pounds salmon fillets, skinned and cut into 1-inch cubes
1½ pounds halibut fillets, skinned and cut into 1-inch cubes
1 large onion, finely grated
1 large carrot, finely grated
3 large eggs, lightly beaten
⅓ cup matzo meal
2 tablespoons vegetable oil
1 tablespoon kosher salt
2 teaspoons freshly ground white or black pepper
1 teaspoon granulated sugar
8 to 10 cups store-bought or homemade fish stock (see Note)
Creamy horseradish, for serving

Place the salmon, halibut, onion, and carrot in the work bowl of a food processor and pulse until the fish is finely ground but not pasty (if your food processor is small, do this in batches). Transfer the chopped fish mixture to a bowl. Add the eggs, matzo meal, 2 tablespoons water, the oil, salt, pepper, and sugar. Mix together until well combined. Place the mixture in the refrigerator, tightly covered, to chill for 1 hour.

Once the mixture has chilled, bring the fish stock to a boil in a large soup pot. Using a ⅓-cup dry measure, lightly scoop up enough of the fish mixture to fill the cup without pressing down and packing it. Use your hands to shape the fish into a small oval. Repeat to form 22 to 24 gefilte fish. Using a slotted spoon, gently drop the gefilte fish pieces into the boiling broth, lowering the heat until it's barely simmering. Simmer the fish, turning once or twice, until the pieces are completely cooked through, 20 to 25

Harry and Maritka Schnitzer from a Passover dinner in the 1950s. He was a kosher butcher in Portland. Their daughter was Edith Zusman, Michael's grandmother, who made great gefilte fish.

minutes. Using a slotted spoon, transfer the gefilte fish to a large baking dish or rimmed platter and set aside to cool for 10 minutes. Tightly cover the dish and refrigerate until thoroughly chilled, about 2 hours.

Serve chilled with creamy horseradish. The gefilte fish can be made up to 1 day in advance.

Note: The fish skin and the trim from the carrot and onion can be used to make a simple stock. Boil them together with 10 cups water in a medium stockpot, then lower the heat to a simmer, skimming off any scum that rises to the surface. Simmer for 1 hour, then strain to remove the solids. The stock can be used immediately, or it can be refrigerated for 1 day or frozen for up to 1 month.

Cream Cheese Schmears

Schmear, the Yiddish word for "grease," was originally slang for a bribe, as in greasing someone's palm. Sounds like great Trivial Pursuit material, but it doesn't answer the burning question: "What kind of cream cheese makes the best bagel schmear?" If it's available, we recommend Gina Marie brand. Produced in California by the Sierra Nevada Cheese Company, it's lighter, fluffier, and easier to spread than the ubiquitous silver brick. We don't know the producer from the man on the moon, but Left Coast food fanatics swear by it and the company's claim that Gina Marie is free from any gums, fillers, preservatives, and other icky stuff. Better still, if there's an artisanally produced, small-batch cream cheese available in your community, use it.

Summer Berry Schmear

Makes about 1¼ cups

If these berry varieties are unavailable fresh from local sources, feel free to substitute. Thawed frozen berries or berries from South or Central America can be used at the risk of losing your locavore street cred.

4 large fresh strawberries, stemmed and chopped
⅓ cup fresh blueberries, chopped
⅓ cup fresh raspberries or blackberries, chopped
1 tablespoon granulated sugar, plus more as needed
1 (8-ounce) package cream cheese, at room temperature
¼ teaspoon pure vanilla extract
Pinch of kosher salt

In a medium bowl, gently mix together all the berries with the sugar. Set aside at room temperature for 30 minutes to allow the berries to soften and absorb some of the sugar.

In the bowl of a stand mixer fitted with the whisk attachment, or in a medium bowl using a handheld electric mixer, whip the cream cheese on medium speed until it is light and creamy, about 2 minutes. Scrape down the sides of the bowl as needed.

Drain the berries in a fine-mesh strainer set over a bowl. Gently press the berries with a rubber spatula to remove any excess juice. (Reserve the juice for another use, such as a mixer with club soda and ice.) Add the strained berries, vanilla, and salt to the cream cheese and beat to combine, about 30 seconds. Taste and add more sugar, if desired, for a sweeter schmear. Transfer to a covered container and refrigerate for at least 1 hour, and preferably overnight, to allow the flavors to meld. Store the schmear in the refrigerator for up to 4 days.

Garlic and Herb Schmear

Makes about 1 cup

For this savory schmear, substitute any fresh herbs for those listed, but take into account that with some strongly flavored herbs, such as rosemary or sage, a little goes a long way.

- 1 (8-ounce) package cream cheese, at room temperature
- 1 large clove garlic
- Pinch of kosher salt
- 1 tablespoon finely snipped fresh chives
- 1 tablespoon finely chopped fresh dill
- 1 tablespoon finely chopped fresh flat-leaf parsley
- 1 tablespoon finely chopped fresh tarragon
- 2 teaspoons freshly squeezed lemon juice

In the bowl of a stand mixer fitted with the whisk attachment, or in a medium bowl using a handheld electric mixer, whip the cream cheese on medium speed until it is light and creamy, about 2 minutes. Scrape down the sides of the bowl as needed.

Mince the garlic and gather it in a small pile on the cutting board. Sprinkle the garlic with the salt. With the edge of your knife positioned at a 30-degree angle, mash the garlic into a smooth paste using a scraping motion.

Add the garlic paste, chives, dill, parsley, tarragon, and lemon juice to the cream cheese and beat to combine, about 30 seconds. Taste and adjust the seasoning. Transfer to a covered container and refrigerate for at least 1 hour, and preferably overnight, to allow the flavors to meld. Store the schmear in the refrigerator for up to 4 days.

Olive and Sun-Dried Tomato Schmear

Makes about 1¼ cups

Though the ingredients for this schmear are available year-round, they make us think of a sunny spring day on the Mediterranean coast. Mixed and pitted marinated olives are widely available at gourmet grocery stores. Make a batch and think warm thoughts.

⅓ cup dry-packed sun-dried tomatoes, finely chopped
1 (8-ounce) package cream cheese, at room temperature
¼ cup chopped marinated black and green olives
2 tablespoons chopped fresh flat-leaf parsley
1 teaspoon freshly squeezed lemon juice
¼ teaspoon kosher salt

Place the sun-dried tomatoes in a small bowl of warm water and set them aside for 30 minutes to rehydrate.

In the bowl of a stand mixer fitted with the whisk attachment, or in a medium bowl using a handheld electric mixer, whip the cream cheese on medium speed until it is light and creamy, about 2 minutes. Scrape down the sides of the bowl as needed.

Drain the sun-dried tomatoes through a fine-mesh strainer, gently pressing them with a rubber spatula to remove any excess water. Add the tomatoes, olives, parsley, lemon juice, and salt to the cream cheese and beat to combine, about 30 seconds. Taste and adjust the seasoning. Transfer to a covered container and refrigerate for at least 1 hour, and preferably overnight, to allow the flavors to meld. Store the schmear in the refrigerator for up to 4 days.

Roasted Red Pepper and Onion Schmear

Makes about 1¼ cups

In autumn, fresh peppers of all shapes and sizes flood the farmers' markets. That makes this schmear ideal when the leaves are in full color and the days begin to shorten.

1 (8-ounce) package cream cheese, at room temperature
½ cup coarsely chopped Roasted Red Peppers (page 15)
1 large shallot, finely grated (about 1 tablespoon)
2 tablespoons chopped fresh flat-leaf parsley
1 teaspoon freshly squeezed lemon juice
¼ teaspoon kosher salt

In the bowl of a stand mixer fitted with the whisk attachment, or in a medium bowl using a handheld electric mixer, whip the cream cheese on medium speed until it is light and creamy, about 2 minutes. Scrape down the sides of the bowl as needed. Add the roasted red peppers, shallot, parsley, lemon juice, and salt to the cream cheese and beat to combine, about 30 seconds. Taste and adjust the seasoning. Transfer to a covered container and refrigerate for at least 1 hour, and preferably overnight, to allow the flavors to meld. Store the schmear in the refrigerator for up to 4 days.

Smoked Salmon Schmear

Makes about 1½ cups

This is not—we repeat, not—the redheaded stepchild of the classic lox and cream cheese bagel ensemble. Unlike premium-priced lox, the flakiness of smoked salmon lends itself perfectly to a cream cheese blend.

1 (8-ounce) package cream cheese, at room temperature
3 ounces smoked salmon, flaked with a fork
¼ cup thinly sliced scallions
2 teaspoons freshly squeezed lemon juice
Pinch of kosher salt

In the bowl of a stand mixer fitted with the whisk attachment, or in a medium bowl using a handheld electric mixer, whip the cream cheese on medium speed until it is light and creamy, about 2 minutes. Scrape down the sides of the bowl as needed. Add the flaked salmon, scallions, lemon juice, and salt to the cream cheese in the bowl. Beat until combined, about 30 seconds. Taste and adjust the salt, if needed. Transfer to a covered container and refrigerate for at least 1 hour, and preferably overnight, to allow the flavors to meld. Store the schmear in the refrigerator for up to 4 days.

Loxter Roll

Makes 4 rolls

If the ability to update and playfully adapt traditional Jewish delicatessen dishes is the hallmark of today's modern artisan delis, this dish from Mile End epitomizes that ethos. Lox with bagel, cream cheese, and accompaniments is a foundational Jewish deli menu item. These tasty filled rolls are about as distant from the traditional presentation as can be. Inspired by the Maine-style lobster roll, Mile End's Loxter Rolls are at once a simple-to-throw-together, summer-on–Cape Cod lunch and a great practical way to use up the last of the lox left over from Sunday brunch. If you need to use up a batch of Gravlax, it can be substituted for the lox. One of our testers recommends "a nice, off-dry Riesling" with these rolls. Why not?

8 ounces lox or Gravlax (page 119), cut into ¼-inch pieces
¼ cup mayonnaise, preferably homemade
¼ cup finely diced celery
2 tablespoons finely diced red onion
1 tablespoon plus 1 teaspoon finely chopped fresh dill
4 potato hot dog buns, split lengthwise
2 tablespoons unsalted butter, melted
¼ cup finely diced pickled red peppers

In a small bowl, gently mix the lox, mayonnaise, celery, red onion, and 1 tablespoon of the dill. Take care not to mash the lox.

Heat a large skillet over medium heat. Brush the outsides, top and bottom, of each bun with the butter. Toast both sides of the buns in the hot skillet until golden brown, 1 to 2 minutes per side. Fill each bun with the lox mixture, dividing it evenly. Garnish with the remaining 1 teaspoon dill and the pickled red peppers. Serve immediately.

Bagels and Lox

Serves 4

Seemingly any round-shaped bread that holds a sandwich filling suffices as a "bagel" these days. And while the authenticity of these modern rolls with holes can be criticized, it's hard to argue with their mass appeal. Still, in the realm of traditional Jewish deli craft, there is nothing as simple and satisfying as a proper bagel topped with first-quality cream cheese, a few silky slices of lox, and an array of complementary accompaniments. Though we recommend our Traditional Bagels (page 180), if you must use the bigger, softer ones (or day-olds), toast the halves first and allow them to cool for 5 minutes before using. Thinly sliced cucumbers and heirloom tomatoes can be added to the ensemble when in season.

4 bagels, halved
¾ cup cream cheese, at room temperature
16 slices lox (about 12 ounces)
½ cup drained and loosely packed Pickled Red Onions (page 9)
3 tablespoons drained capers
3 tablespoons chopped fresh dill
Freshly ground black pepper

Spread the cut sides of each bagel half with cream cheese and add 2 slices lox. Distribute the remaining ingredients evenly over the lox in the following order: pickled onions, capers, and dill. Sprinkle with black pepper and serve immediately, open-face.

Cured Meat
Sold by the Pound

Cup or B
$4.9

LI

BEEF

BOLOGNA	
HER	$8.99
MAN	$4.99
HAM	$4.49
SKAY	$3.99
/PEPPERONI	
HER	$8.99
LIAN	$5.99
ARD	$5.99
RONI	$7.49
KED	$4.99

CORNED BEEF
HOME-OVEN PASTRAMI
BACKYARD BARBECUE PASTRA
RARE ROAST BEEF
PASTRAMI REUBEN SANDWICH
PASTRAMI BURGERS
STEAK'N (PORKLESS BACON)
BRISKET WITH SEASONAL VEC
KISHKE
CABBAGE ROLLS IN TOMATO S

Chapter 5

With this chapter, you have reached the delectable heart of the Jewish delicatessen. Ask ten people what one menu item truly defines the deli, and the answer will almost certainly be some type of smoked or cured meat. Several recipes that fill the bill are included here. Our personal favorite is pastrami, which can be made as a home-oven version (page 142) or by using a backyard barbecue or smoker (page 144). Other deli aficionados will surely select corned beef (page 138), which in many ways is a simplified, mellower version of pastrami. Though these cured meat recipes tend to be a bit more involved than most, the payoff is handsome: no need to fork over big money for something you can make at home—assuming you can buy something that even begins to approach the hand crafted quality of your very own deli meats.

Throughout this book, we have showcased several classic deli dishes, but supplemented them with seasonal variations so that the finest local ingredients of the moment can make the recipes sing year-round. Four versions of the humble brisket pot roast are included in this chapter (pages 153–161). If you ever thought summer just wasn't the right time for a family-size chunk of slow-braised beef, then you have never tasted one with a sunny attitude that includes tomato, fennel, lots of herbs, and even a touch of beer.

While perusing the next pages, please do your part to help maintain the modern revival of old-line Jewish deli craft. If ever there was an obscure deli dish worthy of a comeback, it is the old-country stuffed derma (beef intestine) creation known as *kishke* (page 164), as offered to us by dedicated new-wave Toronto deli man Zane Caplansky. This fantastic dish will forever dispel your fear of what David Letterman jokingly refers to as "variety meats."

There's a whole lot more here, too. For those inclined to skip the hearty, meaty dishes offered in this chapter, we laud your sentiments (and goodness knows, we could lose a few pounds), but in the true community spirit of the traditional Jewish deli, we urge you to consider making these great-tasting, traditional foods for a special occasion to share with your extended family and dearest friends. It would be a mitzvah (loosely translated from Hebrew as "an act of charity").

Corned Beef

Makes 2 to 3 pounds

If there's one deli meat that's universally known and mostly loved, it is corned beef. Though Jews and Irish can argue over who first popularized the stuff, no one can dispute that it's simple to prepare and makes a great sandwich and accompaniment to cabbage or eggs. It also serves admirably as the meaty component in hash alongside potatoes and onions. Corned beef even has a special place in the trivia books: In 1965, a corned beef sandwich was smuggled into space by astronaut John Young on the flight of Gemini 3, making corned beef the only deli meat ever to have orbited the earth. You, too, can eat like an astronaut by following the brining and boiling steps described in this recipe.

Brine

2 cups Diamond Crystal (or other large-crystal) kosher salt

¼ cup (2 ounces) pink salt (see Sources and Resources, page 240)

1 cup granulated sugar

½ cup firmly packed dark or light brown sugar

¼ cup honey

2 tablespoons pickling spice

1 tablespoon whole coriander seeds

1 tablespoon whole yellow mustard seeds

4 cloves garlic, minced

Meat

3 to 4 pounds beef brisket

1 tablespoon pickling spice

1 tablespoon whole coriander seeds

1 tablespoon whole yellow mustard seeds

¼ cup kosher salt

To make the brine, fill a medium to large stockpot with 3 quarts water. Add the kosher and pink salts, granulated and brown sugars, honey, pickling spice, coriander and mustard seeds, and garlic. Bring to a boil over high heat, stirring often to fully dissolve the salt and sugar. Once the brine boils, immediately remove the pot from the heat. Add 3 quarts ice water to a 2-gallon or larger food-safe container that will fit into your home refrigerator. Pour the brine into the container and place the container, uncovered, in the refrigerator until completely cool.

To brine the brisket, trim the fat from the brisket until the fat layer is about ¼ inch thick. Submerge the brisket in the cooled brine, cutting it into two pieces, if needed, to submerge it. Allow the brisket to brine for 5 days, flipping it daily top to bottom and stirring the brine. Make sure that if any of the brisket pieces are touching one another they are turned regularly to eliminate the contact and that all surfaces of the brisket are exposed to the brine.

To cook the brisket, remove the meat from the brine and thoroughly rinse it. Discard the brine. Add 2 gallons water, the brisket, pickling spice, coriander and mustard seeds, and salt to a large pot. Place the pot over high heat and bring to a light boil. Cook uncovered for 2 to 3 hours, until the beef reaches an internal temperature of 200°F and is quite tender and easily punctured with a fork. A ¼-inch-thick slice of fully cooked corned beef should pull apart easily.

To serve, carve the corned beef into ¼-inch-thick slices, or cut as thin as possible without the meat falling apart. Keep tightly wrapped in aluminum foil or plastic wrap in the fridge for up to 1 week or frozen for up to 6 months.

What Is . . . Pastrami?

A few years ago, I had my first taste of pastrami at its very best. It was lavishly smoked, salty with a hint of sweetness, not quite too fatty, and a deep blush hue. The cut of beef from which it was crafted, a section of the brisket called the deckle, was rubbed with crushed coriander and black pepper, among a pantry of other spices. After brining, rubbing, and smoking, a process that unfolds over several days, the pastrami still had to be steamed before serving. The end result: tender, juicy meat, awaiting a few deft flicks of a sharp knife to cascade in thin leaves and be gathered between mustard-lacquered slices of rye bread.

This pastrami was a revelation, I thought. It had only a name in common with the rubbery, characterless packaged products sold at the grocery store and in too many indifferent restaurants. It had far more in common with the kind of pastrami that had largely passed into history, as I have since learned.

Pastrami has Eastern European roots in Romania. It made its way there with the Ottoman Empire. The Ottoman Turks followed the practice of drying and salt-curing meat, then rubbing it with a spice paste. This preserved meat resembling beef jerky was called *basturma*. Romanian Jews tinkered with the recipe, commonly substituting goose for more expensive beef.

Pastrami did not evolve to peak form until the Jewish migrations to America. David Sax, author of *Save the Deli*, recounted in a November 2010 *Saveur* magazine article that once the Ashkenazic Jews arrived in New York City's Lower East Side, "beef was more plentiful and replaced goose as the protein of choice, and pastrami started to be served hot, as a sandwich, so that the local garment workers could eat it on the job." Gil Marks, in his *Encyclopedia of Jewish Foods*, explains another characteristic of peak pastrami: "In the late nineteenth century, the advent of refrigeration allowed for the use of a weaker salt brine for curing, leading to the development of the softer form of pastrami." With these refinements, it's no wonder pastrami became the sovereign of deli meats by the early twentieth century.

Almost as quickly, this paragon of protein retreated, beset by the labor-intensive process it took to make it and the dubious wonders of modern technology that predominate even today—think brine injectors and liquid smoke. My parents and grandparents may

have considered this progress, but now many of us know that mass production and clever marketing are no substitute for time and careful attention to detail.

The batch of great pastrami I sampled a few years ago was made by a couple of guys who sold the stuff at the farmers' market under the fitting name Pastrami King. They were Ken Gordon and Nick Zukin, who went on to open Kenny & Zuke's. The founders of the other artisan delis celebrated in this book were simultaneously pioneering similar efforts. The old, slow ways of pastrami making have been enjoying a tasteful revival ever since.

—MCZ

Home-Oven Pastrami

Makes 3 to 4 pounds

Delicatessen aficionados might cringe at the idea of making pastrami in the oven, since wood smoking is supposed to be the customary cooking method. At least that's what they think. In truth, some of the most lauded pastrami and smoked meat involve no wood smoke at all. In his must-read chronicle, *Save the Deli*, David Sax reveals that the smoky flavor in commercially produced pastrami comes from fat dripping down and sizzling on the gas element of the large ovens that are used.

This recipe begins with the same cured ("corned") beef brisket as in our Backyard Barbecue Pastrami (page 144). But here, the brisket is steam-roasted until tender, avoiding the more complex process required to make the barbecued version. Smoked paprika adds its elemental flavor without getting in the way of the traditional coriander and black pepper seasonings. The process to create this deli classic is time-consuming: 5 days to brine plus 3 to 4 hours to cook. But trust us, your patience will be rewarded.

Brine

2 cups Diamond Crystal (or other large-crystal) kosher salt

¼ cup (2 ounces) pink salt (see Sources and Resources, page 240)

1 cup granulated sugar

½ cup firmly packed dark or light brown sugar

¼ cup honey

2 tablespoons pickling spice

1 tablespoon whole coriander seeds

1 tablespoon whole yellow mustard seeds

4 cloves garlic, minced

3 to 4 pounds beef brisket

Spice Rub

¼ cup ground coriander

2 tablespoons freshly ground black pepper

2 tablespoons smoked paprika

To make the brine, fill a medium to large stockpot with 3 quarts water. Add the kosher and pink salts, granulated and brown sugars, honey, pickling spice, coriander and mustard seeds, and garlic. Bring to a boil over high heat, stirring often to fully dissolve the salt and sugar in the water. Immediately remove the pot from the heat once the brine boils.

Add 3 quarts ice-cold water to a 2-gallon or larger food-safe container that will fit in your refrigerator. Pour the brine into the container and place the container, uncovered, in the refrigerator until completely cool.

Trim the fat from the brisket until the fat layer is about ¼ inch thick. Submerge the brisket in the cooled brine, cutting it into two pieces, if needed, to submerge it.

Allow the brisket to brine for 5 days, flipping it daily top to bottom and stirring the brine. Make sure that if any of the brisket sides are touching one another you regularly turn them away from each other to expose all of the sides to the brine.

To cook the brisket, pour 4 cups water into the bottom of a 12 by 15-inch roasting pan. Set a rack inside the pan and place the brisket on the rack, fatty side down.

To make the spice rub, mix together the coriander, pepper, and paprika in a small bowl. Evenly rub ¼ cup of the mixture onto the top of the brisket, then flip the brisket and rub the remaining spice mixture onto the fatty side. Allow the brisket to come to room temperature, about 2 hours.

Preheat the oven to 300°F with a rack low enough to fit the pan holding the brisket. Tightly cover the brisket and pan with a double layer of aluminum foil. Bake until the meat reaches an internal temperature of 200°F, about 1 hour per pound, or 3 to 4 hours total.

Without trimming the fat, carve the pastrami into ¼-inch-thick slices, or cut as thin as possible without the meat falling apart. Keep tightly wrapped in aluminum foil or plastic wrap in the fridge for up to 1 week or frozen for up to 6 months.

Backyard Barbecue Pastrami

Makes 3 to 4 pounds

While this pastrami takes more time to produce than the Home-Oven Pastrami on page 142, the resulting depth of flavor makes it worth the extra effort. With the wide variety of smokers and barbecue grills available on the market, we can only offer general instructions on how to perfect this superior pastrami. As with all successful meat smoking, the key is low and slow.

Brine

2 cups Diamond Crystal (or other large crystal) kosher salt

¼ cup (2 ounces) pink salt (Sources and Resources, page 240)

1 cup granulated sugar

½ cup packed dark or light brown sugar

¼ cup honey

2 tablespoons pickling spice

1 tablespoon whole coriander seeds

1 tablespoon whole yellow mustard seeds

4 cloves garlic, minced

3 to 4 pounds beef brisket

¼ cup ground coriander

2 tablespoons freshly ground black pepper

To make the brine, fill a medium to large stockpot with 3 quarts water. Add the kosher and pink salts, granulated and brown sugars, honey, pickling spice, coriander and mustard seeds, and garlic. Bring to a boil over high heat, stirring often to fully dissolve the salt and sugar in the water. Once the brine boils, immediately remove the pot from the heat.

Add 3 quarts ice-cold water to a 2-gallon or larger food-safe container that will fit in your refrigerator. Pour the brine into the container and place the container, uncovered, in the refrigerator until completely cool.

Trim the fat from the brisket until the fat layer is about ¼ inch thick. Submerge the brisket in the cooled brine, cutting it into two pieces, if needed, to submerge it.

Allow the brisket to brine for 5 days, flipping it daily top to bottom and stirring the brine. Make sure that if any of the brisket sides are touching one another you regularly turn them away from each other to expose all of the sides to the brine.

To prepare the brisket for smoking, mix together the coriander and pepper in a small bowl. Evenly rub ¼ cup of the spice mixture onto the top of the brisket, then flip the brisket and rub the remaining spice mixture onto the fatty side. Allow the brisket to come to room temperature, about 2 hours.

In an outdoor smoker or barbecue grill, smoke the meat at 225°F for 6 to 8 hours, or until it reaches an internal temperature of 160°F to 175°F. Oak, maple, pecan, hickory, or fruitwoods may be used, depending on availability and preference. Avoid mesquite, as it gives a harsh flavor to long-smoked meats.

Preheat the oven to 300°F with a rack low enough to fit the pan holding the brisket. Tightly cover the brisket and pan with a double layer of aluminum foil. Bake until the meat reaches an internal temperature of 200°F, 1½ to 2 hours.

Without trimming the fat, carve the pastrami into ¼-inch-thick slices, or cut as thin as possible without the meat falling apart. Keep tightly wrapped in aluminum foil or plastic wrap in the fridge for up to 1 week or frozen for up to 6 months.

Corned Beef Tongue

Makes about 3 pounds

Appearances can be deceiving. Though the sight of a whole beef tongue can be repellent to those who have never cooked one before, the payoff is as handsome as the first encounter can be disconcerting. Prepared properly, tongue has an incomparably delicate, yielding texture and mild, beefy flavor. There is none of the "mineral taste" often associated with organ meat such as liver. No wonder beef tongue, especially corned as in this recipe, has been a Jewish deli favorite for generations. It is likewise a popular protein in Mexican cooking, known as lengua. A meat injector is a useful tool to have for this recipe. It allows the brine's flavor to penetrate deeply into the dense-grained meat. Meat injectors can be found at hunting supply and gourmet kitchen stores.

Brine

1 ½ cups kosher salt

¼ cup (2 ounces) pink salt (see Sources and Resources, page 240)

1 cup packed light brown sugar

1 tablespoon pickling spice

1 tablespoon coriander seeds

2 tablespoons whole yellow mustard seeds

8 cloves garlic, finely chopped

2 bay leaves

1 teaspoon crushed red pepper

1 (2½- to 3½-pound) whole beef tongue

1 tablespoon whole yellow mustard seeds

1 tablespoon coriander seeds

1 tablespoon pickling spice

2 bay leaves

4 cloves garlic, thinly sliced

¼ cup kosher salt

To make the brine, place the kosher and pink salts, brown sugar, pickling spice, coriander and mustard seeds, garlic, bay leaves, and crushed red pepper, along with 3 quarts water, in a large stockpot. Bring to a boil over high heat, stirring occasionally so that nothing sticks to the bottom of the pot.

While the brine is heating, add 3 quarts ice water to a 2-gallon or larger food-safe container that will fit in your refrigerator.

Once the brine comes to a boil, pour it into the food-safe container with the ice water. Stir the diluted brine until all the ice melts. Once the liquid cools to room temperature, add the tongue. (At this point, if you have a meat injector, inject the thicker part of the tongue with approximately 6 ounces of the brine.) Use a small plate to keep the tongue submerged in the brine. Refrigerate for 5 days, rotating the tongue top to bottom every day.

Rinse the tongue thoroughly and place it in a large stockpot with 6 quarts water or enough to cover the tongue by 2 inches or more. Discard the brine. Add the mustard and coriander seeds, pickling spice, bay leaves, garlic, and salt to the pot and bring the contents to a boil over high heat. Decrease the heat to low and simmer for 3 to 4 hours, until tender. Tongue is very dense, so it is difficult to judge its tenderness. Pull it from the brine and slice a piece off the thickest end to test it. Using a clean kitchen towel for added grip and protection, peel away the thick skin from the upper part of the still warm tongue.

Tongue can be served warm or cold, in sandwiches or on its own. Keep tightly wrapped in aluminum foil or plastic wrap in the fridge for up to 1 week or frozen for up to 6 months.

Rare Roast Beef

Makes 3½ pounds

In Woody Allen's *Annie Hall*, perfectly Protestant Annie orders her deli sandwich on white bread with mayonnaise, lettuce, and tomato as Allen's quintessentially Jewish character casts a sidelong glance of bemused revulsion. But for all its focus on traditional Ashkenazic dishes, the Jewish deli has equally been a place of warm hospitality for all. Roast beef is not a dish with roots in the Slavic shtetls; it was too expensive. But it is a long-standing deli standard offering a tamer alternative to the more vibrant varieties of deli meat such as pastrami and tongue. The round roast called for in this recipe is very lean, so overcooking will result in dry, tough meat. Be sure to use a meat thermometer and remove the beef from the oven at 115°F for rare or 120°F medium-rare. The internal temperature of the roast will rise another 10°F or so as it rests.

1 (3½-pound) eye of round roast
1 tablespoon extra-virgin olive oil
1 tablespoon kosher salt
1 tablespoon garlic powder
1 tablespoon onion powder
1½ teaspoons yellow mustard powder
1½ teaspoons ground fennel
1½ teaspoons sweet paprika
1 teaspoon freshly ground black pepper

Pat the beef dry with paper towels and rub it all over with the olive oil. In a small bowl, mix together the salt, garlic powder, onion powder, mustard powder, fennel, paprika, and pepper. Sprinkle the beef on all sides with the spice mixture and rub it in well. Refrigerate the beef covered overnight or for at least 8 hours to marinate.

At least 1 hour before roasting, remove the beef from the refrigerator to allow it to come to room temperature. Preheat the oven to 275°F.

Roast the beef until an instant-read thermometer inserted in the thickest part registers 100°F, 40 to 50 minutes. Increase the oven temperature to 500°F and continue roasting until it registers 115°F and the outside is browned and crusty, about 15 minutes longer. (For an even crustier exterior, put it under the broiler for the last 3 to 5 minutes of cooking.)

Allow the beef to rest for at least 30 minutes before slicing. (To keep roast beef as juicy as possible, it is always best to let it cool completely before cutting into it.) Store the beef, tightly wrapped, in the refrigerator for up to 1 week.

Pastrami Reuben Sandwich

Makes 4

Ah . . . the Reuben. Eating one at Kenny & Zuke's is practically a religious experience: pastrami (subbing for classic corned beef), sauerkraut, and Swiss on fresh-baked rye bread slathered with sweet-tangy Russian dressing, grilled to warm, melty transcendence. The delicious (literally) irony is that the Reuben has become synonymous with Jewish deli grub even though its shameless combination of meat and dairy would have disqualified it from the kosher menus that dominated the early New York City Jewish deli scene. Competing claims attribute the early twentieth-century invention of the Reuben to either serial New York City restaurateur Arnold Reuben or Reuben Kulakofsky, a Lithuanian-born, poker-playing Omaha, Nebraska, grocer. We'd arrange a debate, but both claimants are long deceased. For those without a griddle large enough to handle four sandwiches at once, finished ones can be held in a 200°F oven while the others are being heated.

½ cup (1 stick) salted butter, softened, plus more as needed
8 slices Classic Deli Sandwich Rye (page 190)
12 ounces Swiss cheese, sliced
1½ pounds hand-sliced pastrami
1 cup sauerkraut, rinsed and drained
½ cup Russian Dressing (page 24)

Heat a large griddle over medium heat. Generously butter a slice of the bread and set it butter side down on the griddle. Repeat with 3 more slices of bread. Divide the Swiss cheese equally between the bread slices on the griddle. Next add equal portions of the pastrami, about two layers of slices, to each sandwich. Next add ¼ cup of the sauerkraut to each. Finally, dress the remaining 4 slices of bread with 2 tablespoons of Russian dressing each and place the bread, dressing side down, on the grilling sandwiches. Place a baking sheet weighted with something heavy, such as cans of food or a cast-iron skillet, on top of the sandwiches to press their contents together. Cook for 5 to 8 minutes, until the bottoms of the sandwiches are well crisped and dark golden brown.

Remove the baking sheet. Generously butter the tops of each of the sandwiches and carefully flip them one by one using a large pancake turner. A second turner or spatula pressed firmly against the top of the sandwich as you flip it will make the job much easier. If some of the cheese or meat slips out, just shove it back into the sandwich. Place the weighted baking sheet back on top of the sandwiches and cook them for another 5 to 8 minutes, until the underside is crisp and dark.

Transfer the sandwiches to a cutting board and cut diagonally with a very sharp or serrated knife. Serve immediately.

Pastrami Burgers

Makes 4 burgers

Consider this dish, a Kenny & Zuke's favorite, the love child of traditional Jewish deli and classic Americana—one part old-school New York City Reuben sandwich, one part L.A. drive-in burger post–World War II. For best results, make sure the hamburger meat has no less than 20 percent fat content so that the cooked patty ends up nice and juicy. If you have a meat grinder, grind your own beef using half chuck and half short rib meat. Make the buns with challah dough (page 199) or choose a sturdy store-bought bun, such as a Kaiser roll or, in a pinch, potato buns. Imported, aged Swiss is the most flavorful (if not the cheapest) choice of cheeses. For the '57 Chevy Bel-Air of burgers, make your own pastrami, Russian dressing, and pickles from the recipes found in these pages.

8 ounces Swiss cheese, sliced

12 ounces sliced pastrami, cut into pieces no more than 4 inches in length

1½ pounds ground beef

Vegetable oil

Kosher salt and freshly ground black pepper

4 sturdy burger buns, halved and toasted

½ cup Russian Dressing (page 24)

16 Zesty Zucchini Bread-and-Butter Pickles (page 10)

4 leaves romaine lettuce, cut into pieces no more than 4 inches in length

Preheat the oven to 175°F.

Divide the Swiss cheese and pastrami each into 4 equal piles. Fill a glass with water and set it next to the stove. Divide the ground beef into 4 equal pieces and form each into a patty about 5 inches in diameter, just under ½ inch thick.

Heat a large skillet, preferably cast iron, with tall sides and a cover over medium-high heat. Add 1 tablespoon of vegetable oil to the pan. When the oil begins to smoke, liberally season 2 of the patties on one side with salt and pepper. Place the patties seasoning side down in the pan and season the tops of the burgers with salt and pepper. Cook for 2 minutes, until a dark crust forms on the cooked side of the patties.

Flip the patties, and top each with a pile of the Swiss followed by a pile of the pastrami. Pour a small amount of water, about 2 tablespoons, into the skillet. Immediately cover the pan. Cook for 2 minutes or until the burgers reach an internal temperature of approximately 135°F on an instant-read thermometer.

Remove the burgers from the pan and place them in the oven on a plate or tray to stay warm until the other two burgers are cooked. Wipe out the skillet, then cook the remaining patties in the same way.

Coat the insides of the toasted bun halves with the Russian dressing, using about 1 tablespoon per bun half. Place 4 of the pickle slices on the bottom of each bun. Set the topped burgers over the pickle slices, add the lettuce on top, and top with the remaining bun halves. Do not serve or cut into the burgers until they have had 2 minutes to rest after cooking.

Steak'n

Makes about 2¼ pounds

Keeping kosher involves compliance with many rules sometimes seen as synonymous with Judaism itself. None of the restrictions is better known or more widely followed than the ban on eating pork. For our Jewish brothers and sisters who adhere to this particular ritual and must refrain from the peerless porcine pleasure of bacon, do we have good news for you. The demented geniuses at Stopsky's have created the perfect cure for pork envy and were gracious enough to share it with us. Be sure to use pink salt for this recipe rather than curing salt, which already has sugar in it. Stovetop smokers and applewood chips are commonly available where barbecue supplies are sold.

1 cup pure maple syrup
¾ cup firmly packed light brown sugar
¾ cup kosher salt
½ teaspoon pink salt (see Sources and Resources, page 240)
3 pounds boneless beef short ribs, cut into 2 large pieces, each about 4 by 9½ inches

Mix together the maple syrup, brown sugar, kosher salt, and pink salt in a medium bowl. Place the short ribs in a 9 by 13-inch glass baking dish and rub them with the curing mixture. Pour any remaining curing mixture over the top of the short ribs and let it pool around the edges and underneath. Cover tightly and refrigerate the beef to cure for 3 days.

On the third day, turn the beef over in the dish. The curing mixture will have separated, so stir it and then spread it over the top of the beef, allowing it to pool as it did before. Cover and refrigerate for 2 days longer.

Remove the beef from the curing mixture and rinse it well under cold water. Dry it with paper towels. Set up a stovetop smoker with about 2 cups applewood chips scattered on the bottom and the drip tray set on top. Wrap the wires of the smoker's wire rack (not the entire rack) in aluminum foil and set it over the drip tray. Arrange the cured beef on the wire rack. Close the lid and place the smoker over medium heat. Smoke the meat until it reaches an internal temperature of 150°F in the thickest part, about 1 hour.

Remove the beef from the smoker and set it aside to cool to room temperature. If not using immediately, wrap the Steak'n tightly in plastic wrap and store it in the refrigerator for up to 2 weeks. It can also be wrapped in plastic, then placed in a large resealable freezer bag and stored in the freezer for several months.

To serve, slice the Steak'n to the desired thickness and fry it in a large skillet set over medium-high heat until crisp on both sides, 2 to 3 minutes per side.

Spring Brisket: Leeks and Wild Mushrooms

Serves 6

Early spring brings first-of-the-season mushrooms, including yellowfoot chanterelles, hedgehogs, and morels. Whichever varieties are native to your area will be best, of course. Yellowfoots are more delicate than hedgehogs and will become very soft if overcooked. If fresh fungi are in short supply or too expensive, substitute ¼ ounce of dried chanterelles for the 8 ounces of wild mushrooms that go into the pot with the roast. If desired, you may thicken the pan sauce with a cornstarch slurry or a roux after it has reduced. Accompany the brisket with mashed potatoes, egg noodles, or last-of-winter roasted root vegetables.

3 pounds beef brisket

Kosher salt and freshly ground black pepper

1 tablespoon vegetable oil

1 pound wild spring mushrooms, torn or sliced in half

3 large leeks (white and light green parts only), halved lengthwise and thinly sliced into half-moons

8 sprigs fresh thyme, plus 2 tablespoons fresh thyme leaves

1 bay leaf

½ cup dry vermouth

2 cups Homemade Chicken Broth (page 4) or canned low-sodium chicken broth

Preheat the oven to 300°F.

If needed, trim the excess fat from the brisket so that there is about a ¼-inch-thick layer remaining. Pat the brisket dry with paper towels and season it generously with salt and pepper. Select a Dutch oven or stainless-steel roasting pan that will be large enough to accommodate the brisket, vegetables, and braising liquid. Heat the pan over medium-high heat, and then add the oil. When the oil just begins to smoke, add the brisket, fat side down first, and brown it on both sides, 4 to 6 minutes per side. Remove the brisket from the pan and set aside.

Carefully pour off and discard all but about 1 tablespoon of fat from the pan, just enough to leave a thin coating. Lower the heat to medium and add half the mushrooms and half the leeks to the pan. Cook until tender, about 8 minutes, scraping up any browned bits left from searing the brisket as the leeks and mushrooms release their liquid. Add the thyme sprigs, bay leaf, vermouth, and chicken broth. Return the meat to the pan, fat side up, along with any accumulated juices. Nestle the meat into the liquid. If necessary, add enough water so that the liquid in the pan is at least halfway up the side of the meat. Increase the heat to high and bring the liquid to a boil. Cover the pan tightly with a lid or aluminum foil and transfer it to the oven.

continued on next page

Braise the meat for 1½ hours, then turn it over in the pan. Cover and return the brisket to the oven. Continue cooking until the meat is very tender and easily shreds, 1½ to 2 hours longer. To test the brisket for doneness, use two forks to gently pull the meat apart in the center. The internal temperature should be 195°F for lean brisket, or 205°F if it is a fattier brisket. When the brisket is done, transfer it to a cutting board, fat side up.

Strain the braising liquid into a small bowl, pressing down on the solids to extract any juices, then discard the solids. Allow the fat to separate, and then skim and discard all but 2 tablespoons of the fat. Place the pan back over medium-high heat and add the liquid. Boil the liquid until it reduces to about 1 cup, 15 to 20 minutes. Season with salt to taste. Pour the sauce into a bowl and cover to keep it warm.

Place the pan back over medium heat. Add the 2 tablespoons reserved fat and the remaining leeks. Cook until the leeks are tender, about 10 minutes. Add the remaining mushrooms and the thyme leaves. Cook until the mushrooms are just cooked through, about 5 minutes.

Cut the brisket against the grain into ½-inch-thick slices, or, if it is too tender to slice, pull it apart into large chunks. Serve the meat topped with the mushroom-leek mixture and the sauce spooned over the top.

Summer Brisket: Tomatoes, Fennel, and Summer Herb Sauce

Serves 6

Those who believe pot roast isn't suitable for summer, think again. Our low and slow braised summer brisket is appreciably lightened with the flavors of the season. It incorporates red, ripe summer tomatoes, both the Roma variety and super-sweet little cherry tomatoes. The addition of lager or pilsner-style beer to the braising liquid continues the light and luscious summer theme. Even the sauce for the brisket, in the style of a tart, fresh herb–packed South American chimichurri, is ideal for a festive and easy-to-make warm weather meal with family or friends.

3 pounds beef brisket

Kosher salt and freshly ground black pepper

1 tablespoon vegetable or canola oil

1 large yellow onion, thinly sliced

8 large cloves garlic, thinly sliced

2 tablespoons red wine vinegar

1 cup lager or pilsner-style beer

1 pound plum (Roma) tomatoes, chopped (about 3 cups)

1 tablespoon granulated sugar

2 cups cherry tomatoes, halved

1 large bulb fennel, trimmed and cut into ¾-inch-wide wedges

½ cup loosely packed fresh basil leaves

Summer Herb Sauce (recipe follows)

Preheat the oven to 300°F.

If needed, trim the excess fat from the brisket so that there is about a ¼-inch-thick layer remaining. Pat the brisket dry with paper towels and season it generously with salt and pepper. Select a Dutch oven or stainless-steel roasting pan that will be large enough to accommodate the brisket. Heat the pan over medium-high heat, and then add the oil. When the oil just begins to smoke, add the brisket, fat side down first, and brown it on both sides, 6 to 8 minutes per side.

Remove the brisket from the pan and set aside. Carefully pour off and discard all but about 1 tablespoon of the fat. Lower the heat to medium and add the onion, garlic, and vinegar. Scrape the bottom of the pan to release any browned bits. Cook, stirring occasionally until the onion is tender, 5 to 7 minutes. Pour in the beer and stir in the plum tomatoes and sugar. Return the meat to the pan, fat side up, with any accumulated juices; nestle it in so that it is partially covered by the vegetables and liquid. Increase the heat to high and bring the liquid to a boil. Cover the pan tightly with a lid or aluminum foil and transfer it to the oven.

Braise the brisket for 2 hours, and then turn the meat over in the pan. Cover and return the brisket to the oven. Braise for another 1¾ hours, and then add the cherry tomatoes, fennel, and basil, nestling them under and around the brisket.

Continue cooking until the fennel is tender when pierced with a fork and the meat is very tender and easily shreds, 30 to 45 minutes longer. To test the brisket for

continued on next page

doneness, use two forks to gently pull the meat apart in the center. If it is still a bit tough, continue to braise the brisket for about 15 minutes more, and then retest. The internal temperature should be 195°F for lean brisket, or 205°F if it is a fattier brisket.

When the brisket is done, transfer it to a cutting board, fat side up. Use forks to pull it apart into large chunks. Taste the vegetables and braising liquid and season them with salt and pepper, if needed. Spoon the vegetables and liquid onto a large serving platter. Arrange the brisket in the center of the platter. Spoon the herb sauce over the brisket and serve immediately, passing any remaining sauce at the table.

Summer Herb Sauce

1 cup lightly packed fresh basil leaves

1 cup lightly packed fresh flat-leaf parsley leaves

1 cup lightly packed mixed leaves of other fresh summer herbs, such as mint, tarragon, marjoram, and oregano

¼ cup extra-virgin olive oil

2 tablespoons red wine vinegar

2 tablespoons freshly squeezed lemon juice

2 large cloves garlic, peeled

½ teaspoon crushed red pepper

½ teaspoon kosher salt

Place the basil, parsley, mixed herbs, oil, vinegar, lemon juice, garlic, crushed red pepper, and salt in the bowl of a food processor. Process the mixture until the herbs and garlic are finely minced, about 10 seconds. Transfer the sauce to a small bowl, cover, and refrigerate it until needed. The sauce will keep for up to 2 days.

Fall Brisket: Cider and Butternut Squash

Serves 6

Once summer clicks over to autumn, the seasonal merry-go-round brings fresh apples and a multiplicity of winter squash varieties into the farmers' markets and grocery stores. Our fall brisket recipe uses apple cider and the sweet, orange flesh from butternut squash. The acidity from the cider and wine work together during braising to break down the tough fibers in the brisket. The cooking vapor, fragrant with thyme, bay leaf, and garlic, will work like a snake charmer's music to entice household members and invited guests to the dinner table. The earthy fall flavors and textures of the squash and pot roast will do the rest.

3 pounds beef brisket

Kosher salt and freshly ground black pepper

1 tablespoon vegetable or canola oil

4 cups apple cider

2 cups dry red wine, such as Merlot, Syrah, Zinfandel, or Côtes-du-Rhône

6 sprigs fresh thyme, plus 1 tablespoon minced fresh thyme

4 large cloves garlic, smashed

2 bay leaves

1 (2-pound) butternut squash, peeled, seeded, and cut into 2-inch chunks

3 medium red onions, peeled and quartered, leaving the root intact

Position a rack in the center of the oven and preheat it to 300°F.

If needed, trim the excess fat from the brisket so that there is about a ¼-inch-thick layer remaining. Pat the brisket dry with paper towels and season it generously with salt and pepper. Select a Dutch oven or stainless-steel roasting pan that will be large enough to accommodate the brisket, vegetables, and braising liquid. Heat the pan over medium-high heat, and then add the oil. When the oil just begins to smoke, add the brisket, fat side down first, and brown it on both sides, 4 to 6 minutes per side. Remove the brisket from the pan and set aside.

Carefully pour off and discard all of the fat from the pan. Quickly add the cider, wine, thyme sprigs, garlic, bay leaves, and 1 teaspoon salt and scrape the bottom of the pan to release any browned bits. Return the meat to the pan, fat side up, with any accumulated juices. Nestle the meat into the liquid so it is nearly covered. Increase the heat to high and bring the liquid to a boil. Cover the pan tightly with a lid or aluminum foil and transfer it to the oven.

Cook the meat for 1½ hours, and turn the meat over in the pan. Cover and return the brisket to the oven. After another 1¾ hours of cooking, add the squash and onions to the pan, nestling them under

continued on page 159

and around the brisket. Continue cooking until the squash and onions are tender when pierced with a fork and the meat is very tender and easily shreds, 30 to 45 minutes longer. To test the brisket for doneness, use two forks to gently pull the meat apart in the center. If it is still a bit tough but the squash and onions are done, transfer the vegetables to an ovenproof dish using a slotted spoon; set them aside, covered with aluminum foil to keep warm. Continue to braise the brisket for about 15 minutes more, and then retest. The internal temperature should be 195°F for lean brisket, or 205°F if it is a fattier brisket.

When the brisket is done, transfer it to a cutting board, fat side up, while you finish the sauce. Decrease the oven temperature to 200°F. Remove the butternut squash and onions from the braising liquid using a slotted spoon and place them in an ovenproof dish (if you did not do this earlier). Taste the vegetables and season them with salt, if needed. Cover the dish and put the vegetables in the oven to stay hot.

Strain the braising liquid into a small bowl, discarding the solids. Allow the fat to separate, and then skim and discard it. Clean out the pan and pour the braising liquid back in. Bring the liquid to a boil over high heat, and cook, stirring occasionally, until it is reduced to a thickened sauce that coats the back of a spoon, 15 to 20 minutes. Taste and adjust the seasoning with salt and pepper.

Cut the brisket against the grain into ½-inch-thick slices, or, if it is too tender to slice, pull it apart into large chunks. Arrange the vegetables on a large serving platter, with the sliced brisket in the center. Spoon the sauce over the brisket and vegetables. Garnish with the minced thyme. Serve immediately, passing any remaining sauce at the table.

Winter Brisket: Riesling Sauerbraten

Serves 6

For impoverished shtetl dwellers, beef was a luxury. Even when it was available and affordable, the Ashkenazis settled for the lesser (and tougher) cuts bypassed by the well-heeled. Brisket—along with offal—became the centerpiece of Ashkenazic beef cookery. This remained the case even after the migrations to America. To tenderize brisket, clever cooks relied on techniques such as marinating and braising—long, slow, low-temperature cooking in liquid. Sauerbraten, meaning "sour beef" in reference to its tangy marinade, is a traditional German preparation in which the brisket gets the benefit of both techniques. Avoid the temptation to trim all the fat from the brisket before cooking. The fat helps ensure a flavorful and tender cut of meat on the dinner table.

Marinade

1 (750-milliliter) bottle dry Riesling wine
1 cup white wine vinegar
1 large yellow onion, thinly sliced
1 celery stalk, coarsely chopped into ½-inch pieces
1 carrot, peeled and coarsely chopped into ½-inch pieces
1 teaspoon black peppercorns
6 juniper berries
6 whole cloves
1 bay leaf
3 pounds center-cut beef brisket

Braise

Kosher salt and freshly ground black pepper
2 tablespoons vegetable oil
2 leeks (white and light green parts only), halved lengthwise and thinly sliced into half-moons
1 large yellow onion, thinly sliced
3 cloves garlic, chopped
1 tablespoon fresh thyme leaves
1 bay leaf
2 Granny Smith apples, peeled, cored, and cut into ½-inch dice
1 cup golden raisins

Sauce

1 cup homemade beef stock or Homemade Chicken Broth (page 4) or canned low-sodium beef or chicken broth
¼ cup chopped fresh flat-leaf parsley
Kosher salt and freshly ground black pepper

To marinate the brisket, place the wine, vinegar, onion, celery, carrot, peppercorns, juniper berries, cloves, and bay leaf in a large nonreactive pot or Dutch oven and bring the marinade to a boil. Decrease the heat to medium and simmer for 5 minutes. Remove from the heat and cool to room temperature.

Add the brisket to the marinade and push it down so that it is completely submerged. Cover and refrigerate for 4 days, turning the meat once each day.

To braise the brisket, remove the meat from the marinade. Pat it dry with paper towels, and season it generously with salt and pepper. Strain and reserve the marinade; discard the solids.

Position a rack in the center of the oven and preheat it to 300°F.

Select a Dutch oven or stainless-steel roasting pan that will be large enough to accommodate the brisket, vegetables, and braising liquid. Heat the pan over medium-high heat, and then add the oil. When the oil just begins to smoke, add the brisket, fat side down first, and brown it on both sides, 4 to 6 minutes per side. Remove the meat and set aside.

Pour off all but about 2 tablespoons of the fat from the pan. Decrease the heat to medium and add the leeks and onion. Cook, stirring occasionally, until they are tender and golden brown, about 15 minutes. Add the garlic and cook for 1 minute more. Pour in the reserved marinade and scrape the bottom of the pan to release any browned bits. Add the thyme, bay leaf, and 1 teaspoon salt and stir to combine. Return the meat to the pan, fat side up, along with any accumulated juices. Nestle the meat into the liquid so that it is almost covered. Increase the heat to medium-high and bring the liquid to a boil. Cover the pan tightly with a lid or aluminum foil and transfer it to the oven.

Cook the meat for 1½ hours, then turn the meat over and stir the apples and raisins into the liquid. Return the brisket to the oven to braise for 1½ to 2 hours longer. To test for doneness, use two forks to gently pull the meat apart in the center of the brisket. If it is still a bit tough, continue to braise for about 30 minutes more, and then retest. If it is tender and easily shreds apart, it is done. The internal temperature should be 195°F for lean brisket, or 205°F if it is a fattier brisket.

When the brisket is done, remove it from the oven and allow it to rest in the braising liquid at room temperature for at least 30 minutes and up to 1 hour. (At this point, it can be cooled to room temperature and then refrigerated, covered, for up to 5 days before reheating, finishing, and serving.)

Transfer the brisket to a cutting board while you prepare the sauce. Add the stock to the pan and bring to a simmer over medium-high heat. Cook until it is reduced to a thickened sauce, about 10 minutes. Stir in 2 tablespoons of the parsley, and season the sauce with salt and pepper to taste.

To serve, cut the brisket against the grain into ½-inch-thick slices. Select and warm a large serving platter. Spoon some of the sauce in the center of the platter and arrange the sliced brisket over the top. Spoon a bit more of the sauce over the brisket and garnish with the remaining 2 tablespoons parsley. Serve immediately.

Caplansky's Delicatessen: A Throwback in Toronto

One of the stained-glass window-style posters adorning an exposed brick wall inside Caplansky's Delicatessen in Toronto reads: "Kickin' It Old Shul." The slogan suits the place. Owner and chef Zane Caplansky's Jewish food destination is old school for sure and, like so many Jewish delicatessens, it ranks second only to the *shul*, Yiddish for "synagogue," as a place for the Jewish community to gather. While the shul is all about religious ritual, Caplansky's is nondenominational hallowed ground for disciples of the almighty smoked meat sandwich (the Canadian variation on pastrami) and a dozen other deli menu icons.

The smoked meat is hand-carved to order, leaner or fattier, as customers dictate. Caplansky smokes his briskets for eight hours for an old-world flavor that mass-produced meats can't match. Schmaltz, the classic Ashkenazic frying medium and harbinger of deliciousness, is used unapologetically and often. Everything that can be made in-house is. There's even *kishke*, Jewish haggis of sorts that time has nearly left behind. Beyond deli classics, Caplansky's offers riffs on the old ways to delight the serious *fresser*—and make his cardiologist cringe. Case in point: smoked meat poutine, with the flavor-packed protein joined by French fries, cheese, and gravy. Another latter-day glory is the smoked meat knish combining Caplansky's flagship product with mashed potatoes and herbs, all encased in flaky puff pastry.

Caplansky's is decked out in the blue and white colors of the Israeli flag and the City of Toronto. It has linoleum-square floors; salamis hanging behind the deli counter stocked with mustard, pickles, and rye bread; and pithy slogans posted throughout. Caplansky—who legally changed his Anglicized surname of Caplan back to that of his grandfather—originally sold his sandwiches from the back of a second-story dive bar. Following critical acclaim and long lines, he moved to this clean, bright space near Kensington Market, the historic center of Jewish life in Toronto. The kitsch collection may offer homey comfort here, but it's Caplansky's kitchen craft that is the star.

After the food, the highlight at this popular eatery is Caplansky himself. He's there leading his gastronomic house of worship both in person and on a poster showing the portly, curly-haired chef with arms crossed, striking a deli man's *Iron Chef* pose, still nerdy with big black horn-rimmed glasses, white T-shirt, and throwback diamond-shape disposable cook's cap. Caplansky looks like a comic book superhero in everyday disguise, a kitchen-connected Clark Kent. What distinguishes him above all is his passion for his craft. As with the other artisan deli operators we met as this book took shape, it is easy to tell from a few minutes of conversation that Zane Caplansky thinks and cares deeply about the food—its origin and history, where the cuisine is headed, and the role he's playing to carve out a future for the Jewish delicatessen in the robust Toronto food community and beyond. And it is plain that Caplansky relishes his time-machine ride to revive an anachronism.

Kishke

Serves 4

Getting kicked in the kishkes refers to taking a shot to the gut, but eating a kishke means chomping into a pork-free, patty-shaped Jewish sausage that's been stuffed into a segment of beef intestine, or derma (a "gut" of sorts). Kishke stuffing was inexpensively made with bread crumbs, eggs, onion, schmaltz, and seasonings. Kishke were customarily pan-fried or slowly braised in a pot of tzimmes similar to our Ginger- and Orange-Glazed Carrot and Fruit Tzimmes (page 48) and served for Friday night Shabbat dinner. Caplansky's, the revivalist deli in Toronto, has resurrected and updated this rarely served comfort food classic. Our adaptation dispenses with the derma, opting instead for simple free-form patties.

8 ounces pastrami (mostly fatty parts, if available), sliced

5 tablespoons vegetable oil

1 small red onion, finely diced

1 large clove garlic, minced

1 medium Yukon Gold potato, finely grated

1 medium carrot, peeled and finely grated

½ cup all-purpose flour

½ cup matzo meal

2 tablespoons instant oatmeal

1 teaspoon ground coriander

1 teaspoon ground cumin

1 teaspoon ground ginger

1 teaspoon sweet paprika

1 teaspoon freshly ground black pepper

1 teaspoon kosher salt

½ teaspoon ancho chile powder

Place the pastrami in the freezer for about 1 hour before use. It should be semi-frozen so the fat does not melt.

Heat 1 tablespoon of the oil in a small skillet set over medium heat. Add about two-thirds of the onion and cook, stirring often, until it begins to brown, then decrease the heat to medium-low and stir more frequently to avoid burning until the onion is evenly browned and very sweet, about 25 minutes total. Add the garlic and continue cooking until the garlic is aromatic but has not begun to color, about 2 minutes. Transfer the caramelized onion and garlic mixture to a large bowl and stir in the remaining raw onion, the potato, and carrot. Set aside.

In a medium bowl, mix together the flour, matzo meal, instant oatmeal, coriander, cumin, ginger, paprika, black pepper, salt, and chile powder.

Place the semi-frozen pastrami in the bowl of a food processor and pulse until it is chopped into pea-size pieces, 10 to 20 seconds. Add the pastrami to the onion and garlic mixture and stir to combine. Next, add the flour-matzo mixture in three batches, stirring to combine after each addition. Shape the raw *kishke* into 8 round patties, each about 3½ inches in diameter.

Line a platter with paper towels. Heat the remaining 4 tablespoons oil in a large skillet over medium heat. When the oil is hot, add 4 of the patties and cook, turning once, until they are browned on both sides and cooked through in the center, 5 to 7 minutes per side. Transfer the cooked *kishke* to the platter and cover to keep warm. Fry the remaining 4 patties in the same manner. Serve 2 of the fried kishke per person on warmed plates.

Cabbage Rolls in Tomato Sauce

Serves 6

Cabbage rolls, also known as stuffed cabbage or in Yiddish as prakes, are an old-time Jewish deli favorite that, sadly, are seldom seen except on the most traditionalist menus. Variations of moist-heat-softened cabbage leaves rolled around meat and grain have roots going back millennia. The dish lends itself superbly to home cooking; day-old leftovers taste even better than the freshly made rolls. As with so many traditional dishes enjoyed by the Ashkenazis and other impecunious populations, this one begins with cheap and abundant cabbage and makes a little ground beef go a long way with the addition of rice, onion, eggs, and raisins. The paprika adds a piquant Hungarian accent to the ensemble.

Cabbage rolls

Kosher salt

1 extra-large head savoy cabbage (about 3 pounds)

½ cup long-grain white rice

1 ¼ pounds ground beef

1 medium yellow onion, grated on the coarse side of a box grater

½ cup raisins

2 large eggs, beaten

¼ cup chopped fresh flat-leaf parsley

1 clove garlic, minced

½ teaspoon freshly ground black pepper

Tomato sauce

2 tablespoons extra-virgin olive oil

1 large yellow onion, thinly sliced

¼ cup firmly packed light brown sugar

½ cup dry red wine

1 (28-ounce) can crushed tomatoes, including the liquid

1 ½ teaspoons kosher salt

1 teaspoon Hungarian sweet paprika

Juice of ½ lemon

To make the cabbage rolls, preheat the oven to 325°F. Fill a large pot two-thirds full of water, season it generously with salt, and bring it to a boil over high heat. Line a rimmed baking sheet with a clean kitchen towel.

Core the cabbage and carefully lower it into the boiling water. Boil the cabbage, covered, until the outer leaves are tender, about 5 minutes. Using tongs, begin peeling away the outermost leaves from the cabbage as they are cooked, and transfer them to the baking sheet. Continue cooking the cabbage until all of the leaves that are large enough to fill have been removed. You should have about 12 leaves. Remove the center of the cabbage from the water and thinly slice it, discarding any remnants of the core. Scatter the sliced cabbage in the bottom of a large, shallow baking dish (a 10 by 15-inch glass dish is ideal). Remove the large, white center ribs from the whole cabbage leaves. Set the cabbage aside to cool while you prepare the filling.

continued on next page

Cook the rice in a small pan of salted boiling water for 3 minutes; drain well. In a large bowl, mix together the beef, onion, raisins, eggs, parsley, garlic, pepper, and 1 tablespoon plus 1 teaspoon of salt. Stir in the rice.

Working with one cabbage leaf at a time, fill each leaf with about ⅓ cup (¼ cup for smaller leaves) of the meat mixture. Place the meat toward the tip of the leaf, opposite the core end. Fold the sides over the filling and roll it up to completely encase the filling. Arrange the cabbage rolls in the baking dish, seam side down.

To make the sauce, heat the oil in a large saucepan over medium-high heat. Add the onion and cook, stirring occasionally, until golden brown, 8 to 10 minutes. Stir in the brown sugar until it is dissolved. Pour in the wine and cook, stirring occasionally, until it is almost completely evaporated, 3 to 5 minutes. Add the tomatoes, salt, paprika, and lemon juice and bring the mixture to a boil. Lower the heat to medium, and simmer for 5 minutes.

Pour the sauce over the cabbage rolls. Cover the baking dish tightly with aluminum foil (or a lid if it has one), and bake the cabbage rolls for 1 hour. Portion the cabbage rolls onto warmed plates and top with the sauce. Serve immediately.

Grandma's Goulash

Serves 6

Everyone in Nick's family makes a version of their ancestral goulash. "Grandma's Quick & Easy Goulash," as it is titled in Grandma Zukin's own hand, was passed down from Nick's great-grandmother. As recorded in the 1950s, it is made with bell pepper flakes and chili powder. No one can remember the more "difficult" recipe that preceded World War II. Our version is a throwback capturing the spirit of old-world Hungary, using fresh ingredients and traditional spices. Substitute jarred roasted red peppers to save time if you wish, though Grandma Zukin (and Nick) would tell you that the flavor won't be quite the same.

6 medium to large Roasted Red Peppers (page 15)
3 pounds boneless beef chuck
Kosher salt
Vegetable oil, as needed
2 medium white onions, finely diced (about 3 cups)
6 cloves garlic, halved
1 teaspoon caraway seeds
1 bay leaf
¼ cup Hungarian sweet paprika
½ teaspoon cayenne pepper (optional)
½ cup red wine vinegar
1 tablespoon granulated sugar
Cooked potatoes or egg noodles, for serving

Puree the peppers in a blender or food processor until smooth. Set aside.

Trim the fat from the beef and cut it into ¾-inch cubes. Put the meat into a bowl and toss it with 1 tablespoon salt.

Set a large Dutch oven or wide saucepan over medium-high heat and add 1 tablespoon oil. When the oil begins to shimmer and smoke, add as much of the beef as will fit in one uncrowded layer. Sauté until the meat is well browned on all sides, about 8 minutes. Transfer the beef to a bowl, add another 1 tablespoon oil to the pan, and repeat the cooking process until all the beef has been browned.

Lower the heat to medium and add 2 tablespoons oil to the pan. Add the onions, garlic, and 1 teaspoon salt and sauté until the onions are translucent and soft, about 10 minutes, scraping up the browned bits from the bottom of the pan. Add the caraway seeds and bay leaf, stirring until fragrant.

Nick's great-grandmother Helen Zukin, surrounded by family and friends, in the late '60s.

Return the beef to the pan. Add the paprika and cayenne, if using, stirring to coat the beef. Add ¼ cup of the red wine vinegar and the sugar. Cook over medium heat to reduce the liquid until the harsh vinegar smell dissipates, about 5 minutes. Add 4 cups of the red pepper puree (reserve any remaining for another use), thoroughly mixing to combine everything in the pan. Bring the goulash to a simmer, decrease the heat to low, cover, and simmer, stirring every 20 to 30 minutes, for 2½ to 3 hours or until the beef is fork-tender. Stir in the remaining ¼ cup vinegar and add salt to taste.

Serve hot over potatoes or egg noodles.

RINKS

E...$1.50
E...$1.75
K...$1.75
....$1.75
....$1.75
....$3.75
...........80¢

Bagels Bialys and Breads

CH

WICH...$4.50
.........$5.50
RAMI...$5.50
AGE....$6.20
BALL...$3.20
DER....$3.20
RYE....$6.40

TODAY'S SPECIA

Traditional Bagels
Pumpernickel Bagels
Roasted Onion-Poppy Seed
Confetti Bialys
Hearty Rye Bread
Classic Deli Sandwich Ry
Pumpernickel Rye
Pastrami and Cheddar Sc

Chapter 6

Michael has always lived in Portland, Oregon, the third generation of his family born and raised there. When Michael was little, Harry Mosler, the baker—venerated with the nickname "Old Man Mosler"—was still alive and baking. If you wanted a bagel or bialy, a loaf of fragrant Jewish rye, or a challah for Shabbat, you went to his shop, the last of its kind in Portland.

After Harry Mosler died around the High Holidays in 1969, somebody bought the shop, but they couldn't pry loose Mosler's recipes. Without them, the quality of the breads went straight downhill. Like so many heritage Jewish foods, the once wonderful breads that Michael's parents and their parents took for granted soon vanished from view, replaced by whatever pale imitations could conveniently be found at one of the big new supermarkets that sprouted in the suburbs.

While the old ways are long gone, they are not forgotten. To the contrary, they are being revived or reinvented. With few exceptions, the recipes included in this chapter rely on Jewish bread formulations from old texts, exploration of artisan techniques common to many traditional breads, much trial and error, and Michael's own taste memories going back to the days when Harry Mosler was alive.

Michael's recipes became the foundation for Kenny & Zuke's bread selection. His pride and joy are the bagels (page 180), which he is confident are the best anywhere. But be sure and try the other recipes in this chapter, too: the honey-sweet challah (page 199) is especially nice, whether for Shabbat or as the foundation for French toast (page 102) or a simple sandwich.

Making bread can be intimidating for the novice, but have no fear. All you need is some decent equipment and good basic ingredients (see Sources and Resources, page 239), plus enough patience to let the magic of bread yeast happen. To make the task even easier, the recipes in this chapter are expressed in both weight and volume. Using a small kitchen scale to measure your baking ingredients adds an extra level of assurance that your breads will come out right every time.

Kitchen Equipment for the Jewish Baker

Too many good cooks are afraid to make bread. They shouldn't be. Though the process is a little different from other types of cooking, making great bread is neither highly technical nor difficult. And just to squelch any spurious rumors, successful bread baking does not involve magic or benevolent fairies. All it takes is the right equipment and ingredients, plus a bare amount of skill. Where to find particular ingredients is addressed in Sources and Resources (page 239). For the bread baker's specialized equipment needs, read on.

Kitchen Scale: One of the most vital components in a bread baker's kitchen (beyond the bare essentials, such as an oven and baking sheets) is a kitchen scale. The most useful ones can measure either in grams or ounces (for flexibility) and have a tare function, so you can reset the weight to zero even after you place a bowl or one or more ingredients on the scale.

Your first impulse might be to resist purchasing a scale. Don't. When it comes to bread baking, weight has it all over volume. A fundamental reason to use a scale is to standardize flour measurements. The amount of flour in a bread recipe determines how much of every other ingredient goes into the dough. This is technically known as "bakers' percentage," referring to the fact that every ingredient in a bread recipe is measured in proportion to the weight of flour in the recipe. If the basic flour measurement is screwed up, then the entire recipe will be out of whack. The problem arises from the fact that volume measurements of flour can vary widely depending on how it's measured. By weighing the flour, and other ingredients, you are far less likely to end up with either inexplicably dry dough or a mixing bowl full of goo.

A second reason to buy a scale is to help you standardize the size of your bagels, bialys, and other breads. Even if you have been making bread for a long time, it is still no sure thing to eyeball with precision two pieces of dough or, in the case of bagels and bialys, several small pieces. Equal weight will result in a standard-size piece of dough, and a standard size will result in a uniform baking time. Using a scale takes the guesswork out of the process.

Finally, by using weight as your guideline, any bread recipe becomes infinitely and easily scalable.

Stand Mixer: Unless you have the strength of Superman, you should have a heavy-duty stand mixer with which to combine your bread dough ingredients. Especially with bagel or bialy dough, you will not be able to do as good a job combining the ingredients and developing the dough as a good mixer can in 10 minutes. Plus, hand mixing is incredibly messy with the ingredients some of these breads require: sourdough starter, barley malt syrup, honey, and rye flour, to name a few. Do you really want to end up with sticky bits all over your body and clothing? That is not the fun part of bread baking, unless you happen to be ten years old.

A good mixer has the superior ability to develop the gluten in dough. Gluten is what gives dough its stretchy quality. In finished bagels, for example, gluten development also has a lot to do with the dense chewiness that sets them apart from most breads. Mixing by hand cannot compete with a mixer for developing gluten.

A heavy-duty stand mixer is best, with the emphasis on *heavy-duty*. Even though the bread recipes in this chapter come in mixer-friendly quantities, your mixer will still work hard. It will heat up and it may even struggle as the gluten develops and the dough becomes stiffer. A heavy-duty mixer, preferably a 6-quart or larger size, should be up to the challenge. Whatever mixer you use, if it starts to strain or buck, stop it and scrape the dough down the sides of the bowl or divide the dough into two pieces and mix one at a time.

Oven (or Pizza) Stone: The benefit of using a stone is that a large piece of ceramic will absorb a lot of heat as the oven warms up. Once that happens, it tends to hold and radiate the heat when the bread is baking. This helps maintain a uniform oven temperature, minimizing hot and cold spots that detract from even coloring. To maximize the benefit of using a stone, buy one as big as your oven can accommodate and position it on the floor of the oven, beneath the lowest rack setting.

Smallwares: A selection of small pieces of equipment will also make your bread-baking adventures easier. One helpful item is a metal bench scraper. Bench scrapers are flat rectangular pieces of stainless steel, roughly 4 by 6 inches, with either a wooden or rolled stainless-steel handle at one of the long ends. A good bench scraper has multiple uses, from the eponymous task of scraping bits of dough or other crud from the work surface to cutting the dough into pieces for weighing, shaping, and rolling out.

Plastic scrapers in various sizes and shapes are also useful tools, and they are inexpensive. My favorite has one long end that is straight and a second that gently curves. They can substitute for a metal bench scraper in a pinch. Because they are flexible, they are also useful for scraping dough from the sides of the mixer partway through mixing.

Another must-have is a cooling rack or two. Usually made of a wire grid on stubby legs, the cooling rack allows freshly baked breads to rest until they are cool enough to eat. The raised wire grid ensures good air circulation to speed cooling and to prevent moisture from becoming trapped underneath the bottom, which can ruin the crust texture.

Silicone baking mats are a tremendous innovation for making bread-baking projects easier and reducing waste. They are mostly made in France and are not cheap, but their positive qualities justify what you have to pay for them. Nothing sticks to them, their ability to conduct heat rivals that of metal, and they can be used over and over again, indefinitely. Michael has several that have endured more than 10 years of regular use, making parchment paper nearly obsolete. Breads baked on silicone sheets brown beautifully on the bottom, and there is no need to sprinkle the sheets with anything to prevent sticking. And finished loaves readily separate from them.

Michael is also a big fan of silicone pot holders, but you could probably guess that. They may look like rubber, but they do not melt like it. You can hardly tell that you are holding a red-hot baking sheet even as you are doing so. Silicone is amazing stuff.

One last item: a baker's *lame* is the perfect tool for slashing the top of bread loaves just before they go in the oven. Though a sharp knife may suffice, the *lame* works better. A *lame* looks like a stick with a razor blade on the end. The blades can readily be replaced once they become dull with use.

Now start baking.

Sourdough Starter

Sourdough starter is a fundamental building block for making all manner of artisan-style breads. At its simplest, starter is a pasty combination of flour and water that has sat around for a while. But as it sits, an amazing thing happens. It begins to ferment with the help of useful strains of bacteria in the lactobacillus family and wild yeasts in the air and on the surface of grains. Together the chorus line of microbes create flavor. There is the obvious tartness that comes from acidification, but more subtle tastes also develop from exotic compounds such as esters, flavonoids, and enzymes. World Bread Baking Olympics silver medalist and baking instructor Tim Healea was the first head baker at Kenny & Zuke's and now runs Little T American Baker, a bakery in Portland. Tim says, "Treat your starter like a pet. It's happiest when it's fed before going to sleep and right after it wakes up." He shared his method to make and maintain a vigorous starter. Follow the steps and don't be discouraged if nothing much happens until a few days into the process.

Creation

- 1¼ cups / 7 ounces / 200g whole wheat flour
- 1¼ cups / 7 ounces / 200g organic whole (or dark) rye flour
- 1 heaping teaspoon / ⅛ ounce / 4g barley malt powder
- 1¾ cups / 14 ounces / 400g pineapple or orange juice

In a large bowl, blend the flours, malt powder, and juice with a sturdy whisk. Allow the starter to sit out, uncovered, for 24 hours at about 80°F or 36 hours at about 70°F.

First Meal

- ¾ cup / 7 ounces / 200g Creation starter
- 1¼ cups / 7 ounces / 200g unbleached bread or high-gluten flour
- Heaping ½ teaspoon / Generous pinch of / 2g barley malt powder
- ⅞ cup / 7 ounces / 200g pineapple or orange juice

Reserve the required quantity of starter from the Creation step, disposing of the balance. Combine the flour, malt powder, and juice with the starter using a heavy-wired whisk. Allow the starter to sit out, uncovered, for 8 hours at about 80°F or 12 hours at about 70°F.

continued on next page

Second Meal

¾ cup / 7 ounces / 200g First Meal starter

1 ¼ cups / 7 ounces / 200g unbleached bread or high-gluten flour

⅞ cup / 7 ounces / 200g pineapple or orange juice

Reserve the required quantity of starter from the First Meal step, disposing of the balance. Combine the flour and juice with the starter using a heavy-wired whisk. Allow the starter to sit out, uncovered, for 8 hours at about 80°F or 12 hours at about 70°F.

Third Meal

¾ cup / 7 ounces / 200g Second Meal starter

1 ¼ cups / 7 ounces / 200g unbleached bread or high-gluten flour

⅞ cup / 7 ounces / 200g pineapple or orange juice

Reserve the required quantity of starter from the Second Meal step, disposing of the balance. Combine the flour and juice with the starter using a heavy-wired whisk. Allow the starter to sit out, uncovered, for 8 hours at about 80°F or 12 hours at about 70°F.

After this step, or perhaps the next—the exact timing is not predictable—the starter should begin to activate. That is, the starter will expand and take on a pleasantly yeasty smell. Continue feeding through the following additional steps to foster and stabilize the still-fragile culture.

Fourth through Sixth Meals

¾ cup / 7 ounces / 200g starter from the previous Meal

1 ¼ cups / 7 ounces / 200g unbleached bread or high-gluten flour

⅞ cup / 7 ounces / 200g lukewarm (75°F to 85°F) water

Reserve the required quantity of starter from the prior Meal step, disposing of the balance. Combine the flour and water with the starter using a heavy-wired whisk. Allow the starter to sit out, covered with plastic wrap, for 8 hours at about 80°F or 12 hours at about 70°F.

At this point, a healthy, active, and stable starter culture should have taken hold. Feed one more time, as in the prior Fourth through Sixth Meal steps, and use the starter in any recipe that calls for it once it has expanded to about double its original volume and just begun to fall back. Alternatively, refrigerate the starter until needed.

To Use the Starter after Refrigeration

3 tablespoons / 2 ounces / 50g Starter

1 ¼ cups / 7 ounces / 200g unbleached bread or high-gluten flour

⅞ cup / 7 ounces / 200g lukewarm (75°F to 85°F) water

Reserve the required quantity of starter from the amount that has been refrigerated and dispose of the balance. Combine the flour and water with the starter using a heavy-wired whisk. Allow the refreshed starter to sit out, covered with plastic wrap, for 8 hours at about 80°F or 12 hours at about 70°F.

Use whatever quantity of refreshed starter is needed in the recipe you are using. **But always reserve enough (at least 2 ounces or 50g) to keep the starter going for future use.**

After using the starter in your recipe, feed 2 ounces of the reserved amount (disposing of any excess) with the same quantities of flour and water used after refrigeration, then refrigerate again until needed. Repeat this process for any recipe that requires starter. A stable starter culture will keep well in the refrigerator for up to 2 weeks. If the starter remains unused after 2 weeks, remove it from the refrigerator, reserve the minimum (disposing of any excess), feed it with flour and water, and refrigerate again. By following a proper feeding schedule, a starter can be maintained indefinitely. The longer the starter is maintained, the more stable and easy to activate it tends to be.

What Are . . . Bagels?

Unlike challah, the bagel lacks a biblical provenance. So, unfortunately, there is neither ancient myth nor prophetic symbolism to go along with the bagel. There are at least a couple of stories about its invention that, while heartwarming, are false. The most prominent is that the bagel was invented by Jewish bakers in late seventeenth-century Vienna as a tribute to the Polish troops who saved the day from marauding Turks. This tale might make sense until you consider that historical relations between Jews and the Polish military were never terribly warm. It is far more likely to imagine a little old Jewish baker using a stale bagel like a Japanese throwing star to dispatch one of the despised Cossacks. More telling still are the facts that, according to Matthew Goodman in his book *Jewish Food*, (a) Jewish community ordinances in Krakow, Poland, refer to bagels as early as 1610, well before the alleged act of Polish chivalry; and (b) roughly the same story of Polish military prowess has also been cited to explain the origin of the French croissant and a second Jewish baked item, rugelach. Another good story ruined by facts.

What, then, is the bagel's origin? To put it bluntly, there is no uniformly accepted theory. The authorities are in accord that, in terms of its linguistic heritage, the bagel is a German product, with its etymology traceable to Yiddish and Middle High German words for "ring" and "bracelet." The most clinical recounting of the bagel's history is in Allan Davidson's *The Oxford Companion to Food*: "The bagel is a Jewish bread, apparently originating in S. Germany, migrating to Poland and thence to N. America, where it has become the most famous and archetypal Jewish food." Makes your mouth water, doesn't it?

Another question is, Why the ring shape? Here, pragmatism and symbolism may be at odds. For the baker, it is easy to imagine an early colleague enjoying an epiphany, suddenly discerning that, if he left a hole in the middle of his rolls, he could store or carry a whole bunch of them on a stick or package them simply by running a string through the middle of the customer's desired quantity and tying it off before sending his patron off to home and family.

The more romantic notion, however, according to Marcy Goldman in *A Treasury of Jewish Holiday Baking*, is that the round shape accords with "the ceaseless, never-ending continuity of the life cycle." This is a

superficially sensible explanation. The proof offered is that bagels are served in connection with both Jewish death and birth rituals. Maybe so, but in Michael's experience as a lifelong Jew and dining maven, large platters of food, including bagels, are commonly served at *every* Jewish milestone event. The hockey puck and the doughnut have the same circular shape as a bagel, but no one seems to wax poetic about their relationship to the human life cycle.

The cross-cultural popularity of the bagel is a recent phenomenon, a mixed blessing courtesy of a bagel-making machine perfected in 1962 and put into widespread use by Lender's a year later. Other innovations in the mass marketing of the bagel: flash freezing, upsizing, and the reformulation of bagel dough by Lender's to make bagels spongy-soft. Others have taken things even further, eschewing boiling as part of the bagel production process.

On the one hand, modernization has made bagels ubiquitous in North America. On the other, what they sell at the grocery store today would be barely recognizable by our Eastern European ancestors—and they would make a pretty lousy weapon besides.

—MCZ

Traditional Bagels

Makes about 18

Michael created his bagel recipe shortly after he started baking in 1996. The malty, lightly tangy flavor, crunchy-on-the-outside-chewy-in-the-middle texture, and deep golden color from a short but intense bake set these bagels apart from the crowd. They take a day or two from start to finish, but most of that is to allow for cold, slow flavor development in your refrigerator before boiling and baking. They are worth the wait and they freeze well, too.

6 cups / 2 pounds / 900g unbleached white bread flour

3 teaspoons / ¼ ounce / 10g instant or bread machine yeast (or 1 packet active dry yeast)

2 tablespoons / 1 ounce / 30g kosher salt

¼ cup / 2 ounces / 60g granulated sugar

⅓ cup / 2 ounces / 60g nonfat dry milk powder

1 cup / 12 ounces / 350g Sourdough Starter (page 175)

⅓ cup / 3 ounces / 100g barley malt syrup, plus more for boiling

1½ cups / 12 ounces / 350g lukewarm (75°F to 85°F) water

Semolina flour, for dusting

Toppings, such as sesame or poppy seeds, dehydrated onions, or kosher salt (optional)

In the bowl of a stand mixer fitted with the dough hook attachment, place the flour, instant or bread machine yeast, salt, sugar, and milk powder. (Alternatively, if using active dry yeast, stir it into ½ cup of the lukewarm water to proof for 15 minutes, or until the water begins to bubble or foam.) Add the starter and the ⅓ cup / 3 ounces barley malt syrup to the dry ingredients in the bowl. Add the 1½ cups lukewarm water, holding back a tablespoon or two. (Alternatively, if using active dry yeast, add all the water in which the yeast was proofing plus the remaining 1 cup lukewarm water, holding back a tablespoon or two.) Mix on the lowest speed to combine for 2 to 3 minutes, scraping down the sides of the bowl once or twice, if necessary. Increase the mixer speed to medium-low and mix for another 2 to 3 minutes. If needed, add the remaining tablespoon or two of water (and more, if necessary), a little at a time, until a fairly firm but tacky and elastic dough has formed. Continue to mix for another 2 to 3 minutes to develop the dough. (If the mixer begins to strain or stops altogether, remove the dough from the mixer, divide in half, and finish mixing the dough one half at a time.)

Turn the dough out onto an unfloured work surface. (If the dough is too sticky to handle easily, lightly flour the work surface.) Using a bench scraper or similar implement and a kitchen scale, divide the dough and weigh it into 3½- to 3¾-ounce pieces.

Line each of two baking sheets with a silicone baking mat or parchment paper. Dust with semolina. On an unfloured work surface, use two hands to gently but firmly roll out each piece of dough into a 10- to 12-inch rope. If the dough begins to pull back, allow it to rest for a minute or two before resuming. Form each bagel ring by encircling the back and open palm of one hand with the dough rope, with the two ends overlapping by about an inch. On the work surface, firmly roll the overlapping ends back and forth under your palm until an unbroken ring is formed. As each ring is formed, place it on one of the baking sheets. Each baking sheet should have space for a dozen rings spaced ½ to 1 inch apart. Once all the rings are on the baking sheets, cover each sheet with a dry linen or other lint-free cloth and refrigerate. (While forming the bagel rings, take care to keep other dough pieces from drying out by covering them with a damp towel or by spraying them lightly with water from a spray bottle.)

Refrigerate the bagel rings for 12 to 48 hours, the longer the better to allow the surface to dry out. The dry surface will help promote a thicker, crispier crust on the bagels once they are boiled and baked. The long rest also promotes yeast activity (the bagel rings will puff up slightly) through slow fermentation.

Once the refrigeration period is complete, position racks in the top and bottom thirds of the oven and preheat to 475°F. Fill a stockpot about three-quarters full of water, set it over high heat, and bring the water to a rolling boil. Add the ⅓ to ½ cup barley malt syrup. The water should have the medium caramel color of cola.

Near the stockpot, place one or two clean, lint-free cloths, folded in half or quarters. If using seeds or dried onions as a topping, fill a small, wide bowl half full with each topping. If using salt, pour a tablespoon or two into a small bowl or ramekin. Place the topping bowls near the cloths. Prepare additional baking sheets for use, lining with silicone baking mats or parchment. Place near the cloths and topping bowls, if using. The proximity of stockpot, towels, toppings, and baking sheets should form an easy-to-maneuver assembly line to allow bagels to move quickly from the boiling kettle to the oven.

Transfer the chilled bagel rings (one or two at a time) directly from the refrigerator to the boiling water. Boil each side for 10 seconds, flipping the bagel rings with a slotted spoon, wide-mesh strainer, or similar utensil. Transfer the rings from the water to the cloth to drain briefly.

If using seeds or onions as a topping, place each ring top down in the topping bowl, then transfer carefully to the baking sheet. If topping with salt, sprinkle lightly on top of the bagel ring, then transfer carefully to the baking sheet. Once one sheet is full (6 is the ideal number, spaced 1 to 2 inches apart), lower the oven heat to 450°F and place the sheet in the oven. Bake for 17 to 20 minutes, rotating once or twice to bake as evenly as possible, until the bagels are a deep golden brown.

Transfer the hot bagels from the baking sheet to a cooling rack. Allow them to cool for at least 30 minutes before eating. Bagels are best if eaten within a day if left out, or they can be wrapped well in aluminum foil and frozen for up to 1 month, then thawed as desired. Putting them in plastic or the refrigerator may lengthen edible life but will ruin their crispy crust texture. Toasting previously stored bagels will restore the crust texture.

Note: To make these bagels without sourdough starter, add an additional 6 ounces of flour and 6 ounces of water to the quantities listed in the recipe. The bagels will not have quite the same flavor as the original, but the result will still be satisfactory.

Pumpernickel Bagels

Makes about 18

Rye flour and caraway seeds add a flavor twist, and caramel coloring—sugar that has been commercially cooked down to a deep, dark brown, almost black, color—lends a rich cocoa appearance to these bagels. Once you have learned the basic craft of bagel baking, the trickiest part about making these is tracking down the caramel coloring, since it is primarily a commercial ingredient. Determined home bakers can obtain caramel coloring with a few mouse-clicks or a phone call or two (see Sources and Resources, page 239). The recipe calls for liquid caramel coloring, though 2 tablespoons of powdered can be substituted and combined with the other dry ingredients. Pumpernickel bagels are delicious unadorned but taste best with a light sprinkling of salt baked on top.

3 cups / 1 pound / 450g unbleached white bread flour

3 cups / 1 pound / 450g light rye flour

3 teaspoons/ ¼ ounce / 10g instant or bread machine yeast (or 1 packet active dry yeast)

2 tablespoons / 1 ounce / 30g kosher salt

¼ cup / 2 ounces / 60g granulated sugar

⅓ cup / 2 ounces / 60g nonfat dry milk powder

1½ cups / 12 ounces / 350g lukewarm (75°F to 85°F) water

1 cup / 12 ounces / 350g Sourdough Starter (page 175)

⅓ cup / 3 ounces / 100g barley malt syrup, plus more for boiling

3 tablespoons / 2¼ ounces / 65g liquid caramel coloring

⅛ cup / ½ ounce / 15g ground caraway seeds

Semolina flour, for dusting

Kosher salt, for topping (optional)

In the bowl of a stand mixer fitted with the dough hook attachment, place the flours, instant or bread machine yeast, salt, sugar, and milk powder. (Alternatively, if using active dry yeast, stir it into ½ cup of the lukewarm water to proof for 15 minutes, or until the water begins to bubble or foam.) Add the starter, the barley malt syrup, and liquid caramel coloring to the dry ingredients. Add the 1½ cups lukewarm water, holding back a tablespoon or two. (Alternatively, if using active dry yeast, add all the water in which the yeast was proofing plus the remaining 1 cup lukewarm water, holding back a tablespoon or two.) Mix on the lowest speed to combine for 2 to 3 minutes, scraping down the sides of the bowl once or twice, if necessary. Increase the mixer speed to medium-low and mix for another 2 to 3 minutes. If needed, add the remaining tablespoon or two of water (and more, if necessary), a little at a time, until a fairly firm but tacky and elastic dough has formed. Continue to mix for another 2 to 3 minutes to develop the dough. Add the ground caraway seeds (plus a few more drops of water) and mix on the lowest speed just long enough to incorporate and distribute them evenly in the dough, 1 to 2 minutes. (If the mixer begins to strain or stops altogether, remove the dough from the mixer, divide in half, and complete mixing the dough one half at a time.)

Turn the dough out onto an unfloured work surface. (If the dough is too sticky to handle easily, a distinct possibility when using rye flour, you may flour the work surface lightly.) Using a bench scraper or similar implement and a kitchen scale, divide the dough and weigh it into 3½- to 3¾-ounce pieces.

Line each of two baking sheets with a silicone baking mat or parchment paper. Dust with semolina. On the work surface, use two hands to gently but firmly roll out each piece of dough into a 10- to 12-inch rope. If the dough begins to pull back, allow it to rest for a minute or two before resuming. Form each bagel ring by encircling the back and open palm of one hand with the dough rope with the two ends overlapping by about an inch. On the work surface, roll the overlapping ends back and forth under your palm until an unbroken ring is formed. (While forming the bagel rings, take care to keep the other dough pieces from drying out by covering them with a damp towel or by spraying them lightly with water from a spray bottle.) As each ring is formed, place it on one of the baking sheets. Each baking sheet should have space for a dozen rings spaced ½ to 1 inch apart. Once all the rings are on the baking sheets, cover each sheet with a dry linen or other lint-free cloth and refrigerate.

Refrigerate the bagel rings for 12 to 48 hours, the longer the better to allow the surface to dry out. The dry surface will help promote a thicker, crispier crust on the bagels once they are boiled and baked. The long rest also promotes yeast activity (the bagel rings will puff up slightly) and flavor development through slow fermentation.

Once the refrigeration process is complete, position racks in the top and bottom thirds of the oven and preheat to 475°F. Fill a stockpot about three-quarters full of water, set it over high heat, and bring the water to a rolling boil. Add ⅓ to ½ cup barley malt syrup. The water should have the medium caramel color of cola.

Near the stockpot, place one or two clean, lint-free cloths, folded in half or quarters. If using salt for topping, pour a tablespoon or two into a small bowl or ramekin and place near the cloths. Prepare additional baking sheets for use, lining with silicone baking mats or parchment. Place near the cloths and topping bowls, if using. The proximity of stockpot, towels, toppings, and baking sheets should form an easy-to-maneuver assembly line to allow the bagels to move quickly from the boiling kettle to the oven.

Transfer the chilled bagel pieces (one or two at a time) directly from the refrigerator to the boiling water. Boil each side for 10 seconds, flipping the bagel rings with a slotted spoon or wide-mesh strainer or similar utensil. Transfer the rings from the water to the cloth to drain briefly.

Sprinkle salt lightly on the bagel, then transfer carefully to a baking sheet. Once one sheet is full (6 is the ideal number, spaced 1 to 2 inches apart), lower the oven temperature to 450°F and place the sheet in the oven. Bake for approximately 20 minutes, rotating once or twice to bake as evenly as possible, until the bagels are a deep dark brown, nearly black.

Transfer the hot bagels from the baking sheet to a cooling rack. Allow them to cool for at least 30 minutes before eating. Bagels are best if eaten within a day if left out, or they can be wrapped well in aluminum foil and frozen for up to 1 month, then thawed as desired. Putting them in plastic or the refrigerator may lengthen edible life but will ruin their crispy crust texture. Toasting previously stored bagels will restore the crust texture.

Note: To make these bagels without sourdough starter, add an additional 6 ounces of flour and 6 ounces of water to the quantities listed in the recipe. The bagels will not have quite the same flavor as the original, but the result will still be satisfactory.

Roasted Onion-Poppy Seed Bialys

Makes 8

Bialys are one of the classic Jewish breads, along with bagels, rye bread, and challah, but most people, including a lot of bakers, have never heard of them. Maybe they need a better publicist. These bialys look a little like mini pizzas, thick rimmed and about 5 inches in diameter, though the topping hews to traditional simplicity: roasted onion with a sprinkling of poppy seeds and kosher salt. Fresh from the oven with a pat of butter or chunk of cream cheese melting on top, they make a transcendent anytime nosh. The generally held wisdom is that bialys were named for Bialystok, a town in Poland where they were especially popular among the large pre–World War II Jewish population there. From Bialystok to New York City, bialys remain a Jewish deli specialty best enjoyed fresh from your home oven.

Dough

3 cups / 1 pound / 450g bread or high-gluten flour

2 tablespoons / 1 ounce / 30g granulated sugar

3 teaspoons / ¼ ounce / 10g instant or bread machine yeast (or 1 packet active dry yeast)

1 tablespoon / ½ ounce / 15g kosher salt (we use Morton's kosher salt)

1 cup / 8 ounces / 225g lukewarm (75°F to 85°F) water

½ cup / 5 ounces / 150g Sourdough Starter (page 175)

Vegetable oil, as needed

Topping

2 medium yellow onions, coarsely chopped

2 tablespoons vegetable oil

Poppy seeds, for sprinkling

Kosher salt, for sprinkling

To make the dough, in the bowl of a stand mixer fitted with the dough hook attachment, place the flour, sugar, yeast, and salt. (Alternatively, if using active dry yeast, stir it into ½ cup of the lukewarm water to proof for 15 minutes, or until the water begins to bubble or foam.) Combine for a few seconds with a spoon or by hand. Add most of the 1 cup lukewarm water to the dry ingredients, holding back a tablespoon or two. (Alternatively, if using active dry yeast, add all the water in which the yeast was proofing plus the remaining ½ cup lukewarm water to the dry ingredients, holding back a tablespoon or two.) Add the Sourdough Starter. Mix on the lowest speed to incorporate all the ingredients, 1 to 2 minutes. Increase the speed to medium and mix for another 8 to 10 minutes, stopping once or twice to scrape down the side of the mixing bowl, if necessary, and to check the consistency of the dough. The finished dough should be soft, smooth, supple, and slightly tacky but not sticky. If the dough is too dry, add the remaining tablespoon or two of water a little at a time until the proper consistency is achieved. Start the mixer on low speed after each addition of water to avoid splashing before returning to medium speed to complete the mixing time.

continued on next page

Turn the dough out onto a lightly floured work surface. Knead by hand for 1 to 2 minutes, shaping the dough into a rough ball. Lightly oil a large bowl and place the dough in the bowl, turning to coat all over with the oil. Cover the bowl with plastic wrap and allow the dough to rise in a warm place (such as an oven with the light on or a warming drawer) for 1½ to 2 hours, or in the refrigerator for 6 to 8 hours (or overnight), until doubled. (If refrigerating, leave the dough out at room temperature for 30 minutes to allow the yeast to begin to work before transferring to the refrigerator.)

Position oven racks in the top and bottom thirds of the oven and preheat to 450°F.

To make the topping, peel and coarsely chop the onions. Place the chopped onions in a medium bowl. Add the oil. Using a rubber spatula, fold the onions repeatedly until thoroughly coated with oil. Turn the onions out onto a rimmed baking sheet and spread into an even layer. Roast the onions for 10 minutes. Remove the pan from the oven, and using a large, heatproof spatula, gather the onions into a pile in the middle of the pan, turn the onions over, then spread once again in an even layer. Roast for another 10 minutes, or until the onions have softened and some of the pieces have begun to darken. Remove the pan from the oven and transfer the onions to a medium bowl to cool. Once cooled, the onions are ready to use, or cover the bowl and refrigerate. The onions can be kept in the refrigerator, tightly covered, for up to 3 days before using.

Increase the oven temperature to 475°F.

To make the bialys, once the dough is fully risen, turn it out onto a lightly floured work surface, patting away any excess oil with a paper towel, and roll it out into a 16- to 18-inch log. Cut the dough into 8 equal pieces of approximately 4 ounces each. On an unfloured surface, roll each piece into a ball by using a cupped hand with medium pressure until the dough looks smooth. Flatten each piece into a thick 2- to 3-inch diameter disk. Set aside and cover lightly with plastic wrap. Let the disks rest for 15 to 20 minutes.

As the disks of dough are resting, line two rimmed baking sheets with silicone baking mats or parchment paper and set aside. Remove the onions from the refrigerator if the onions were made ahead and chilled. Pour a few teaspoons of poppy seeds into a small bowl or ramekin. In a separate small bowl or ramekin, pour a few teaspoons of kosher salt.

Generously flour your work surface. Roll each dough disk in the flour to coat. Using a rolling pin, roll each piece out into an approximately 5-inch disk.

Next, hand-shape each disk by holding it up with your hands in the 11 and 1 o'clock positions. Rotate clockwise around the circumference, pinching and pulling to form a 1-inch rim around the edge. After forming the rim, hold the thin disk flat and use your fingers under the back side of the dough to gently pull and stretch from the center outward so that the centermost portion of each piece is very thin, but not quite translucent. Take care not to tear the dough. (If there is a tear, gently stretch and press a little of the adjacent dough over it to repair.)

Next, use the bottom of a half-cup measure or similar flat-bottomed utensil, like a glass, to press down the center of each disk to discourage the dough from bubbling during baking.

Top each of the bialys with 2 rounded tablespoons of the roasted onions, then press down lightly and spread to cover the central portion of the bialy.

Sprinkle a generous pinch or two of the poppy seeds on top of the onions, followed by a pinch of the salt.

After topping all the bialys, place them in the oven and bake for about 20 minutes, rotating the baking sheets about halfway through the baking time, if necessary, to ensure even baking. If the onions appear to be darkening too rapidly, lower the oven temperature to 450°F. The rims of the finished bialys should be a medium to dark golden color with any residual flour tempering the color slightly and giving a rustic appearance. Bits of the onions should be darkly colored, but there should still be plenty of soft, uncolored onions as well. With a large, heatproof spatula, transfer the bialys to a cooling rack. Allow to cool for at least 5 minutes before consuming. Bialys do not keep well at room temperature, so they are best eaten immediately or within a day. If left for more than a few hours, toast briefly to refresh the texture. They can also be wrapped well in aluminum foil and frozen for up to 1 month, then thawed as desired. After thawing, toast briefly to refresh the texture.

Garlic Bialys

Prepare the dough as in the main recipe. Instead of the onions, peel and finely chop 2 small heads of garlic or an equivalent amount of larger, sweet cloves of elephant garlic. Pour 1 tablespoon vegetable oil into a medium skillet set over medium heat. Sauté the garlic for about 3 minutes, or until it just begins to color. Transfer the garlic to a small bowl to cool. Once cooled, the garlic is ready to use, or cover and refrigerate for up to 3 days before using. Top each bialy with a generous teaspoon or two of the garlic, and then bake as directed in the main recipe.

Confetti Bialys

Prepare the dough as in the main recipe. Prepare half the quantity of onions called for in the main recipe. Prepare the garlic as in the Garlic Bialys variation. With a sharp knife, remove the stem end, then halve lengthwise 2 to 4 medium fresh red and green chiles. Jalapeños and serranos are a good moderately hot choice, though personal preference and heat tolerance should dictate selection. It is preferable to use both red and green chiles to give good color to these decidedly nontraditional bialys. Wearing rubber gloves, use your fingers and a paring knife in tandem to remove the seeds and ribs from the interior of the chiles and discard. Coarsely chop the chiles. Add another 1½ teaspoons oil to the same skillet in which the garlic was sautéed, returning the heat to medium, then sauté the chiles for about 3 minutes, until softened. Once cooled, the chiles are ready to use, or cover and refrigerate for up to 3 days before using. In a medium bowl, combine the onions, garlic, and chiles. Top each bialy with 2 rounded tablespoons of this colorful and robustly flavored topping mixture and bake as directed in the main recipe.

Bagel Daze

From the turn of the twentieth century through the 1950s, most of the Jews in my hometown of Portland, Oregon, lived clustered in and around an area remembered as Old South Portland. In those days, there were plenty of good bagels. According to my favorite local history book, *The Jews of Oregon 1850–1950*, three Jewish bakeries competed for the local trade during the first half of the twentieth century. There was the Star, Gordon's, and Mosler's. After World War II, only Mosler's remained.

Harry Mosler was a tough guy, and his bagels, it is said, were the best anyone ever tasted. There were many other Jewish-owned food businesses in Portland in those days: Mrs. Levine's Fish Market (her husband, Mr. Levine, was a *shochet*, a man who slaughtered cows and chickens in the kosher way); Korsun's grocery and Mink's grocery; Calistro and Halperin's delicatessen; and the competing meat markets run, respectively, by Simon Director, Isaac Friedman, and Joseph Nudelman. Mrs. Neushin, smoldering cigarette a fixture between her lips, made her famous dill pickles; and Louis Albert was the soda-pop king.

Harry Mosler was a tiny man. His diminutive stature may explain his big personality. In the photograph of him I once had tacked up at work, he wore a plain white T-shirt and a once-white apron. Below his bald dome, there was a smudge of a mustache, half-moon ears, and bags under his eyes so prominent they announced, "I am a sleep-deprived bread baker." Two stories about Harry Mosler begin to illustrate the man. One is that he never had change for a dollar—you could only get an extra bagel. At the same time, if you were a child, there was always a free bagel for you. The other story, bittersweet and true, is that as he aged, his grandson Darrell—who had worked for Mosler and even attended a fancy baking school in Chicago—begged him for his recipe to assure at least another generation of great bagels. Mr. Mosler refused. He told Darrell what his weary face expressed, "The work is too hard. Do something else."

By the 1960s, the first clumsy urban renewal efforts that had begun in Portland a decade earlier were in full swing. They gave the town a shiny new freeway that bounded the central city on two sides. But at what cost? Much of Old South Portland was obliterated and its insular Jewish community dispersed. At the time, no one gave much thought to the cultural displacement. *Progress* was the watchword of the day; political correctness had not yet emerged as a moral imperative; and neighborhood activism was in its infancy. There was another nasty war going on, the civil rights movement was dawning, and the only food revolution in America at the time involved regrettable innovations such as TV dinners, Tang, and Space Food Sticks. Besides, the prosperous local Jewish community was already assimilating at a rapid pace and heading to the suburbs with everyone else.

The original Old South Portland location of Mosler's Bakery was overrun in the late 1950s. The second location, not far from the first, lasted only a few years before the bulldozers came. Mr. Mosler's last days as a professional baker were spent—emblematically—in a suburban shopping center. When Harry Mosler died in 1969, he took his bagel recipe to the grave. May he rest in peace. No one should have to work so hard.

—MCZ

Classic Deli Sandwich Rye

Makes 2 (1½-pound) loaves

Perfect for pastrami, sublime for salami, can't miss for corned beef—this simple deli rye bread is the marriage-made-in-heaven foundation for any proper Jewish deli sandwich. When we were searching for just the right rye to use for sandwiches at Kenny & Zuke's, a version from which this recipe is adapted came out on top. Proving yet again that there's truly nothing new under the sun, the Kenny & Zuke's recipe is itself a variation on a rye bread recipe from Jeffrey Hamelman's bread-baking treatise, *Bread: A Baker's Book of Techniques and Recipes.*

Rye sour

1 tablespoon / ½ ounce / 15g Sourdough Starter (page 175)

Scant ½ cup / 3¼ ounces / 100g water

Scant ½ cup / 4½ ounces / 125g light rye flour

Dough

4 cups / 1¼ pounds / 600g bread or high-gluten flour

3 teaspoons / ¼ ounce / 10g instant or bread machine yeast (or 1 packet active dry yeast)

2 tablespoons / ½ ounce / 15g kosher salt

1½ cups / 12 ounces / 350g lukewarm (75°F to 85°F) water

⅛ cup / ½ ounce / 15g whole or ground caraway seeds

Vegetable oil, as needed

Cornmeal or polenta, for sprinkling

To make the rye sour, in a medium bowl, place the Sourdough Starter and water, combining with a heavy-wired whisk until most of the starter has dissolved into the water. Add the flour using the whisk in tandem with a plastic scraper to combine into a thick, pasty mass. Cover and set aside at room temperature for 6 to 8 hours or overnight. During this rest period, the rye sour should puff up slightly.

To make the dough, once the sour is ready, transfer it to the bowl of a stand mixer fitted with the dough hook attachment. Add the flour, instant or bread machine yeast, and salt. (Alternatively, if using active dry yeast, stir it into ½ cup of the lukewarm water to proof for 15 minutes, or until the water begins to bubble or foam.) Add most of the 1½ cups of the lukewarm water to the bowl, holding back a tablespoon or two. (Alternatively, if using the active dry yeast, add all the water the yeast was proofing in to the bowl, plus the remaining 1 cup lukewarm water, holding back a tablespoon or two.) Mix on the lowest speed to incorporate the ingredients for 1 to 2 minutes. Increase the speed to medium-low and mix for another 3 to 4 minutes, adding the remaining water a little at a time, if necessary, until a soft, sticky dough forms. Add the seeds and mix on low speed to incorporate, 1 to 2 minutes. Increase the mixer speed to medium to complete mixing, another 2 to 3 minutes. The finished dough should be slightly sticky, with a slight gloss and elastic feel. If the dough seems too sticky, sprinkle a little extra bread flour into the mixing bowl and mix for 1 to 2 minutes longer, until the proper texture is achieved.

Turn the dough out onto a lightly floured work surface. If the dough still seems too sticky, sprinkle a little more bread flour over the top and hand-knead to incorporate. Bear in mind that rye dough tends to be somewhat sticky compared to dough made with all wheat flour. Form the dough into a rough ball. Lightly oil a large bowl and place the dough in the bowl, turning to coat all over with the oil. Cover the bowl with plastic wrap and allow the dough to rise in a warm place (such as an oven with the light on or a warming drawer) for 1½ to 2 hours, or in the refrigerator for 6 to 8 hours (or overnight), until doubled. (If refrigerating, leave the dough out at room temperature for 30 minutes before transferring it to the refrigerator to allow the yeast to start working.)

Preheat the oven to 450°F.

Once the dough is fully risen (and brought to room temperature if refrigerated, about 1 hour), turn it out onto a lightly floured work surface and pat away any excess oil with a paper towel.

Divide the dough in half into roughly square or rectangular pieces. Using both hands, gently flatten and shape each piece of dough. To form each loaf, fold the dough over itself in thirds, as one would fold a business letter. Pinch the seam that forms to seal the bottom of the loaf and roll back and forth once or twice on the work surface. Allow the initially formed loaves to rest seam side down, covered, for 15 to 20 minutes.

After the rest period, tuck and press the ends under the formed loaf to seal and shape the ends. Using friction between the loaf and work surface, roll the loaf back and forth to tighten and complete shaping. The finished loaves should look like 8- to 10-inch cylinders with rounded ends and a well-sealed seam on the bottom.

Line a baking sheet with a silicone baking mat or parchment paper and sprinkle lightly with cornmeal. Gently place each loaf crosswise or at a slight angle on the baking sheet, leaving at least 3 to 4 inches between the loaves. Allow the loaves to rise, covered, at room temperature for 45 minutes to 1 hour, until they have begun to expand but have not doubled. (Avoid over-rising; over-risen loaves tend to fall due to the weak gluten structure in rye dough.)

With a very sharp knife or *lame*, cut two or three parallel slashes about ½ inch deep and 1 inch apart along the length of the top of the loaves. Immediately transfer the loaves to the oven and bake for 40 to 45 minutes, rotating the loaves halfway through the baking time, until the loaves are a uniform dark brown color and the internal temperature reads at least 190°F on an instant-read thermometer. Remove the loaves from the oven and carefully transfer them from the baking sheet to a cooling rack. Allow the loaves to cool thoroughly before slicing, at least 1 hour.

The loaves are best if eaten within 2 days. If left out, store in a paper bag or bread box. Putting the loaves in plastic or the refrigerator may lengthen edible life by a day or two but will ruin their crust texture. Toasting slices of previously stored rye bread will restore the crust texture. Whole or partial loaves can be wrapped well in aluminum foil and frozen for up to 1 month, then thawed.

Hearty Rye Bread

Makes 2 (1½-pound) loaves

Becoming a Jewish baker means learning the quirks of rye bread, the Jewish deli sandwich standard. Rye flour has much less stretchy gluten than wheat, so it's tricky to get the dough to form into springy loaves that rise high in the oven. But rye was cheap and readily available in the Slavic lands, and wheat flour scarce and expensive, so budget-strapped Jewish bakers learned how to work with what they had. They brought their rye bread know-how to America and the Jewish deli. Rye bread has a wonderfully complex aroma and flavor, especially with the addition of caraway and charnushka (also known as nigella) seeds. This hearty bread, with both rye flour and whole-grain rye, may produce a low-rise loaf, but it's as good on its own as it is accompanying pastrami or corned beef.

Soaker

¾ cup / 4½ ounces / 125g cracked rye or rye meal

½ cup plus 2 tablespoons / 4½ ounces / 125g warm (90°F to 100°F) water

Thick rye sour

Scant ½ cup / 4½ ounces / 125g Sourdough Starter (page 175)

½ cup plus 2 tablespoons / 4½ ounces / 125g water

1½ cups / 7 ounces / 200g light rye flour

Dough

2 cups / 9 ounces / 250g bread or high-gluten flour

¾ cup / 2½ ounces / 75g light rye flour

3 teaspoons / ¼ ounce / 10g instant or bread machine yeast (or 1 packet active dry yeast)

1 tablespoon / ½ ounce / 15g kosher salt (we use Morton's kosher salt)

½ cup / 4 ounces / 125g lukewarm (75°F to 85°F) water

¼ cup / 1 ounce / 30g caraway seeds

1½ tablespoons / ½ ounce / 15g charnushka seeds (optional; see Sources and Resources, page 239)

Vegetable or other neutral oil, as needed

Cornmeal or polenta, for sprinkling

1 large egg

To make the soaker, in a small bowl, place the cracked rye, then add the water and combine so all the rye is just immersed in the water. Cover and set aside to stand at room temperature for about 8 hours or overnight.

To make the rye sour, in a medium bowl, combine the Sourdough Starter and water, stirring them together with a heavy-wired whisk until most of the starter has dissolved into the water. Add the flour using the whisk and a plastic scraper in tandem to completely combine into a shaggy dough-like mass. Cover and set aside at room temperature for about 8 hours or overnight. During this rest period, the rye sour should puff up noticeably.

To make the dough, once the soaker and rye sour are ready to use, place them in the bowl of a stand mixer fitted with the dough hook attachment. Add the bread flour, rye flour, instant or bread machine yeast, and salt. (Alternatively, if using active dry yeast, stir it into the ½ cup of the lukewarm water to proof for 15 minutes, or until the water begins to bubble or foam.) Add most of the ½ cup lukewarm water to the dry ingredients, holding back a tablespoon or two. (Alternatively, if using active dry yeast, add only the water that the yeast was proofing in to the dry ingredients.) Mix on the lowest speed to incorporate the ingredients, 1 to 2 minutes. Increase the speed to medium-low and mix for another 3 to 4 minutes, adding the remaining water a little at a time, if necessary, until a soft, sticky dough forms. Add the seeds and mix on low speed to incorporate, 1 to 2 minutes. Increase the mixer speed to medium to complete mixing, another 3 to 4 minutes. The finished dough should be moderately sticky, with a slight gloss and elastic feel. If the dough seems too sticky, sprinkle a little extra bread flour into the mixing bowl and mix for 1 to 2 minutes longer, until the proper texture is achieved.

Turn the dough out onto a lightly floured work surface. If the dough still seems too sticky, sprinkle a little more bread flour over the top and hand-knead to incorporate. Bear in mind that rye dough tends to be somewhat sticky compared to dough made with all wheat flour. Form the dough into a rough ball. Lightly oil a large bowl and place the dough in the bowl, turning to coat all over with the oil. Cover the bowl with plastic wrap and allow the dough to rise in a warm place (such as an oven with the light on or a warming drawer) for 1½ to 2 hours, or in the refrigerator for 6 to 8 hours (or overnight), until doubled. (If refrigerating, leave the dough out at room temperature for 30 minutes before transferring it to the refrigerator to allow the yeast to start working.)

Preheat the oven to 450°F.

Once the dough is fully risen (and brought to room temperature if refrigerated, about 1 hour), turn it out onto a lightly floured work surface and pat away any excess oil with a paper towel. Divide the dough in half into roughly square or rectangular pieces. Using both hands, gently flatten and shape each piece of dough. To form each loaf, fold the dough over itself in thirds, as one would fold a business letter. Pinch the seam that forms to seal the bottom of the loaf and roll back and forth once or twice on the work surface. Allow the initially formed loaves to rest seam side down, covered, for 15 to 20 minutes.

After the rest period, tuck and press the ends under the formed loaf to seal and shape the ends. Using friction between the loaf and work surface, roll the loaf back and forth to tighten and complete shaping. The finished loaves should look like 8- to 10-inch cylinders with rounded ends and a well-sealed seam on the bottom.

continued on next page

Line a baking sheet with a silicone baking mat or parchment paper and sprinkle lightly with cornmeal. Gently place each loaf crosswise or at a slight angle on the baking sheet, leaving at least 3 to 4 inches between the loaves. Allow the loaves to rise, covered, at room temperature for 45 minutes to 1 hour, until they have begun to expand but have not doubled. (Avoid over-rising; over-risen loaves tend to fall due to the weak gluten structure in rye dough.)

Make an egg wash, beating together the egg and 2 tablespoons water. Brush the fully risen loaves all over with the egg wash. Transfer the loaves to the oven and bake for 40 to 45 minutes, rotating the loaves halfway through the baking time, until the loaves are a uniform golden brown color and the internal temperature reads at least 190°F on an instant-read thermometer. Remove the loaves from the oven and carefully transfer them from the baking sheet to a cooling rack. Allow to cool thoroughly before slicing.

The rye loaves are best if eaten within 2 days. If left out, store in a paper bag or bread box. Putting the loaves in plastic or the refrigerator may lengthen edible life by a day or two but will ruin their crust texture. Toasting slices of previously stored rye bread will restore the crust texture. Whole or partial loaves can be wrapped well in aluminum foil and frozen for up to 1 month, then thawed.

Pumpernickel Rye

Makes 2 (1½-pound) loaves

There's no delicate way to say it: Pumpernickel is a German word meaning "devil's fart." It's supposedly a seventeenth-century appellation referring to the flatulence-causing properties of the dark whole-rye peasant breads first produced in the German state of Westphalia during a famine. Ashkenazic immigrants to America adapted traditional pumpernickel, melding it with their own recipes for rye bread and incorporating wheat flour that was readily available in the New World. This bread gets its dark color and depth of flavor from a combination of cocoa powder, molasses, caramelized onions, and natural caramel coloring. Pumpernickel can be substituted for light rye in any deli meat sandwich, though it's also sublime spread simply with peanut butter or canned tuna mixed with mayo.

Rye sour

1 tablespoon / ½ ounce / 15g Sourdough Starter (page 175)

Scant ½ cup / 3¼ ounces / 100g water

Scant ½ cup / 4½ ounces / 125g light rye flour

Dough

4 cups / 1¼ pounds / 600g bread or high-gluten flour

3 teaspoons / ¼ ounce / 10g instant or bread machine yeast (or 1 packet active dry yeast)

2 tablespoons / ½ ounce / 15g kosher salt (we use Morton's kosher salt)

¼ cup / 1¼ ounces / 35g cocoa powder

Scant ¼ cup / 2½ ounces / 50g dark molasses

2 tablespoons / 1½ ounces / 40g liquid caramel coloring (see Sources and Resources, page 239)

⅓ cup / 3½ ounces / 100g Caramelized Onions (page 8, prepared omitting the salt, sugar, and vinegar)

1½ cups / 12 ounces / 350g lukewarm (75°F to 85°F) water

⅛ cup / ½ ounce / 15g whole or ground caraway seeds or charnushka seeds (see Sources and Resources, page 239), or a mixture of both

Vegetable oil, as needed

Cornmeal or polenta, for sprinkling

1 large egg

continued on next page

To make the rye sour, in a medium bowl, place the Sourdough Starter and water, combining with a heavy-wired whisk until most of the starter has dissolved into the water. Add the flour using the whisk in tandem with a plastic scraper to combine into a thick, pasty mass. Cover and set aside at room temperature for 6 to 8 hours or overnight. During this rest period, the rye sour should puff up slightly.

To make the dough, once the sour is ready, transfer it to the bowl of a stand mixer fitted with the dough hook attachment. Add the flour, instant or bread machine yeast, salt, cocoa powder, molasses, caramel coloring, and onions. (Alternatively, if using active dry yeast, stir it into ½ cup of the lukewarm water to proof for 15 minutes, or until the water begins to bubble or foam.) Add most of the 1½ cups lukewarm water, holding back a tablespoon or two. (Alternatively, if using active dry yeast, add all the water the yeast was proofing in, plus the remaining 1 cup lukewarm water, holding back a tablespoon or two.) Mix on the lowest speed to incorporate the ingredients for 1 to 2 minutes. Increase the speed to medium-low, and mix for another 3 to 4 minutes, adding the remaining water, a little at a time if necessary, until a soft, sticky dough forms. Add the seeds and mix on low speed to incorporate, 1 to 2 minutes. Increase the mixer speed to medium to complete mixing, another 2 to 3 minutes. The finished dough should be slightly sticky, with a slight gloss and elastic feel. If the dough seems too sticky, sprinkle a little extra bread flour into the mixing bowl and mix for 1 to 2 minutes longer, until the proper texture is achieved.

Turn the dough out onto a lightly floured work surface. If the dough still seems too sticky, sprinkle a little more bread flour over the top and hand-knead to incorporate. Bear in mind that rye dough tends to be somewhat sticky compared to dough made with all wheat flour. Form the dough into a rough ball. Lightly oil a large bowl and place the dough in the bowl, turning to coat all over with the oil. Cover the bowl with plastic wrap and allow the dough to rise in a warm place (such as an oven with the light on or a warming drawer) for 1½ to 2 hours, or in the refrigerator for 6 to 8 hours (or overnight), until doubled. (If refrigerating, leave the dough out at room temperature for 30 minutes before transferring it to the refrigerator to allow the yeast to start working.)

Preheat the oven to 475°F.

Once the dough is fully risen (and brought to room temperature if refrigerated, about 1 hour), turn it out onto a lightly floured work surface and pat away any excess oil with a paper towel.

Divide the dough in half into roughly square or rectangular pieces. Using both hands, gently flatten and shape each piece of dough. To form each loaf, fold the dough over itself in thirds, as one would fold a business letter. Pinch the seam that forms to seal the bottom of the loaf and roll back and forth once or twice on the work surface. Allow the initially formed loaves to rest seam side down, covered, for 15 to 20 minutes.

After the rest period, tuck and press the ends under the formed loaf to seal and shape the ends. Using the friction between the loaf and work surface, roll the loaf back and forth to tighten and complete shaping. The finished loaves should look like 8- to 10-inch cylinders with rounded ends and a well-sealed seam on the bottom.

Line a baking sheet with a silicone baking mat or parchment paper and sprinkle lightly with cornmeal. Gently place each loaf crosswise or at a slight angle on the baking sheet, leaving at least 3 to 4 inches between the loaves. Allow the loaves to rise, covered, at room temperature for 45 minutes to

1 hour, until they have begun to expand but have not doubled. (Avoid over-rising; over-risen loaves tend to fall due to the weak gluten structure in rye dough.)

In a small bowl, make an egg wash by lightly beating the egg together with 2 tablespoons water. Using a light touch, brush the egg wash all over the exposed surfaces of the fully risen loaves.

With a very sharp knife or *lame*, cut three parallel slashes about ½ inch deep and 2 inches apart widthwise across the top of the loaves. Immediately transfer the loaves to the oven and bake for about 45 minutes, rotating the loaves halfway through the baking time, until the loaves are a uniform deep, dark chocolate brown color and the internal temperature reads at least 190°F on an instant-read thermometer. Remove the loaves from the oven and carefully transfer them from the baking sheet to a cooling rack. Allow the loaves to cool thoroughly before slicing, at least 1 hour.

The loaves are best if eaten within 2 days. If left out, store in a paper bag or bread box. Putting the loaves in plastic or the refrigerator may lengthen edible life by a day or two but will ruin their crust texture. Toasting slices of previously stored rye bread will restore the crust texture. Whole or partial loaves can be wrapped well in aluminum foil and frozen for up to 1 month, then thawed.

Note: Two tablespoons of dry caramel coloring may be substituted for liquid. Another coloring alternative is food gel, which is produced by several companies. Unlike caramel coloring, which is obtained from natural sugars, food gels are synthetic. Also, using food gel can be tricky because it is difficult to tell from a small concentrated container how the color will turn out once it is mixed with a batch of dough and how much should be used. Use the darkest shade of brown food gel available, starting with ¼ teaspoon and adding another ¼ to ½ teaspoon as needed to obtain the darkest possible shade of brown achievable with that color.

Three-Strand Braided Challah

Makes 2 (2-pound) loaves

The subtle honey-sweet flavor of this braided Jewish festival bread makes it a favorite anytime. We love to use a single-flower honey, such as blackberry, or, when we can find it, a variety called meadow foam, which has a unique, memorable flavor resembling marshmallows. Traditionalists pull their challah (pronounced with a hard "ch" sound) apart in chunks for casual eating, but it also makes fine sliced sandwich bread. And day-old challah is on par with brioche to make the most divine French toast, if the fresh loaves don't disappear first. If you intend to make Chocolate Babka (page 224) or Challah Sticky Buns (page 227), prepare a sweeter version of this dough by increasing the quantity of brown sugar to ½ cup and decreasing the salt to 2 teaspoons. Mix the dough and allow it to rise as instructed in this recipe, and then follow the respective recipes for their particular shaping and baking instructions.

- 7 cups / 1¾ pounds / 850g unbleached all-purpose or bread flour
- Scant 5 tablespoons / 2 ounces / 50g light or dark brown sugar
- 6 teaspoons / ½ ounce / 20g instant or bread machine yeast (or 2 packets active dry yeast)
- 2¼ teaspoons / ¾ ounce / 25g kosher salt
- ½ cup / 6 ounces / 200g honey
- 6 tablespoons (¾ stick) / 3 ounces / 100g unsalted butter, melted
- 3 large eggs, lightly beaten, plus 2 large eggs for egg wash
- 1 cup / 8 ounces / 225g lukewarm (75°F to 85°F) water, plus more as needed
- Vegetable oil, as needed
- 4 teaspoons sesame seeds or poppy seeds (optional)

Whisk together the flour, brown sugar, instant or bread machine yeast, and salt in the bowl of a stand mixer fitted with the dough hook attachment. (Alternatively, if using active dry yeast, stir it into ½ cup of the lukewarm water to proof for 15 minutes, or until the water begins to bubble or foam.) Add the honey, melted butter, and 3 eggs. Add 1 cup of the lukewarm water to the center of the dry ingredients. (Alternatively, if using active dry yeast, add all the water the yeast was proofing in, plus the remaining ½ cup lukewarm water, to the center of the dry ingredients.) Mix the dough on low speed to moisten the dry ingredients and create a tacky, slightly sticky dough. If the dough is too dry, add up to ½ cup more water, 1 tablespoon at a time, until the dough reaches the proper consistency. Increase the speed to medium-low and mix for about 3 minutes, until the dough is glossy and elastic. (Alternatively, this dough may be mixed by hand. After initially

continued on next page

combining the dry and wet ingredients, knead for 20 to 30 minutes, until the proper consistency is achieved.)

Lightly oil a large bowl. Shape the dough into a ball and place it into the bowl, turning to coat all sides of the dough with oil. Cover the bowl with plastic wrap and set in a warm place (such as an oven with the light on or a warming drawer set to 80°F) to rise until doubled in size, about 2 hours.

Line a baking sheet with a silicone baking mat or parchment paper.

Divide the dough in half and set one piece aside, covered with a cloth. Divide the other piece into 3 equal pieces and roll each on a lightly floured work surface into a rope about 12 inches long. Set the 3 strands parallel to one another with about 1 inch between them.

Pinch the tips of the strands together at one end to seal them. Starting at the pinched end, braid the strands, placing left over middle, right over middle, left over middle, and so on, until the entire length of strands is braided. Pinch together the remaining ends, then fold both ends slightly under the loaf to ensure an attractive appearance. Repeat with the remaining dough ball.

Carefully transfer the loaves to the prepared baking sheet, arranging them so that they have as much room as possible to expand and spread. Cover the loaves with a towel and let rise for 45 minutes, or until nearly doubled in size.

About 30 minutes before baking, preheat the oven to 375°F.

Whisk the remaining 2 eggs in a small bowl with 2 tablespoons water to make an egg wash. Remove the towel from the loaves and brush them generously with the egg wash. Place the baking sheet in the oven and lower the temperature to 350°F. Bake for 20 minutes. Remove the baking sheet from the oven and generously brush the loaves one more time with the egg wash. Immediately sprinkle the sesame seeds, if desired, over the loaves.

Return the loaves to the oven, rotating the pan 180 degrees, and bake for 15 to 20 minutes longer, until the loaves are dark golden brown. (If you have an instant-read thermometer, the loaves should register at least 190°F.) Transfer the loaves to a wire rack to cool completely before serving, at least 1 hour.

The loaves are best if eaten within 2 days. If left out, store in a paper bag or bread box. Putting the loaves in plastic wrap or the refrigerator may lengthen edible life by a day or two. Whole or partial loaves can be wrapped well in aluminum foil or plastic wrap and frozen for up to 1 month, then thawed.

Stopsky's Pretzels

Makes six 5-ounce pretzels

At Stopsky's Deli in Seattle, they make a pretzel to die for. Happily, they shared the recipe with us to share with you. We've adapted the recipe for the home baker, but it still relies on food-grade lye (see Sources and Resources, page 240) to make the perfect dark, leathery crust. That means science lab precautions are required: rubber gloves and eye protection or don't even think about it! (If lye comes into contact with your skin, it will burn. It should be rinsed off with vinegar immediately to neutralize it.) While baking, the lye loses its caustic properties and becomes safe to consume.

3 teaspoons / ¼ ounce / 10g active dry yeast (1 package)

1 cup / 8 ounces /225g warm (90°F to 100°F) water

About 1 tablespoon / ¼ ounce / 10g malt powder (see Sources and Resources, page 240) or firmly packed dark brown sugar

About 3¼ cups/ 1¼ pounds/ 625g unbleached bread flour

2 tablespoons / 1 ounce / 30g unsalted butter, cubed and at room temperature, plus more for greasing the bowl

About 2 teaspoons / ¼ ounce / 7g kosher salt

Cooking spray

2 tablespoons food-grade lye, or ¼ cup baking soda, treated (see Note)

Coarse salt, such as pretzel salt, for topping

To make the dough, sprinkle the yeast over the warm water in the bowl of a stand mixer fitted with the paddle attachment. Stir in the malt powder until it is dissolved. Allow the yeast to proof for about 15 minutes, or until the water begins to bubble or foam. Add the flour, butter, and salt to the yeast mixture and mix on low speed until a ball forms. The dough should be quite firm and may be slightly tacky but should not be sticky. If it is sticky, add a little more flour, about 1 tablespoon at a time, and mix it in until the dough is smooth. If the dough is too dry to come together, add more water, 1 teaspoon at a time, until the proper consistency is reached. Continue kneading on medium-low speed until the dough is elastic, 5 to 7 minutes. Alternatively, mix the dough by hand in a large bowl and then turn it out on an unfloured work surface and knead it for 8 to 10 minutes.

Lightly grease a large bowl with butter. Place the dough ball in the bowl, coat it all over, and cover it with plastic wrap. Set the dough in a warm place (such as an oven with the light on or a warming drawer set to 80°F) to rise until doubled in size, about 2 hours.

Spray two rimmed baking sheets with cooking spray and set aside.

continued on next page

Turn the dough out on an unfloured work surface and firmly press it down to deflate. Cut the dough into 6 equal portions. Working with one piece of dough at a time and keeping the rest covered, pat the dough down and shape into a rectangle and then tightly roll it up lengthwise, forming it into a little loaf. Pinch the resulting seam together. Shape the dough into a rope by rolling it against the work surface using your palms and applying mild pressure, working from the center of the dough out. If you need more friction, spray the counter with a little water from a squirt bottle or drizzle a few drops of water and spread it with your hand. Once you can feel that the dough rope doesn't want to stretch any farther (usually when it is 12 to 16 inches long), set it aside to rest and begin shaping another piece in the same manner. Repeat this process with the remaining pieces of dough and cover.

Return to the first dough rope and continue rolling it out to a length of 34 to 38 inches, leaving the center about 1 inch in diameter and tapering the ends by applying a little more pressure as you work your way out. Position the dough rope into a U shape with the ends pointing away from you. Holding one of the ends in each hand, cross the dough and then cross it again. Fold the ends down and press them into the U at about 4 and 8 o'clock. Place the pretzel on one of the prepared baking sheets. Repeat this process with the remaining dough, spacing the pretzels out on the baking sheets a few inches apart.

Allow the pretzels to rise in a warm spot until they have increased in size by half, about 30 minutes. Transfer the pretzels to the refrigerator, uncovered, for at least 8 hours and up to 24 hours for the flavor to develop and a skin to form on the outside of the dough. (This will help promote a chewy crust.)

About 30 minutes before baking, position racks in the top and bottom thirds of the oven and preheat it to 450°F. Bring 1 cup water to a boil over high heat. With gloves on and eye protection in place, place the lye in a large stainless-steel bowl. Slowly pour in 3 cups room temperature water and stir to dissolve. Next, pour the boiling water into the bowl, being careful not to breathe in any of the steam.

Using a large skimmer or your gloved hands, gently dip the pretzels in the lye solution. Leave them in the solution for about 20 seconds, carefully turning once after 10 seconds. Avoid any splashing. Remove one of the pretzels from the liquid, drain over the bowl, and return it to the baking sheet. Repeat with the remaining pretzels. While each pretzel is being dipped, spray the baking sheet with more nonstick spray to ensure that the pretzels won't stick when they are baked. After dipping, use a sharp paring knife or a razor blade to cut a deep slit in the thickest part of each pretzel. Sprinkle the pretzels with coarse salt.

Bake the pretzels until they are deeply browned, 12 to 15 minutes, rotating the pans halfway through the baking time to ensure even browning. Transfer the pretzels to a rack to cool for about 5 minutes before serving.

The pretzels are best the day they are made, but they can be stored, covered, at room temperature for up to 2 days. Reheat them in a 350°F oven for about 5 minutes to refresh the crust.

Note: As a substitute for lye, spread ¼ cup baking soda on a pie plate and bake at 300°F for 1 hour. Use as instructed to create the dipping liquid for the pretzels. Lye solution can easily be neutralized for safe disposal by adding 2 tablespoons of distilled white vinegar.

Pastrami and Cheddar Scones

Makes 12

These amazingly moist and full-flavored scones come to us from Mile End Deli, where they use Montreal smoked meat instead of pastrami, relying on the recipe devised by Mile End co-founder (and resident sardonic wit) Noah Bernamoff. At Mile End, they are always looking for ways to use the non-sandwich-worthy shards of smoked meat that flake off during carving, according to Mile End's other founder, Rachel Cohen. One use is Mile End's version of poutine, the Canadian one-course-weight-gain plan made with French fries, cheese curds, gravy, and bits of meat. These scones are a less outrageous, French fry– and gravy-free, play on poutine that can be eaten out of hand.

3 cups unbleached all-purpose flour, plus more for dusting
6½ tablespoons cold unsalted butter, cubed
3 tablespoons cornmeal
2 teaspoons kosher salt
1½ teaspoons baking powder
1 teaspoon baking soda
¼ teaspoon smoked paprika
⅛ teaspoon freshly ground black pepper
1½ cups diced pastrami
1 cup cold diced sharp cheddar cheese (about 4 ounces)
1 cup cold buttermilk
½ cup cold heavy cream

Position one rack in the upper third and another rack in the lower third of the oven and preheat it to 375°F. Line two baking sheets with silicone baking mats or parchment paper.

Place the flour and butter in the bowl of a food processor. Process until the butter is incorporated into the flour in small pieces, with the largest about pea-size and the smallest like grains of rice. Transfer the mixture to a large mixing bowl and stir in the cornmeal, salt, baking powder, baking soda, paprika, and black pepper. Stir in the pastrami and cheese. Add the buttermilk and cream and gently combine the mixture with a large rubber spatula or wooden spoon until it forms a moist dough.

Transfer the dough to a well-floured work surface. Dust your hands and the top of the dough with flour and form the dough into a large ball. Divide the ball of dough in half and shape each half into a large disk about 1 inch thick. Cut each disk into 6 wedges, as if you were cutting a pie. Arrange the wedges about 2 inches apart on the baking sheets. Bake until they are golden brown, 17 to 20 minutes, rotating the baking sheets in the oven halfway through the baking time. Transfer the scones to a wire rack to cool. They are best enjoyed the day they are made, though they will keep in a covered container at room temperature for up to 3 days.

Delica

Pastries, Desserts and Drinks

DAY'S
ECIAL

RAMI
BEN
&
DMA'S
LASH
95

bout
to Go!

Classic Brown Sugar and Cinnamon Rugelach

Hamantaschen
Chocolate-Dipped Coconut Macar
Chocolate Babka
Challah Sticky Buns
Passover Honey Cake
Apple Cake
Sweet Noodle Kugel
Cheesecake with Shortbread Crus

Celery Soda
Egg Cream
Spicy Ginger Ale

Chapter 7

Every meal deserves a sweet finish, which is why it's hard to find a Jewish delicatessen worth its salt (or sugar, as the case may be) that doesn't pride itself on a slate of specialty desserts. On the typical deli menu, the house baker's skills are showcased in one or more varieties of crescent-shaped rugelach (pronounced *ROO-guh-lakh*). Home bakers can replicate the feat with our classic brown sugar–cinnamon rugelach or seasonal fruit-filled variations (pages 209–215). Jiggly, rich cheesecake (page 230) is another deli tradition that can be made in your home kitchen, but promise to let it cool ever so slowly, as the recipe requires, to avoid a cracked top.

Naturally, we couldn't avoid tinkering with the old ways to create something that is at once thoroughly modern but still harkens back to the traditional. There is no finer (or sweeter) example than our Challah Sticky Buns (page 227).

Sweets made for Jewish holidays frequently appear on deli menus, but they are accessible to anyone with the desire and a few basic ingredients. Triangle-shaped Hamantaschen (page 219) have a great story behind them from the Old Testament's Book of Esther and a flavor that melds a sweet pastry crust and a poppy or prune filling. No one is 100 percent sure how northern European Jews began to bake coconuty macaroons (page 222) that look like miniature haystacks. What we do know is that they are moist and delicious (especially when dipped in dark chocolate) and, with no flour in the recipe, have long been a family Passover favorite.

A handful of deli-specific drinks are likewise sure to satisfy any sweet tooth. Consider the Egg Cream (page 237), which is made with neither egg nor cream, or a strangely satisfying Celery Soda (page 233). Try one or all. These beverages are a cinch to make and serve as a refreshing alternative to the usual soda suspects.

Rugelach with Seasonal Fillings

On the sweets side of a Jewish deli menu, rugelach is a mid-twentieth-century creation that has achieved broad cross-cultural popularity. Adapted from the traditional crescent-shaped central European *kipfel*, they are made with an enriched pastry dough and any number of fillings. The dough is cut into disks, which are then dabbed with the filling, cut into wedges, and rolled up pinwheel-style into crescent shapes. A short stint in the oven and, voilà: A star is born. We offer the full recipe for traditional brown sugar– and cinnamon-filled rugelach, plus filling variations to suit each season. For the seasonal rugelach, the only difference from the main recipe is the filling and an increase in cooking time, as directed.

Classic Brown Sugar and Cinnamon Rugelach

Makes 16

This is similar to the rugelach served at Kenny & Zuke's Delicatessen. The pastry, using both butter and cream cheese, is a synthesis of two recipes, one by fabled Jewish cookbook author Joan Nathan and another that appeared in *Cook's Illustrated* magazine.

Dough

1 cup all-purpose flour

¼ cup confectioners' sugar

Pinch of kosher salt

½ cup (1 stick) cold unsalted butter, coarsely chopped

4 ounces (½ cup) cold cream cheese, broken into about 4 pieces

½ teaspoon freshly squeezed lemon juice

½ teaspoon pure vanilla extract

Filling

2 cups packed dark brown sugar

2 teaspoons ground cinnamon (see Sources and Resources, page 239)

½ teaspoon ground ginger

½ cup raisins

½ cup chopped walnuts

Topping

1 large egg

½ cup turbinado sugar

To make the dough, pulse the flour, confectioners' sugar, and salt in a food processor to combine them. Add half the butter and pulse until the mixture becomes dry and pebbly. Add the remaining butter and pulse again until combined. Add half the cream cheese and pulse until it is fully incorporated. Add the remaining cream cheese, lemon juice, and vanilla and pulse until the mixture clumps up around the blade in a ball. Remove the dough from the food processor and divide it in half. Flatten each half into a disk about 4 inches in diameter. Wrap the disks separately in plastic wrap and refrigerate for at least 15 minutes.

continued on page 211

Roll one of the chilled dough disks between sheets of parchment paper into a 10-inch round. Repeat with the second disk. Refrigerate for at least 30 minutes.

To make the filling, combine the brown sugar, cinnamon, ginger, raisins, and walnuts in a bowl and thoroughly mix. Set aside.

Line a baking sheet with a silicone baking mat or parchment paper.

Place one of the dough rounds on a lightly floured work surface (a cold stone slab is best, if available). Peel off the top sheet of parchment, then flip the dough over and remove the second sheet of parchment.

Spread half the filling mixture evenly over the dough. With a pizza cutter, cut the dough into quarters. Then, bisect each quarter to make 8 equal wedges. Tightly roll each wedge, starting at the wide, outside edge and rolling toward the center, to form 8 crescent-shaped rugelach.

Evenly space the rugelach on the prepared baking sheet, leaving at least 1 inch between them. Repeat with the second dough round. Refrigerate the rugelach for 30 minutes, or freeze them for 15 minutes.

While the rugelach chill, preheat the oven to 350°F.

To make the topping, in a small bowl, whisk the egg with 1 tablespoon water to make an egg wash. Generously brush 4 of the rugelach at a time with egg wash and sprinkle generously with the turbinado sugar. Repeat until all are topped.

Bake the rugelach for about 25 minutes, until they are dark golden brown, rotating the pan front to back after the first 15 minutes to ensure even baking. Transfer the baking sheet to a wire rack to cool completely.

When cool, remove the rugelach from the baking sheet with a spatula and store in an airtight container or plastic bag for up to 3 days.

Spring: Strawberry-Rhubarb Filling

Makes enough filling for 16 rugelach

A harbinger of spring, rhubarb is invariably the first local fruit to be found at early season farmers' markets. A few weeks later, spring sun permitting, come the first-of-the-year strawberries. These seasonal rugelach take full advantage of both early spring fruit flavors.

- 1 rhubarb stalk, thinly sliced (about 1 cup)
- 8 ounces strawberries, sliced (about 2 cups)
- ½ cup granulated sugar
- Pinch of kosher salt
- 2 tablespoons cornstarch

Place the rhubarb, half the strawberries, the sugar, and salt in a small saucepan over medium heat. Cover and cook until the sugar is dissolved and the fruit is very soft and swimming in simmering liquid, about 10 minutes.

Combine the cornstarch with 2 tablespoons water in a small bowl, stirring to remove all lumps. Pour the slurry into the saucepan and mix with the fruit until thoroughly combined. Add the remaining strawberries and bring the contents to a simmer. Continue to cook for 1 minute, stirring constantly to prevent lumps or scorching, until the sauce thickens to a pudding-like consistency. Remove from the heat and fully cool in the refrigerator before using.

Fill and top the rugelach as directed in the main recipe. The baking time for these rugelach may increase by 5 to 10 minutes due to the increased moisture of the filling.

Summer: Nectarine-Almond Filling

Makes enough filling for 16 rugelach

For optimum results, use only the very ripest nectarines, preferably ones you pick yourself at their absolute summer peak. Nick insists that even farmers' market and farm-stand fruit runs a distant second behind fresh-picked. You may substitute peaches for the nectarines. Additional sugar, up to double the amount, may be added if the fruit is not fully sweet.

4 cups chopped nectarines
¼ cup granulated sugar
Pinch of kosher salt
2 tablespoons cornstarch
¼ teaspoon pure vanilla extract
1 cup slivered almonds

Place the fruit, sugar, and salt in a small saucepan over medium heat. Cover and cook until the sugar is dissolved and the fruit is soft and swimming in simmering liquid, about 10 minutes. It may be necessary to mash the fruit, but the liquid should remain somewhat chunky for best results.

Combine the cornstarch with 2 tablespoons water in a small bowl, stirring to remove all lumps. Pour the slurry into the saucepan and mix with the fruit until thoroughly combined. Bring the contents to a simmer. Continue to cook for 1 minute, stirring constantly to prevent lumps or scorching, until the sauce thickens to a pudding consistency. Stir in the vanilla, remove from the heat, and fully cool in the refrigerator before using.

After spreading the fruit filling on the rugelach dough, evenly sprinkle ½ cup of slivered almonds per sheet of dough before slicing and rolling up into pinwheels. Top as directed in the main recipe.

The baking time for these rugelach may increase by 5 to 10 minutes due to the increased moisture of the filling.

Fall: Huckleberry-Cinnamon Filling

Makes enough filling for 16 rugelach

For a glorious few weeks in early fall, huckleberries carpet the forest floors in the mountain foothills of the Pacific Northwest. During their brief season, they can also be purchased at area farmers' markets. And they freeze well for later use. If huckleberries are unavailable, substitute fresh or thawed frozen blueberries.

Filling

4 cups huckleberries

¾ cup granulated sugar

½ teaspoon ground cinnamon (see Sources and Resources, page 239)

Pinch of kosher salt

2 tablespoons cornstarch

Topping

¼ cup turbinado sugar

½ teaspoon ground cinnamon

To make the filling, place the berries, granulated sugar, cinnamon, and salt in a small saucepan over medium heat. Cover and cook until the sugar is dissolved and the fruit is soft and swimming in simmering liquid, about 10 minutes. It may be necessary to mash the berries, but the liquid should remain somewhat chunky for best results.

Combine the cornstarch and 2 tablespoons water in a small bowl, stirring to remove all lumps. Pour the slurry into the saucepan and mix with the fruit until thoroughly combined. Bring the contents to a simmer. Continue to cook for 1 minute, stirring constantly in order to prevent lumps or scorching, until the sauce thickens to a pudding-like consistency. Remove from the heat and fully cool in the refrigerator before using.

To make the topping, which will highlight the cinnamon flavor in the filling, mix together the turbinado sugar and the cinnamon. Use this mixture instead of the turbinado sugar alone used in the main recipe. The baking time for these rugelach may increase by 5 to 10 minutes due to the increased moisture of the filling.

Winter: Chocolate-Fig Filling

Makes enough filling for 16 rugelach

Alan Lake, a friend of Nick's who is also Jewish and a Chicago chef, helped with this filling. He suggested blending chocolate with dried fruit to avoid chocolate's tendency to turn crumbly or burn when baked into the cookies. It worked using dried figs, and the combination of flavors is brilliant. A tart Madagascar chocolate, like those from top U.S. chocolate makers Patric, Amano, or Rogue Chocolatier (see Sources and Resources, page 239), works especially well.

1 cup dried Mission figs, stemmed
1 cup bittersweet chocolate chips
½ cup granulated sugar

Place the figs and chocolate chips in the bowl of a food processor and process to make a thick paste. Add the sugar and pulse until the mixture is crumbly. Fill and top the rugelach as directed in the main recipe and then bake according to the main recipe.

Kenny & Zuke's: An Artisan Deli to Brighten Gray Portland Skies

Kenny & Zuke's founders, Ken Gordon and Nick Zukin, were unprepared for the crowds that swept in when the deli's doors first swung open in the fall of 2007. Employees sought to keep up with the pent-up demand for pastrami and corned beef, which sold out before the dinner hour. Even in a trend-setting city known for quirky establishments offering hand-prepared dishes and small-batch specialties, Kenny & Zuke's set a new standard for detail-driven fare.

The brains behind Kenny & Zuke's make an interesting yin-yang of personalities and backgrounds. Ken Gordon is a New Yorker by birth but a classically trained French chef who has lived and cooked in Portland for more than 20 years. Nick Zukin is a notorious local food-obsessive and blogger. Gordon is brash and confident; Zukin is more introspective and analytical. Despite their differences, they came together over the pastrami that they first sold at farmers' markets and Gordon's previous restaurant before hatching the idea of a full-service Jewish delicatessen.

Their ability to advance Jewish deli culture—or more accurately, to circle back to the delicatessen's pre-industrial roots—is due to the full-size basement beneath the restaurant that allows for on-premises preparation of almost every item served upstairs. Curious visitors may witness pastrami in its preparatory stages: brining, rubbing with a coriander and black pepper–rich spice mixture, and smoking for ten hours. Nearby, bakers spend their days hand-forming bagels, rolling rugelach, braiding challah, and crafting large, sandwich-ready loaves of rye bread. Suffice it to say, the downstairs ovens are rarely at rest.

Other Kenny & Zuke's specialties are likewise birthed in the basement: from traditional potato knishes, whitefish salad, and chopped liver to modern-leaning bagel dogs and pastrami gravy. Upstairs, pastrami-centered creations such as the pastrami burger (a beef patty joined on a bun by pastrami, sauerkraut, and Russian dressing), pastrami cheese fries, and the hollandaise-topped pastrami Benedict are created. Craft-produced bottled sodas and local microbrews are available, too.

By Portland standards, Kenny & Zuke's is large, with seating for seventy. A core group of original employees still works the floor, though the servers are all too young to sport blue-washed hair or call you "Hon." The crazy crowds and production problems of the early days have given way to a more metered madness, with a predictable weekday lunch rush and standing-room-only crowds that fill weekend brunch seats for hours.

How to explain the Kenny & Zuke's phenomenon? Gordon tried: "We knew Portland was a fertile place to create the kind of artisanal framework we saw the deli fitting into—it was happening all around us with bakers, butchers, cheese makers and winemakers, charcutiers, and pizza makers. We thought customers would respond positively, but we really had no sense of the avalanche that we opened to. We seemed to have touched something in the community, and among food lovers. We provoked responses in people who hadn't tasted the real thing since they were younger and who found something familiar and comforting in what we were doing. It turned us into an institution after a very short time."

Hamantaschen

Makes about 24 cookies

It's not often that the bad guy in a story ends up with all the glory. But somehow the evil Haman, villain in the Old Testament Book of Esther, was the one with a cookie named after him, while good King Ahasuerus and the lovely Queen Esther got bubkes—Yiddish for nothing. Hamantaschen are triangular cookies, most commonly filled with either a honey-sweetened prune or poppy seed mixture. They are traditionally made during the festival of Purim, the Jewish holiday that celebrates Esther's triumph over Haman. Their shape is modeled after the three-sided hat that Haman wore. Michael admits he's a fan of neither Haman nor his eponymous cookie. But the mainstream popularity of hamantaschen bespeaks a strong contrary sentiment.

Dough

½ cup (1 stick) unsalted butter, cubed, at room temperature

½ cup granulated sugar

¼ teaspoon kosher salt

1 large egg

2 teaspoons freshly squeezed orange juice

½ teaspoon pure vanilla extract

2⅓ cups unbleached all-purpose flour

½ teaspoon baking powder

Poppy seed filling

1 cup poppy seeds

½ cup heavy whipping cream

¼ cup honey

1 tablespoon unsalted butter

½ teaspoon pure vanilla extract

¼ teaspoon kosher salt

Prune filling

¾ cup dried prunes

¼ cup freshly squeezed orange juice

⅛ teaspoon kosher salt

1½ tablespoons honey

1 egg white, beaten with 1 teaspoon milk

To make the dough, in the bowl of a stand mixer fitted with the paddle attachment, cream together the butter, sugar, and salt on medium speed until fluffy, about 2 minutes. Stop once to scrape down the sides of the bowl. Beat in the egg, orange juice, and vanilla. In a separate bowl, mix together the flour and baking powder. Add 1 cup of the flour mixture and mix on medium-low speed until it is incorporated. Add the remaining 1⅓ cups of flour mixture and mix just until the dough is moistened and clumpy. Turn the dough out onto a lightly

continued on next page

floured work surface and form it into a flat disk. Wrap the disk in plastic wrap and refrigerate it to chill for at least 1 hour.

To make the poppy seed filling, stir together the poppy seeds, cream, honey, butter, vanilla, and salt in a small saucepan and bring the mixture to a simmer over medium heat. Decrease the heat to medium-low and simmer until the mixture thickens and clumps together, 6 to 8 minutes. Remove the pan from the heat and set it aside to cool.

To make the prune filling, combine the prunes, ¼ cup water, the orange juice, and salt in a small saucepan. Bring the mixture to a simmer over medium heat. Simmer until the liquid reduces by about two-thirds and the prunes are softened, 7 to 10 minutes. Transfer the mixture to a food processor and add the honey. Process it into a smooth puree. Transfer the filling to a small bowl and set aside to cool.

Preheat the oven to 350°F. Line two baking sheets with silicone baking mats or parchment paper. Remove the dough from the refrigerator. If it is too cold and firm to roll, allow it to warm up slightly, about 15 minutes.

Lightly dust your work surface with flour. Use a rolling pin to roll the dough out to a ⅛-inch thickness, dusting the top of the dough and the rolling pin with flour as needed. Using a 3-inch round cookie cutter, cut circles out of the dough and place them a few inches apart on the prepared sheets. Gather the scraps of dough and form them back into a flat disk, wrap it in the plastic, and refrigerate it to chill. When it is chilled but still pliable, roll out the disk to a ⅛-inch thickness and cut more circles of dough. You should end up with a total of 24 circles.

Fill each circle of dough with about 1 tablespoon of filling. (There should be enough of each type of filling for a dozen circles.) Working with one circle at a time, brush the edge of the circles with the egg wash. Fold up the edges to form a triangle that surrounds the filling and slightly covers it. Pinch together the tips of the triangles. Brush the tops and outside edges of the dough with the egg wash.

Bake the hamantaschen until they are golden brown at the tips, 18 to 22 minutes, rotating the pans in the oven halfway through the baking time. Transfer the cookies to a cooling rack and allow them to cool before serving.

Store hamantaschen at room temperature in an airtight container, layered between sheets of waxed paper, for up to 5 days.

Passover Honey Cake

Makes one 9-inch cake

The special dietary rules that prevail during Passover—prohibiting the use of wheat flour, among other items—create a major challenge for pastry bakers. How are you supposed to follow the rules and still bake a cake that tastes good and doesn't have the density of a brick? The key is matzo cake meal, matzo that has been ground to an extremely fine, flour-like powder. Look for it around Passover time at major grocery stores in communities with a substantial Jewish population, or search online. If that doesn't work, sift regular matzo meal into a small bowl or measuring cup to obtain the needed quantity, discarding the larger pieces that collect in the sifter.

- 1 cup honey
- ½ cup freshly brewed hot coffee
- 2 large eggs
- 2 tablespoons vegetable oil
- ½ cup firmly packed light brown sugar
- 1 cup matzo cake meal
- 1 cup potato starch, sifted
- 1½ teaspoons baking powder
- 1½ teaspoons baking soda
- ½ teaspoon kosher salt
- ½ teaspoon ground cinnamon
- ¼ teaspoon ground ginger
- ⅛ teaspoon ground cloves
- ⅛ teaspoon freshly ground nutmeg

Preheat the oven to 300°F. Lightly grease a 9-inch springform pan.

In a small bowl, stir the honey into the hot coffee to dissolve. In a large bowl, beat the eggs, then stir in the oil and brown sugar. In a separate large bowl, mix together the matzo cake meal, potato starch, baking powder, baking soda, salt, cinnamon, ginger, cloves, and nutmeg. Alternatively add the dry mixture and the honey mixture to the egg mixture in 3 batches each, stirring to combine after each addition.

Pour the batter into the prepared pan and place the pan on a rimmed baking sheet (in case it leaks). Bake the cake until it is set in the center and the top is deeply browned, 55 to 60 minutes. Allow the cake to cool before removing the springform. Slice and serve the cake once it reaches room temperature.

The cake will keep at room temperature, covered, for up to 4 days.

Chocolate-Dipped Coconut Macaroons

Makes about 2 dozen cookies

The connection between the coconut, a tropical fruit, and Ashkenazic cooking in Slavic Central and Eastern Europe is elusive. What little is known is that sweets using coconut were featured in an English-Jewish cookbook in 1846 and that a recipe for the coconut macaroon is given in Mrs. Esther Levy's *Jewish Cookery Book* (also known as *The First Jewish-American Cookbook*), published in Philadelphia in 1871. Shredded coconut and coconut oil were in use in Ashkenazic baking in the mid-nineteenth century, and coconut replaced more traditional almonds in Passover macaroon recipes during this time. How exactly the coconut migrated north in the first place remains mysterious, though speculation centers on Italian Jews as the link. Regardless of origin, coconut macaroons, including chocolate-dipped varieties such as these, have become an easy-to-make Jewish deli dessert classic.

1 cup plus 2 tablespoons granulated sugar
3¾ cups unsweetened shredded coconut
3 large egg whites
1 teaspoon pure vanilla extract
Pinch of kosher salt
1 cup bittersweet chocolate chips or buttons
1 teaspoon vegetable oil

Preheat the oven to 350°F. Line a baking sheet with a silicone baking mat or parchment paper.

In a large bowl, combine the sugar, coconut, egg whites, vanilla, and salt. Mix well, preferably using your hands, until all of the shredded coconut is moistened by the egg whites.

Form 2 lightly packed heaping tablespoons of the mixture into a haystack shape on the lined baking sheet or, to make the task quicker and easier, take a single scoop of the mixture with a #30 ice-cream scoop (available at most kitchen and restaurant supply stores). Use the backs of your fingers to gently pat and tighten the base of the haystacks and make an even, crack-free dome on the tops. Repeat with the remaining coconut mixture, placing the macaroons at least ½ inch apart.

Bake until golden brown, about 20 minutes. Transfer the baking sheet to a cooling rack and allow the cookies to cool to room temperature. If you try to remove them before they are cooled, the bottom may stick, leaving part of the cookie on the sheet.

After the macaroons are cooled, mix together the chocolate chips and vegetable oil in a small microwave-safe bowl. Slowly melt the chocolate in the microwave on low power, stirring about every 30 seconds, until the chips are just melted, about 2 minutes.

Dip the bottom of each macaroon in the melted chocolate so that ¼ inch of the sides are coated, scraping the excess chocolate from the bottom of the macaroons before setting them back on the parchment. Use a spoon to drizzle the remaining chocolate in thin streaks over the tops of the macaroons. Let the macaroons sit until the chocolate is set, about 2 hours. Store in an airtight container at room temperature for up to 3 days.

Chocolate Babka

Makes 2 loaves

Picture how sweet and delicious a well-made cinnamon roll can be, then imagine an entire swirly cinnamon loaf with the filling supplemented by dark, oozy, bittersweet chocolate. That is chocolate babka, loosely translated from Yiddish as "grandmother's cake." Quality ingredients are essential for babka to brag about. It begins with freshly made challah dough, enhanced with a little extra brown sugar. For the filling, we recommend Ceylon true cinnamon (as compared to cassia, which is commonly substituted for the real stuff on grocery store shelves), with its subtle flavor and distinctive citrus note (see Sources and Resources, page 239). The chocolate should be top-notch, too. Avoid standard bagged chocolate chips, in which the natural cocoa butter is often replaced by hydrogenated oil. Instead, use a premium brand of chips or buttons (also called coins or, in French, pistoles) for best flavor and texture.

1 recipe Sweet Challah Dough (page 199)

½ cup (1 stick) unsalted butter, melted and hot, plus more for greasing the pans

1 cup granulated sugar

½ cup cocoa powder

1 teaspoon ground cinnamon

All-purpose flour, for dusting

½ cup bittersweet chocolate chips or buttons

1 egg beaten with 1 tablespoon milk or water

When the Sweet Challah Dough is just about fully risen, lightly grease two 9-inch loaf pans with butter. Set aside.

In a medium microwave-safe bowl, whisk together the sugar, cocoa powder, and cinnamon. Set aside.

Turn the fully risen dough out onto a lightly floured work surface. Pat the dough to expel excess gas. Divide it in half. Return half of the dough to the bowl and cover it with plastic wrap. Set it aside while you work with the other half.

Dust a rolling pin and the top of the dough with flour and roll it out to a 9 by 18-inch rectangle about ⅛ inch thick. Cut the dough in half crosswise to create two 9-inch squares of dough.

Add the hot melted butter to the cocoa mixture and stir to form a thick paste. Use an offset frosting knife or rubber spatula to spread about one-quarter of the paste on each square of dough, leaving a ½-inch border around the edges. Sprinkle about 2 tablespoons of the chocolate chips over each square of dough. Brush the edges with some of the egg wash. Working quickly so the egg wash doesn't dry out, roll up each square of dough into a tight log, beginning with the edge closest to you and rolling away from you. Pinch the seams and ends together to prevent the logs from falling apart. Twist the logs together, placing one over the other alternately, 3 times, then gently press together the ends of the two logs to secure. Transfer the twist to one of the prepared pans, tucking the ends under as needed to fit it into the pan. Cover the pan with plastic wrap and set aside. Repeat this process with the other half of the dough and the remaining filling ingredients to make the second loaf. (If the cocoa paste is too firm to spread, it can be warmed in the microwave for 5 to 10 seconds on high power to soften it up.) Reserve the remaining egg wash.

Place both the covered pans in a warm place to rise until they are puffy and, when you gently press a finger into the dough, the impression remains, 30 to 45 minutes. (After the dough rises, the babkas can be refrigerated overnight and baked the following day. Allow them to come to room temperature in a warm spot for about 1 hour before baking.)

While the babkas are rising, preheat the oven to 350°F.

When the loaves are fully risen, uncover them and brush the top of each liberally with the remaining egg wash. Bake the babkas until they are deeply browned and glossy, 50 minutes to 1 hour, rotating the pans in the oven halfway through the baking time. To check the babkas for doneness, insert an instant-read thermometer into the seam formed by one of the twists at the thickest part of the loaf. The temperature should be about 190°F.

After removing the fully baked loaves from the oven, run a table knife around the edges of the pans to free the loaves, then transfer them to a cooling rack. Allow them to cool for at least 30 minutes before slicing so that the loaves have set up, but are still slightly warm to the touch.

The babka will keep, covered at room temperature, for 2 days, or refrigerated for up to 4 days. Once the babka becomes a little stale, it can be used to make exceptional French toast (page 100).

Challah Sticky Buns

Makes 12 buns

Are these buns traditional? Heck, no (well, except for the challah part). Are they delicious? You bet they are, and that's key to the unshackled approach taken in the modern Jewish deli. Just because it wasn't served in 1930 doesn't mean it has no place at today's table. A pan of these sticky buns, made with real maple syrup, is the perfect morning sweet treat to serve a houseful of guests along with their morning cup of coffee. Assemble the buns at night and bake them first thing the next day. Since they rise big and tall, it is important to use a large, deep roasting pan for baking. And try to find grade B maple syrup for the deepest, richest maple flavor. Grade A dark amber is the next best thing.

Filling

¾ cup plus 2 tablespoons (1¾ sticks) unsalted butter, cubed, at room temperature

1 cup firmly packed light brown sugar

1½ teaspoons ground cinnamon

Topping

1 cup (2 sticks) unsalted butter, cubed, at room temperature

1 cup firmly packed light brown sugar

1½ teaspoons kosher salt

1 cup pure maple syrup, preferably grade B

2 cups chopped pecans, lightly toasted

3 pounds (approximately) Sweet Challah Dough (page 199)

All-purpose flour, for dusting

To make the filling, in the bowl of a stand mixer fitted with the paddle attachment, place the butter, brown sugar, and cinnamon. Beat the mixture on medium speed until it is light and fluffy, about 3 minutes. Stop the mixer to scrape down the sides of the bowl once or twice. Transfer the filling mixture to a small bowl and set aside.

To make the topping, place the butter, brown sugar, and salt in a clean bowl of the stand mixer fitted with the paddle attachment. Beat the mixture on medium speed until it is light and fluffy, about 3 minutes, stopping once to scrape down the sides of the bowl. With the mixer running, slowly drizzle in the maple syrup. Continue beating the mixture until it is homogeneous and fluffy, 2 to 3 minutes more. Scrape down the sides of the bowl as needed. Spread the topping mixture on the bottom of a deep 15- to 16-inch roasting pan with sides that are at least 2½ inches high. Sprinkle the pecans over the top and set aside.

continued on next page

Turn the risen dough out onto a lightly floured work surface. Dust a rolling pin and the top of the dough with flour and roll it out to a 10 by 22-inch rectangle about ¼ inch thick. Position the dough so that the long edges are parallel to the edge of the work surface. Gently pull at the corners of the dough to square them off. Use an offset frosting knife or rubber spatula to spread the filling over the surface of the dough, leaving a ½-inch border on the long edge that is furthest away from you. Starting from the long edge of the dough that is closest to you, roll the dough up into a tight log, using pressure from your fingers and hands to tuck and tighten as you roll. If the ends of the log are tapered, pat them in so that the log is about 24 inches long and 3 inches in diameter throughout. Use a tape measure and a sharp knife to score the log into 2-inch-thick buns, and then cut the buns. Re-shape them into round rolls and space them out, 3 by 4, over the topping in the pan. There should be about 1 inch of space between each bun.

Cover the pan with plastic wrap and set the buns in a warm spot to rise until they are puffy and increased in size by about half, 30 minutes to 1 hour. (The time will depend on room temperature.) Refrigerate the rolls, covered, for 6 to 8 hours or overnight.

Remove the buns from the refrigerator and allow them to come to room temperature in a warm spot, covered, for about 1 hour. Before baking, they should be touching, or almost touching, and when you press your finger into the dough, the depression should spring back very slowly.

Preheat the oven to 350°F about 30 minutes before baking. Remove the plastic wrap and bake the buns until they are deep golden brown on top and the center registers 180°F to 185°F on an instant-read thermometer, 40 to 45 minutes. Allow the buns to cool until the caramel has stopped bubbling, about 5 minutes, and then turn the buns out of the pan. Do this by running a table knife around the edges of the pan, and then invert the buns onto a large serving platter or a rimmed baking sheet. Serve the sticky buns warm.

The buns will keep, covered at room temperature, for 2 days, or refrigerate them for up to 4 days. Reheat the buns at 350°F for 8 to 10 minutes before serving.

Apple Cake

Makes one 8- or 9-inch cake

An ancient cultivar, the apple has a time-honored place in the foods of many cultures. In Jewish cooking, apples are used in such holiday specialties as charoset, a spiced fruit-nut relish first served by Ashkenazis on Passover, or simply sliced and dipped in honey on Rosh Hashanah. The symbolic reference in both cases is to the sweetness of life. Apple cake is yet another sweet treat among the range of Jewish baked goods. The recipe calls for Golden Delicious apples, though any softer, sweet variety will suffice. Vietnamese cinnamon (see Sources and Resources, page 239) is worth seeking out for its particularly potent flavor and aroma, a shining match with apples.

3¾ cups all-purpose flour
2⅓ cups granulated sugar
1 tablespoon baking powder
½ teaspoon kosher salt
1 cup vegetable oil, plus more for greasing the pan
4 large eggs, beaten
⅓ cup freshly squeezed orange juice
1 teaspoon pure vanilla extract
2½ teaspoons ground cinnamon
4 medium Golden Delicious apples, peeled, cored, and thinly sliced

Preheat the oven to 350°F.

Sift together the flour, 1⅔ cups of the sugar, the baking powder, and salt into a large bowl. Create a well in the center of the flour mixture and pour in the oil, eggs, orange juice, and vanilla. Stir the wet ingredients into the dry ingredients until they are just combined.

In a separate large bowl, mix together the remaining ⅔ cup of sugar and the cinnamon. Add the apples and gently stir until they are evenly coated with the cinnamon-sugar mixture.

Lightly grease an 8- to 9-inch springform pan with vegetable oil. Place the pan on a rimmed baking sheet (in case it leaks). Pour in half of the cake batter and spread it out to the edges of the pan in an even layer. Scatter half of the apples evenly over the batter. Repeat to create another layer of batter topped with the remaining apples.

Bake the cake until the top layer of apples is deeply browned and leathery and when a table knife inserted into the center of the cake comes out clean, about 1 hour and 45 minutes. Rotate the pan in the oven about halfway through the baking time to ensure even baking.

Allow the cake to cool completely before serving. Run a knife around the edge of the pan to separate the cake from the pan, then remove the springform. Serve at room temperature. The cake will keep at room temperature, wrapped tightly in plastic wrap, for up to 4 days.

Cheesecake

with Shortbread Crust

Makes one 9- or 10-inch cake

The accidental creation of cream cheese in 1872 led to a cheesecake revolution in New York City Jewish delicatessens. By the late 1930s, cheesecake with a graham cracker crumb crust had become the defining deli dessert. Our updated version relies on a sweetened short dough crust, which is every bit as delicious as one made from graham crackers. The most common question among novice cheesecake bakers is: How do you know when it's fully baked? The answer: It's done when the edges show just a hint of golden color and the center is still very jiggly. The center will set as it slowly cools, at first in the oven, then at room temperature. A browned top is undesirable, as it's a sure sign the cheesecake is overdone and will be dry as a bone.

Crust

¾ cup (1½ sticks) unsalted butter, cold, plus more for greasing the pan

⅓ cup granulated sugar

¼ teaspoon kosher salt

1⅔ cups all-purpose flour

Filling

3 (8-ounce) packages cream cheese, preferably Gina Marie brand, at room temperature

1½ cups granulated sugar

3 cups (1½ pounds) sour cream

5 large eggs

1 tablespoon pure vanilla extract

Preheat the oven to 400°F.

To make the crust, place the butter, sugar, and salt in the bowl of a stand mixer fitted with the paddle attachment. Beat the mixture together on medium speed until the sugar is absorbed, scraping down the sides of the bowl as needed. Add the flour and continue mixing just until incorporated and the mixture is still dry and crumbly. Press the dough into the bottom of a 9- or 10-inch springform pan. Bake the crust until it is golden brown, 15 to 20 minutes. Set the crust aside to cool slightly, about 15 minutes. Decrease the oven temperature to 300°F.

To make the filling, place the cream cheese in the bowl of a stand mixer fitted with the paddle attachment and beat it on medium-low speed until it is smooth, scraping down the sides of the bowl as needed, 1 to 2 minutes. Add the sugar and mix until it is incorporated. Scrape down the sides of the bowl, add the sour cream, and continue mixing to combine. With the mixer running, add the eggs,

1 or 2 at a time, mixing just until they are blended in before each new addition. Finally, add the vanilla and continue mixing just until the mixture is smooth and fully combined.

Coat the sides of the springform pan with butter and place the pan on a rimmed baking sheet (in case it leaks). Pour the filling into the pan to cover the crust and smooth the top with a rubber spatula. Bake the cheesecake until the edges are set but still pale in color and the center is still jiggly and appears underdone, 60 to 75 minutes. Turn off the oven. Wedge a wooden spoon in the oven door to crack it open and leave the cheesecake inside for at least 1 hour. (Cooling the cake very slowly in the oven will prevent the top from cracking.)

Remove the cheesecake from the oven and allow it to continue cooling at room temperature, about 2 hours. Cover the pan with aluminum foil, making sure that the foil does not come into contact with the surface of the cake, and transfer it to the refrigerator to chill for at least 4 hours, preferably overnight.

The cheesecake tastes the best when it is cool but not cold, so remove it from the refrigerator about 1 hour before serving. Place the pan on a serving platter. Run a blunt knife between the edge of the cake and the pan to release it, and then remove the springform. Cut the cake into slices and serve. The cake will keep in the refrigerator, covered, for up to 3 days.

Sweet Noodle Kugel

Serves 12 to 16

This is a classic sweet kugel recipe, with raisins, cinnamon, and sugar joining the noodles and customary ensemble of dairy ingredients. The abundance of beaten eggs helps keep the finished product from being overly dense. This dish also ranks high on the simplicity scale, with all the ingredients combined in a single large pot before the kugel mixture is transferred to a baking dish, then the oven.

Cooking spray
18 ounces wide egg noodles (about 1½ packages)
½ cup (1 stick) plus 2 tablespoons unsalted butter, cubed
3 cups small-curd cottage cheese
3 cups sour cream
¾ cup raisins
½ cup milk
6 large eggs, beaten
1½ teaspoons kosher salt
1 cup granulated sugar
2 teaspoons ground cinnamon

Preheat the oven to 350°F. Spray a 9 by 13-inch glass baking dish with cooking spray and set aside.

Fill a large pot with about 5 quarts water and bring to a boil over high heat. Add the egg noodles and cook until they are just underdone, about 5 minutes. Drain the noodles in a colander, shaking to remove excess water, and then transfer the noodles back into the dry pot. Add the ½ cup butter and stir to melt. Allow the noodles to cool slightly, about 5 minutes.

Stir in the cottage cheese, sour cream, raisins, milk, eggs, and salt. In a small bowl, whisk together the sugar and cinnamon. Add about half of the cinnamon-sugar mixture to the noodle mixture.

Pour the noodle mixture into the baking dish and spread it out into an even layer. Sprinkle the top of the kugel with the remaining cinnamon-sugar mixture and dot it with the remaining 2 tablespoons cubed butter. Place the baking dish on a rimmed baking sheet (in case of overflow) and bake until the kugel is set in the center and brown and crunchy on top, 50 minutes to 1 hour. Allow the kugel to cool about 10 minutes before cutting and serving.

Store the leftover kugel in the refrigerator, covered, for up to 3 days. To reheat, add a drizzle of milk to the top of the kugel and bake it at 350°F, covered, until heated through. (The cooking time depends on how much kugel you are reheating.)

Celery Soda

Serves 4

Celery-flavored soda has to be the most unusual of the sharp-tasting specialty drinks crafted to quench the thirst of Jewish deli diners. Making its first appearance in New York City in the late 1800s, Dr. Brown's Cel-Ray is the brand name synonymous with celery soda. But good luck finding it outside New York or maybe Miami. The key ingredient in most celery soda is celery seed, which gives the beverage a slightly bitter, earthy flavor. The lemon and fresh celery in our rendition makes for a more vibrant, summery taste. Try it with a corned beef, Swiss cheese, and chopped liver sandwich or on its own during the next heat wave.

12 ounces celery (10 to 12 stalks), very finely chopped

1 ounce fresh ginger (about 1 knob), peeled and very finely chopped or grated

2 cups granulated sugar

Zest of 1 lemon

Pinch of kosher salt

48 ounces chilled seltzer or club soda

Place 1½ cups water, the celery, and ginger in a saucepan and bring to a boil over medium-high heat. Lower the temperature to medium-low, cover, and simmer for 45 minutes. Remove from the heat and strain into a bowl, pressing down firmly on the solids to extract any remaining liquid.

Pour the liquid back into the saucepan set over medium-high heat and add the sugar. Once the sugar is dissolved, add the lemon zest and salt to the saucepan. Cover and decrease the heat to low.

Simmer the syrup for 15 minutes, remove from the heat, and allow it to stand uncovered until it cools to room temperature. Strain the syrup into a small bowl.

In each tall glass, combine ½ cup of the syrup with 12 ounces (1½ cups) seltzer. If not making all the soda at once, the syrup may be kept in a tightly covered container in the refrigerator for up to 1 month.

Talking Deli with . . . *Nach Waxman*

Anyone with an interest in food and the written word must make a pilgrimage to New York City's Upper East Side. There, among a block of unremarkable storefronts, is Kitchen Arts & Letters, the best shop in the United States, if not the world, to find culinary literature spanning the globe and human history. Its proprietor is Nach Waxman, whose formidable knowledge of all things gastronomic includes the cuisine of his Jewish heritage.

Could you describe your upbringing and how that translated into what you grew up eating?

Nach Waxman: Though both my parents were from New York City (my mother from Rivington Street, Lower East Side; my father from Brooklyn), I grew up in a small town in rural southern New Jersey. Philadelphia and Wilmington were the closest cities; New York City was as remote as Moscow is from Minsk. Once a week, Iz Goldstein, the grocer, got in a supply of bagels, onion rolls, and lox from a source in Philly so the local *yiddische* (Jewish aristocracy) could *fress* (eat heartily) on Sunday mornings. What we drank was seltzer, ginger ale, and hot tea in a glass.

No cured meats were brought in, so my mother had to make her own corned beef, tongue, and—once or twice—pastrami, not to mention chopped liver and all the other specialties. I think Barney Woldar, the kosher butcher on the scene, made a few things like *kishke* and probably brought in kosher *vurst*—hot dogs and salami—from Philadelphia, and little else. But there was no place to go in and have a sandwich or a schmaltz-dappled chicken soup.

Did the foods you ate growing up affect your current dietary preferences?

Nach Waxman: Yes, markedly. Although I no longer keep kosher, my food is distinctly colored by the dishes I just mentioned, and many more. These foods are a source of comfort, pleasure, and well-being—as well as a source of being overweight and having high blood pressure. Happily, medical wisdom and gustatory enthusiasm have now reached a pretty sound balance.

What are your thoughts on the role of the Jewish deli traditionally and today?

Nach Waxman: With a very few exceptions, nearly all of what we call deli dishes were, in my parents' day, made at home, not

purchased. So, when my mother could get fresh herring, she would pickle it herself, slice up lots of onions, and mix it all up in sour cream. She didn't buy the jarred stuff unless she had no other choice. I believe this was true of the homes in which my parents grew up. They didn't get these foods from a deli; the deli got the foods from them and from their contemporaries.

I suspect that as time available for cooking shrank and as cooking skills deteriorated, the deli provided a way of getting approximations of many of these dishes. Some items were not practical to make at home and were always purchased. That is likely true of knishes, for example. My mother's mother in New York could buy them from Yonah Schimmel or one of his competitors, but my mother could not in her small town in New Jersey. And she didn't know how to make them because her mother had never learned how.

So, the deli has an important place in American Jewish history: It saved, at least for another generation or two, we hope longer, the foods that our people couldn't (or were unwilling to) make for themselves. On the other hand, we see people in the store all the time who are trying to learn old processes in food making—Jewish baking, Jewish charcuterie, Jewish preserving, and so on for home and small businesses.

Do you have a favorite deli dish?

Nach Waxman: I suppose pastrami and chopped liver on rye, or maybe tongue and chopped liver. Good pastrami is getting hard to find.

Egg Cream

Serves 4

This iconic deli drink includes neither egg nor cream. Commonly credited to Louis Auster, a Jewish immigrant who ran a candy store and soda fountain on the Lower East Side prior to the turn of the twentieth century, the egg cream is a simple concoction of seltzer water, chocolate syrup, and milk. So, what's the deal with the name? Gil Marks speculates that it comes from the foamy, egg white–like head that resulted when seltzer was squirted at high pressure from a soda siphon into a chocolate milk–filled glass. Alternative theories abound. Fox's U-Bet is the standard brand of syrup for an egg cream, though real chocolate syrup (as opposed to chocolate-flavored), such as Dagoba, produces a better-tasting drink.

2 cups whole milk
48 ounces chilled seltzer or club soda
1 cup chocolate syrup

Pour ½ cup milk in the bottom of a tall soda glass (narrow at the bottom, wide on top), filling it less than one-third of the way. Add seltzer to the glass until the frothy mixture fills the glass to about an inch below the rim. Add ¼ cup of the chocolate syrup to the glass.

Angle a long spoon from one side of the glass's rim to the opposite side of the glass's bottom. Use a rapid up-and-down movement with the spoon while slowly rotating the bottom of the glass with your other hand to mix the chocolate into the milk without stirring, which will ruin the soda's traditional layered appearance. Continue until the lumps of chocolate syrup in the bottom of the glass are fully incorporated and a 1- to 3-inch frothy white head crowns the rich chocolate brown soda below. Add enough additional seltzer to raise the head to the rim of the glass. Repeat for the remaining three sodas.

It's best to consume egg cream without a straw so that the liquid below and the foamy top mix with every sip.

Spicy Ginger Ale

Serves 4

Salty, savory deli food calls for an assertive, refreshing beverage. This ginger ale fills the bill. Traditional ginger ales, such as Vernor's, are light, sweet sodas. Ginger beers—Cock & Bull from Los Angeles or naturally fermented Bundaberg from Australia, for example—are less sweet and have a more intense ginger flavor. For ginger ale fanatics, one of the most beloved brands is Blenheim, a super-spicy version from South Carolina that is difficult to find outside the Deep South. This homemade variation packs all the punch of Blenheim and is perfect paired with pastrami, too.

12 ounces fresh ginger, peeled and finely chopped or grated
2 cups granulated sugar
Zest of 1 lemon
1 habanero chile, stemmed and halved
Pinch of salt
48 ounces chilled seltzer or club soda

Place 2 cups water and the ginger in a saucepan and bring to a boil over medium-high heat. Lower the temperature to medium-low, cover, and simmer for 45 minutes. Remove from the heat and strain into a bowl, pressing down firmly on the ginger to extract any liquid.

Pour the liquid back into the saucepan set over medium-high heat and add the sugar. Once the sugar is dissolved, add the lemon zest, chile, and salt to the saucepan. Cover and decrease the heat to low. Simmer the syrup for 15 minutes, remove from the heat, and allow it to stand uncovered until it cools to room temperature. Strain the syrup into a small bowl.

In each tall glass, combine ½ cup of the syrup with 12 ounces (1½ cups) seltzer. If not making all the soda at once, the syrup may be kept in a tightly covered container in the refrigerator for up to 1 month.

Where to Find What You Need to Know and Buy

Some ingredients are tough to find. We can point you in the right direction. Bookstores and the Internet are teeming with useful publications and information pertinent to Jewish deli food. For those who seek further enlightenment, we offer a sampling of these sources. And finally, for those times when you just don't feel like doing it yourself and you want a meal at one of the great artisan Jewish delis in North America, we list each one, along with contact information.

Sources for Hard-to-Find Ingredients

Barley Malt Syrup

Vital for bagels, the best place to find barley malt syrup is at your local brewers' supply store, where it is often available inexpensively in bulk. Dark or medium barley malt syrup is preferable to light. Natural foods stores and the natural foods section at major grocers are other places to find barley malt syrup, usually in glass jars sharing shelf space with other natural sweeteners.

Caramel Coloring

Essential to obtain that deep, dark cocoa color that distinguishes pumpernickel breads, caramel coloring is amazingly elusive for the home cook. Your best bet for obtaining liquid caramel coloring are local bakery supply or general restaurant food supply companies. Online sources include The Spice Place (for McCormick brand by the pint, see page 241). The most consumer-friendly source is the King Arthur Flour Baker's Catalogue, though only powdered caramel is sold.

Cinnamon, Ceylon and Vietnamese

Most of what you find in the grocery store is Chinese cassia, which may be close to real cinnamon, but it is not the same nor of the same quality. Penzeys carries several cinnamon varieties that can be ordered from its online store (see page 241) if there is no bricks-and-mortar location in your community. Ceylon cinnamon is the most subtle and interesting of them all. Vietnamese has the purest, most powerful cinnamon flavor.

Charnushka (Nigella) Seeds

Caraway seeds will suffice, but for a superior rye bread, smoky-flavored charnushka seeds are a must. Also labeled under the abbreviated version of their scientific name, *Nigella sativa*, look for the seeds at any local spice retailer or online from Penzeys or The Spice House (see page 241).

Chocolate, Specialty

Of course, you can find the usual varieties of waxy chocolate chips at the grocery store, but to find extraordinary chocolate that will elevate the dishes in this book, dig a little deeper. Gourmet grocery stores and baking supply stores are a couple of places to find quality brands in bars, bags, and bulk. In some cities, there are stores dedicated solely to selling fine chocolate. And, of course, a search online can be fruitful too, especially once your Web browser is pointed to Chocosphere (see page 240), a chocolate fancier's dream come true.

Farmer (or Pot) Cheese

It has the flavor of a dry cottage cheese with the texture of a crumbly chèvre. Russian, Middle Eastern, or Scandinavian markets are your best source. It can also be purchased online at amazon.com or russianfooddirect.com.

Food-Grade Lye

Also known as sodium hydroxide, lye for use in making pretzels is most easily found online. Our resident pretzel expert suggests essentialdepot.com, though it can also be ordered from amazon.com.

Malt Powder

Also known as barley flour (but not to be confused with malted milk powder in a jar), this is simply the dried and powdered by-product of sprouted barley. Used for its mildly sweet natural flavor (and dough-enhancing properties in the case of diastatic malt), malt powder can be purchased at most baking supply stores, natural foods stores, and online from either King Arthur or Bob's Red Mill, right.

Pink Salt

Sometimes called curing salt or Prague powder #1. It is a 6.25 percent mixture of sodium nitrite and table salt that helps prevent harmful bacteria from growing and fixes the appetizing reddish color in cured meats. Locally, it can often be purchased from independent butchers who still process meat themselves. Look for a butcher who makes sausages, salami, ham, or bacon. Pink salt can also be purchased online from amazon.com or americanspice.com.

Porcini Powder

The powder made from dried porcini mushrooms (sometimes referred to as cèpes or boletes) adds an intense and luxurious earthy flavor to dishes. It can be found in Italian or gourmet grocers or made by pulverizing dried porcinis in a spice grinder. Other sources include farmers' market vendors and online from several Web sites, including oregonmushrooms.com, thespicehouse.com, and amazon.com.

Smoked Whitefish

Smoked Great Lakes whitefish can be found in Jewish appetizing stores (if you happen to have one near you), Russian markets, or select gourmet seafood markets. Russian markets also carry smoked chubs, which can be substituted for whitefish. Online, whitefish can be found at amazon.com or russianfooddirect.com.

Selected Internet Resources

Bob's Red Mill

bobsredmill.com

Bob's Red Mill produces and sells a vast array of grain products. The company is physically located in the Portland, Oregon, suburb of Milwaukie and has an enormous outlet store there. Select Bob's Red Mill products are also stocked at major grocers and natural foods stores nationwide. Bob's Web site offers convenient online shopping.

Chocosphere

chocosphere.com

This online-only source for chocolate may offer the broadest variety of quality brands anywhere. Though the Web site itself is chaotic, it does offer the chance to browse and shop for whatever top-notch chocolate may suit the moment or the recipe you need to make.

Diane Morgan Cooks

dianemorgancooks.com

Resource Web site and blog for the Portland, Oregon, cookbook author.

The Jewish Daily Forward

Hosting "The Jew & the Carrot" blog (blogs.forward.com/the-jew-and-the-carrot), a multi-contributor blog all about Jewish food and eating.

King Arthur Flour

kingarthurflour.com

Along with Bob's Red Mill, King Arthur is the largest online retailer of goods for use by the home baker. As with Bob's, King Arthur products are often found at major grocers and natural food stores, though the more exotic items, such as caramel coloring, are apt to be available only from the online catalog.

Mostly Foodstuffs

mostlyfoodstuffs.blogspot.com

Blog by Portland, Oregon, food writer (and NPR correspondent) Deena Prichep.

Penzeys Spices

penzeys.com

No doubt about it, Penzeys has the most impressive selection of spices and flavorings anywhere.

Originally, the only brick-and-mortar stores were in Wisconsin, but now there are dozens of outlets around the country, all attractively designed, in addition to the easy-to-navigate online store.

Portland Food Group

portlandfood.org
Portland, Oregon, food and restaurant forum hosted by Nick under his online pseudonym, Extramsg.

Russian Food Direct

russianfooddirect.com
Though a live visit to a Russian market will always be more fun, there are several online sources for goods from Russia and nearby nations. Russian Food Direct has a larger selection and is easier to order from than most, plus the site lets you search specifically for kosher foods.

The Shiksa in the Kitchen

theshiksa.com
Blog by Torey Avey, culinary anthropologist and convert to Judaism, who writes about the history of Jewish food and related topics.

The Spice House

spicehouse.com
A good online alternative to Penzeys, run by a different branch of the Penzey family, The Spice House offers a selection of dried herbs and spices that is in the same league if not as well known as the familial competition.

Our Favorite Artisan Jewish Delicatessens

Caplansky's Delicatessen

356 College Street
Toronto, Ontario M5T 3A9
416-500-3852
caplanskys.com

Kenny & Zuke's Delicatessen

1038 S.W. Stark Street
Portland, Oregon 97205
503-222-3354
kennyandzukes.com

Mile End Delicatessen

97a Hoyt Street
Brooklyn, New York 11217
718-852-7510
mileendbrooklyn.com

Stopsky's Delicatessen

3016 78th Avenue SE
Mercer Island, Washington 98040
206-236-4564
stopskysdelicatessen.com

Wise Sons Delicatessen

3150 24th Street
San Francisco, California 94110
415-787-3354
wisesonsdeli.com

Two other artisan-style Jewish delicatessens that we know of opened after this book was written but before it went to press:

Josh's Delicatessen & Appetizing

9517 Harding Avenue
Surfside, Florida 33154
305-397-8494
joshsdeli.com

DGS Delicatessen

1317 Connecticut Avenue NW
Washington, D.C. 20036
202-293-4400
dgsdelicatessen.com

Russian Markets: Stalking the Secret Source for Elusive Deli Ingredients

Russians began coming to the New World even before there was a United States. Historically, they came to hunt, fish, trap, prospect, and trade. After the Bolshevik Revolution in 1917, Russians and citizens of surrounding nations that became part of the Soviet Union came to escape Communism and seek out opportunity. After the fall of the USSR, still more came, seeking work and a piece of the American Dream.

Where these émigrés have settled, their food markets have become a gathering place serving new Americans ethnically identifiable as Russians, Poles, Ukrainians, Latvians, Romanians, Georgians, Lithuanians, Serbians, Bosnians, and Armenians, to name a handful.

Even though the vast majority of Eastern Europeans who arrived were non-Jewish, centuries of common geography with the Ashkenazic Jews resulted in shared—or at least overlapping—culinary traditions. Many of the specialty goods needed to make traditional Jewish deli dishes—the ingredients not likely to be found at a national grocer or even at your favorite farmers' market—can be obtained at these ethnic food stores.

But where to find these Russian markets (the blanket label we use for want of a better term)? One clue: signs written in Cyrillic lettering, the alphabet of the Russian language. Another telltale sign is in the name of the place. If there is a store with "Odessa" or "Moscow" or another Slavic city in the name, by all means inquire further. Other hints are broad geographic designators such as "European Market," "Euro Foods," or "International Deli."

Naturally, you have to take a look inside. If your instincts steered you right, the shelves (and cold cases) will serve as a great resource for Jewish deli cooking. Basic but otherwise hard-to-find staples readily found here will include: kasha, farmer cheese, canned fish, and hearty dark breads. Pickles will encompass far more than cucumbers: Think pickled tomatoes, squash, mushrooms, and, of course, cabbage. Find roasted red peppers by the jar and many of the condiments made with them, such as *Ajvar* (page 17) and *lutenica*. Also in the aisles: walnuts, sour cherries, rose hips, apricots, and currants, either fresh, as fillings for desserts, or as preserves. Poppy and caraway seeds, caviar, and European chocolate will all be priced less than at your local supermarket.

But the most beguiling bounty at the Russian market is in the cold case. There visitors can find smoked fish of all sorts: trout, salmon, mackerel, sturgeon, and whitefish. Also look for *basturma*, the old-style air-dried beef that is a predecessor to pastrami. Another treat is *evreiskaya*, a Jewish-style Russian dry salami, or cervelat, an all-beef summer sausage. In addition to farmer cheese, you'll find half a dozen different fetas and Goudas.

So, grab a basket and take advantage of the availability and value the Russian markets offer. They are a surefire ticket to creating *Yiddische* deli dishes the Old-World way.

Selected Bibliography

Cook's Illustrated Magazine Editors. *Baking Illustrated*. Brookline: America's Test Kitchen, 2004.

Deutsch, Jonathan, and Rachel D. Saks. *Jewish American Food Culture*. Westport: Greenwood Press, 2008.

Gergely, Anikó. *Culinaria Hungary*. Potsdam: H. F. Ullmann, 2008.

Glezer, Maggie. A *Blessing of Breads: Recipes and Rituals, Memories and Mitzvahs*. New York: Artisan, 2004.

Goldberg, Molly, and Myra Waldo. *The Molly Goldberg Cookbook*. New York: Doubleday, 1955.

Goldman, Marcy. A *Treasury of Jewish Holiday Baking*. New York: Broadway Books, 1998.

Goodman, Matthew. *Jewish Food: The World at Table*. New York: HarperCollins Publishers, 2005.

Greenstein, George. *Secrets of a Jewish Baker*. Freedom: The Crossing Press, 1993.

Hamelman, Jeffrey. *Bread: A Baker's Book of Techniques and Recipes*. Hoboken: John Wiley & Sons, 2004.

Koerner, András. A *Taste of the Past: The Daily Life and Cooking of a 19th Century Hungarian Jewish Homemaker*. Hanover: University Press of New England, 2004.

Labensky, Steven, Gaye G. Ingram, and Sarah R. Labensky. *The Prentice Hall Dictionary of Culinary Arts*. 2nd ed. Upper Saddle River: Pearson Prentice Hall, 2006.

Lang, George. *The Cuisine of Hungary*. New York: Bonanza Books, 1971.

Leonard, Leah. *Jewish Cookery*. New York: Crown Publishing, 1949.

Levy, (Mrs.) Esther, *The First Jewish-American Cookbook*. Minneola: Dover Publications, 2004. Originally published as *Jewish Cookery Book* (Philadelphia: W. S. Turner, 1871).

London, Anne, and Bertha Kahn Bishov. *The Complete American-Jewish Cookbook*. New York: World Publishing, 1971.

Lowenstein, Steven. *The Jews of Oregon, 1850–1950*. Portland: Jewish Historical Society of Oregon, 1988.

Marks, Gil. *Encyclopedia of Jewish Food*. Hoboken: John Wiley & Sons, 2010.

Metzger, Christine. *Culinaria Germany*. Potsdam: H. F. Ullmann, 2008.

Nathan, Joan. *Jewish Cooking in America*. New York: Knopf Books, 1998.

Nathan, Joan. *Joan Nathan's Jewish Holiday Cookbook*. New York: Schocken, 2004.

Ruhlman, Michael, Brian Polcyn, and Thomas Keller. *Charcuterie: The Craft of Salting, Smoking, and Curing*. New York: W. W. Norton & Company, 2005.

Sahni, Julie. *Classic Indian Cooking*. New York: William Morrow and Company, 1980.

Sax, David. *Save the Deli: In Search of Perfect Pastrami, Crusty Rye, and the Heart of the Jewish Delicatessen*. New York: Houghton Mifflin Harcourt Publishing, 2009.

Schwartz, Arthur. *Jewish Home Cooking: Yiddish Recipes Revisited*. Berkeley: Ten Speed Press, 2008.

Sheraton, Mimi. *The German Cookbook*. New York: Random House, 1965.

Stewart, Martha. *The Martha Stewart Cookbook: Collected Recipes for Every Day*. New York: Clarkson Potter, 1995.

Trutter, Marion. *Culinaria Russia: Ukraine, Georgia, Armenia, Azerbaijan*. Potsdam: H. F. Ullmann, 2007.

van Cleef, Henny. *The Israeli Table Kitchen*. Translated by Theresia Riggs. Kearney: Morris Publishing, 2003.

von Bremzen, Anya, and John Welchman. *Please to the Table: The Russian Cookbook*. New York: Workman Publishing, 1990.

Wirkowski, Eugeniusz. *Cooking the Polish-Jewish Way*. Warsaw: Interpress Publishers, 1988.

Ziedrich, Linda. *The Joy of Pickling: 250 Flavor-Packed Recipes for Vegetables and More from Garden or Market*. Boston: Harvard Common Press, 2009.

Metric Conversions and Equivalents

METRIC CONVERSION FORMULAS

To Convert	Multiply
Ounces to grams	Ounces by 28.35
Pounds to kilograms	Pounds by .454
Teaspoons to milliliters	Teaspoons by 4.93
Tablespoons to milliliters	Tablespoons by 14.79
Fluid ounces to milliliters	Fluid ounces by 29.57
Cups to milliliters	Cups by 236.59
Cups to liters	Cups by .236
Pints to liters	Pints by .473
Quarts to liters	Quarts by .946
Gallons to liters	Gallons by 3.785
Inches to centimeters	Inches by 2.54

APPROXIMATE METRIC EQUIVALENTS

Weight

¼ ounce	7 grams
½ ounce	14 grams
¾ ounce	21 grams
1 ounce	28 grams
1¼ ounces	35 grams
1½ ounces	42.5 grams
1⅔ ounces	45 grams
2 ounces	57 grams
3 ounces	85 grams
4 ounces (¼ pound)	113 grams
5 ounces	142 grams
6 ounces	170 grams
7 ounces	198 grams
8 ounces (½ pound)	227 grams
16 ounces (1 pound)	454 grams
35.25 ounces (2.2 pounds)	1 kilogram

Length

⅛ inch	3 millimeters
¼ inch	6 millimeters
½ inch	1¼ centimeters
1 inch	2½ centimeters
2 inches	5 centimeters
2½ inches	6 centimeters
4 inches	10 centimeters
5 inches	13 centimeters
6 inches	15¼ centimeters
12 inches (1 foot)	30 centimeters

Volume

¼ teaspoon	1 milliliter
½ teaspoon	2.5 milliliters
¾ teaspoon	4 milliliters
1 teaspoon	5 milliliters
1¼ teaspoons	6 milliliters
1½ teaspoons	7.5 milliliters
1¾ teaspoons	8.5 milliliters
2 teaspoons	10 milliliters
1 tablespoon (½ fluid ounce)	15 milliliters
2 tablespoons (1 fluid ounce)	30 milliliters
¼ cup	60 milliliters
⅓ cup	80 milliliters
½ cup (4 fluid ounces)	120 milliliters
⅔ cup	160 milliliters
¾ cup	180 milliliters
1 cup (8 fluid ounces)	240 milliliters
1¼ cups	300 milliliters
1½ cups (12 fluid ounces)	360 milliliters
1⅔ cups	400 milliliters
2 cups (1 pint)	460 milliliters
3 cups	700 milliliters
4 cups (1 quart)	0.95 liter
1 quart plus ¼ cup	1 liter
4 quarts (1 gallon)	3.8 liters

COMMON INGREDIENTS AND THEIR APPROXIMATE EQUIVALENTS

1 cup uncooked white rice = 185 grams
1 cup all-purpose flour = 140 grams
1 stick butter (4 ounces • ½ cup • 8 tablespoons) = 110 grams
1 cup butter (8 ounces • 2 sticks • 16 tablespoons) = 220 grams
1 cup brown sugar, firmly packed = 225 grams
1 cup granulated sugar = 200 grams

OVEN TEMPERATURES

To convert Fahrenheit to Celsius, subtract 32 from Fahrenheit, multiply the result by 5, then divide by 9.

Description	Fahrenheit	Celsius	British Gas Mark
Very cool	200°	95°	0
Very cool	225°	110°	¼
Very cool	250°	120°	½
Cool	275°	135°	1
Cool	300°	150°	2
Warm	325°	165°	3
Moderate	350°	175°	4
Moderately hot	375°	190°	5
Fairly hot	400°	200°	6
Hot	425°	220°	7
Very hot	450°	230°	8
Very hot	475°	245°	9

Information compiled from a variety of sources, including *Recipes into Type* by Joan Whitman and Dolores Simon (Newton, MA: Biscuit Books, 2000); *The New Food Lover's Companion* by Sharon Tyler Herbst (Hauppauge, NY: Barron's, 1995); and *Rosemary Brown's Big Kitchen Instruction Book* (Kansas City, MO: Andrews McMeel, 1998).

Acknowledgments

Honestly, if we had known up front how much work would be involved, this cookbook probably would have been pushed aside for other less rigorous pursuits. And though the laboring oar was borne by the two of us, this was a group effort for sure.

From beginning to end, there has been Jean Lucas, our editor, along with the rest of the ever-positive crew at Andrews McMeel. They supported our vision about what this book ought to be and helped us produce a beautifully designed and useful volume.

We are also grateful to Diane Morgan. Diane is a gifted and prolific cookbook writer in her own right who somehow found the time to step in and help us with the huge task of organizing the book and overseeing the first edit. Diane also happens to teach a food-writing course every year or two, which was invaluable in helping plant the seed from which this book sprouted.

We are indebted to Andrea Slonecker for, among other things, her pretzel expertise, turning Michael's family keegal formulation into a real recipe, and, most of all, helping Nick develop recipes when he decided he just had to open another restaurant in the middle of writing a cookbook. Thanks, also, to Deena Prichep for her Jewish-hippie-pescatarian insights and recipe wrangling. Further thanks to others who contributed to the book: Nach Waxman, Joan Nathan, and Sharon Lebewohl, whose love of deli is evident in these pages.

We had what seemed like a legion of willing testers and tasters to whom deepest thanks are owed. We are especially grateful to Jolene George and Liz Crain for taking on many of the book's comparatively technical bread recipes; and not least to the crew on Nick's popular food and restaurant forum, PortlandFood.org, including VJ Beauchamp, Jamie Green, Nadine Fiedler, Jill R. Oppenheim, Veronica Vichit-Vadakan, Jennifer Perrella, Ben Wolff, Pamela Wilkinson, Kathy Mayers, Carin Moonin, Kris Pennella, Kristi Van Damme, Eva Bernhard, Judy Pohutsky, Keith Orr, and Sarah Sugarman.

Also due evolutionary credit is David Sax, author of *Save the Deli.* After reading David's book and getting to know him, it occurred to us that we needed to close the circle that David had begun to draw.

Of course, this book would not exist without the handful of folks who have been foresighted and gutsy enough to buck a longstanding downhill trend by opening Jewish delicatessens over the last several years: Noah Bernamoff, Rachel Cohen Bernamoff, Zane Caplansky, Evan Bloom, Leo Beckerman, Jeff Sanderson, Josh Marcus, Barry Koslow (and his business partners), and Ken Gordon.

Michael also wants to extend thanks to his many professional colleagues who have supported his odd dual passions: judge by day and writer by night. Particular gratitude is due Multnomah County Circuit Court Trial Court Administrator Doug Bray. Among writers and editors who have worked with Michael, no one has been more influential and appreciated than Karen Brooks.

Special thanks to Kelly Zusman for her edit of the book's introduction; Joshua Brody and Juliana Grenzeback for their scouting mission; Gil Marks and Ted Merwin for their scholarship and help and Tim Healea for the sourdough starter recipe.

Michael's final thanks go out to his close friends and family who have put up with him, at a minimum, for decades. The immediate family: Ma and Dad; Steve and Diane, Amanda, Natalie, Cassidy, and Jake; Auntie and Uncle Mel, Bruce, and Lisa; Grace Maritka; and the memories of David and Rose Fertig and Abe and Edith Zusman. The longest-time friends: Gerry Birnbach, David Richenstein, Vince Bernabei, Karl Weist, James Greenblatt, Michael Evans, Victor Richenstein, The Coasters, and the poker circle.

Nick would also like to thank the several online communities and friends that helped him reconnect with his culinary heritage, ultimately leading to Kenny & Zuke's and this book. In particular, it was on eGullet where he first got excited about making artisan pastrami, rugelach, and knishes. The folks at PortlandFood.org, starting with the founding members—Jill-O, Ducky, Amanda, Aristo, and Dimsumdiva—have always been a wonderful sounding board, both encouraging and grounding him. And finally to the folks at LTHForum, the best food forum in the country, a hearty Midwestern thank-you.

Nick has the deepest gratitude, of course, to his friends, family, and, especially, his wife, Lisa, who have supported him in both large and small ways so that his hobby could be his profession.

Both Michael and Nick would like to thank the benefactors of B'nai B'rith Summer Camp.

Index

R

S

T

V

W

Z